WHAT ARCHITECTURE MEANS

What Architecture Means introduces you to architecture and allows you to explore the connections between design ideas and values across time, space, and culture. It equips you to play an active and informed role in architecture either as a professional or as a consumer, client, and citizen. By analyzing famous and everyday buildings while presenting and questioning the positions of important architects and theorists, this book will help you to evaluate and decide what qualities, ideas, and values you believe are important in architecture.

You'll learn:

- how various definitions of "architecture" establish different relationships with all buildings, and even non-buildings;
- how buildings express and accommodate ideas of the sacred, the family, and the community;
- what an architect is, and what priorities he or she brings to design and construction;
- how an architect's expertise relates to that of the engineer, and why these are distinct disciplines;
- about values like beauty, originality, structural expression, and cultural memory and their purpose in architectural design;
- about the interests and ethical values that architects, and architecture, serve and promote.

Topics include sacred spaces, the house, the city, architects and engineers, aesthetics and design, originality and method, technology and form, memory and identity, and ethics and responsibility.

"Inclusive, richly conceived, visually and substantively informative—Denise Costanzo presents the beginning student of architecture with a deft presentation that weaves history and theory into a compelling saga that will both fascinate and inspire."

— Harry Francis Mallgrave, Distinguished Professor Emeritus,
Illinois Institute of Technology, USA

"*What Architecture Means* provides a three-dimensional view of the people, places, and powers of architecture—from its fundamental roles to its highest ambitions. Costanzo interweaves technical and pragmatic matters with aesthetics and ethics, provoking an exploration of the reader's own architectural interests, values, and aspirations."

— Korydon Smith, University at Buffalo,
State University of New York, USA

"Approachable and engaging, *What Architecture Means* offers readers the conceptual tools to investigate their own built environment and decide for themselves what architecture really means, and what it could aspire to for the future."

— A. Krista Sykes, PhD, author of The Architecture
Reader and Constructing A New Agenda, Cambridge, USA

"While most books on architecture tend to illuminate the subject by means of illustrations and descriptive texts alone, Denise Costanzo's profoundly revealing approach explores how conceptual thinking in design impacts on the final results. *What Architecture Means* looks at buildings and spaces from their sources of inspiration, the designer's intent, the culture's evaluation, and the user's response. This is an essential book for anyone who is curious about how human habitat is conceived and its significance."

— James Wines, President of SITE New York
and Professor of Architecture at Penn State University, USA

WHAT ARCHITECTURE MEANS

CONNECTING IDEAS AND DESIGN

DENISE COSTANZO

Routledge
Taylor & Francis Group

NEW YORK AND LONDON

To Vitruvius: Thanks for getting this conversation started.

First published 2016
by Routledge
711 Third Avenue, New York, NY 10017

and by Routledge
2 Park Square, Milton Park, Abingdon, Oxon OX14 4RN

Routledge is an imprint of the Taylor & Francis Group, an informa business

Library of Congress Cataloging in Publication Data
Costanzo, Denise, author.
What architecture means : connecting ideas and design / Denise
Costanzo.
pages cm
Includes bibliographical references and index.
1. Architecture. I. Title.
NA2550.C67 2015
720—dc23
2015002393

ISBN: 978-0-415-73903-0 (hbk)
ISBN: 978-0-415-73904-7 (pbk)
ISBN: 978-1-315-81694-4 (ebk)

Acquisition Editor: Wendy Fuller
Editorial Assistant: Grace Harrison
Production Editor: Hannah Champney

Typeset in Univers LT Std
by Swales & Willis Ltd, Exeter, Devon, UK

Printed and bound in the United States of America by Publishers Graphics,
LLC on sustainably sourced paper.

CONTENTS

ACKNOWLEDGMENTS

This book would not have come to fruition without the help and support of many people. Chief among these is Mehrdad Hadighi, chair of the Department of Architecture at the Pennsylvania State University. I thank Mehrdad for his initial enthusiasm regarding my approach to teaching an introductory course, and his instinct that it might become a book. He created the practical conditions for its realization in many ways, most generously by providing both teaching leave and financial support for otherwise prohibitive image research and publication rights. Both the illustrations and the project as a whole received additional, crucial support from Kelleann Foster, director of Penn State's Stuckeman School of Architecture and Landscape Architecture. Their encouragement, which took many forms, was indispensable to this book's timely completion.

Wendy Fuller and Grace Harrison at Routledge shepherded this project from a set of bloated lecture transcripts into a leaner and, I believe, more powerful discussion. I thank Wendy for her guidance and support through the early phases of this process. I also acknowledge the book proposal's many anonymous reviewers, whose reactions to the project were most incisive and helpful. Many thanks to Grace for both her much-needed editorial wisdom during rewriting, a task that felt like pruning a sequoia into a bonsai, and her faith in the ultimate outcome.

I am extremely grateful to Emma Brown for her expert image research and skilled navigation of the world of illustration rights on a scale I had never yet attempted. Like Grace, Emma both provided practical assistance and served as a much-needed discussant as I tackled numerous issues throughout this process. I also thank Matthew Underwood for providing beautiful and communicative drawings. They are crucial to the book's success as a tool for learning about architecture, and I thank him for the time and thought he dedicated to making them as effective as possible.

This book reflects how I teach, which has been profoundly shaped by my own teachers. Chief among these is Craig Zabel of Penn State's Department of Art History. Craig was instrumental in helping me discern a pedagogical goal of presenting "big ideas" in architecture. Besides his direct influence on my own understanding of the history and significance of the built environment, Craig provided an example of how to engage those new to architecture as a subject: with rigor, humor, and an astute eye for both design and the present moment.

Since first teaching the course that inspired this book, I have also received excellent help from many graduate teaching assistants, who have provided both practical support and helpful insights on the material. I thank one in particular, Aparna Parikh, who is an especially enthusiastic, informed, and invaluable interlocutor from whom I learned (and still learn) a great deal. Although too numerous to name individually, I also wish to thank the many students who have raised their hands, sought me out in person, or e-mailed comments, reactions, and questions (often with intriguing photographs attached) to discuss buildings and ideas with me over the years. Your interest in talking about architecture outside of class, and in applying the concepts we discussed to the buildings you encountered, demonstrated that this approach works.

Other students, current and former, in the Penn State Department of Architecture kindly read drafts of several chapters. Tim Annin, Mahsa Masoud, Bridget Novielli, Stephanie Rakiec, and Melanie Ray all provided extremely helpful suggestions and feedback. Rebecca Henn, my colleague in the Department of Architecture, also generously reviewed the chapter on power and politics. I thank her for her help; our discussions and her insights helped reshape and clarify its content and goals for the better. Henry Pisciotta and Tim AumAn of the Penn State Architecture and Landscape Architecture Library also offered much-needed, greatly appreciated research assistance.

I had the great pleasure of completing final work on the manuscript while on a fellowship at the American Academy in Rome. In addition to enjoying many beneficial conversations about this project with the community's astoundingly gifted artists and scholars, three of them, Claire Catenaccio, Marilynn Desmond, and Michelle DiMarzo, each read a chapter and provided much-appreciated thoughts.

My final, deepest thanks go to my husband, Francesco Costanzo, the primary source of my appreciation for the brilliance of engineers, and our two amazing sons, Gabriel and Gregory. I may not be entirely certain what architecture means, but I do know that you all make my life infinitely more meaningful.

PREFACE

Architecture is often introduced through (1) *architectural history*, which typically presents its development over time and as a facet of cultural history, or (2) *architectural appreciation*, which helps students understand and value the discipline's aesthetic and design goals. Both approaches are crucial for educating future architects, and can also greatly interest and benefit non-specialists. In addition, books on (3) *architectural theory* present the field's conceptual dimension, either as a gateway to the subject for new students or as a more advanced layer of knowledge that enriches, deepens, and activates prior learning.[1]

What Architecture Means: Connecting Ideas and Design incorporates aspects of all three of these approaches. It considers buildings' design and appearance; when, where, and by whom buildings were made; how they were used; whom they serve; and what concepts they embody. But it also turns the "answers" (straightforward or not) into issues that pose further architectural problems: Which beliefs and values should shape our built environment? What are the benefits, and the difficulties, that arise from emphasizing beauty, structure, or originality in design? How do we reconcile architecture's perpetual dependence on power with architects' ancient responsibility to construct healthy, stable societies? These questions all pivot around the architect's creative, professional, and cultural identity, blessed and cursed with what Rem Koolhaas has called "a poisonous mixture of power and impotence."[2]

The book's goal is distinct from those typical of architectural appreciation or history. Presenting what *should* be appreciated necessarily defines, however sensitively and convincingly, architectural quality from a position of authority. This absorbs, rather than questions, established notions of "good architecture." Architectural history overlaps with this issue by presenting buildings that are considered important, exemplary, or both. Historians typically embed their choices in a social, intellectual, and ideological context that often raises the same questions posed in this book. However, history necessarily emphasizes "What happened?" over "What should happen next?" While I am a historian, in this book I will pull the latter question into the foreground.

This is not because I offer a prescription for architecture's future—far from it. But I do believe that deciding what should be built next, and how, deserves participation by a wide constituency. I also believe that we should recognize how diffuse architectural awareness is, and let this inspire curiosity and involvement. We spend our lives living in and around buildings, making choices about them, being shaped by them. Architecture is both exotically esoteric and universally known—as mysterious and tangibly familiar as our own homes can be. An invitation to pay attention to architecture, to observe what the buildings shaping our world accomplish, to explore the motivations and assumptions behind their making, and to consider which of the many reasons for building we consider most valid can prepare any of us to take a more active, thoughtful role in architecture.

This book is intended to provide that opportunity. It asks how buildings reflect, embody, and communicate concepts and values, where those ideas come from, and what their strengths and weaknesses might be. The discussion is organized around a set of nine issues, each explored in a separate chapter. These are the idea that architecture (1) creates locations with a special, "higher" purpose; (2) defines private experience; (3) shapes human community; (4) is produced by certain people with particular knowledge and skills; (5) achieves certain aesthetic goals; (6) embodies creative, original ideas; (7) expresses its own construction; (8) belongs to a particular culture or place; and (9) serves certain people, or everyone.

Neither this list of issues nor my particular supporting examples are exhaustive. The latter in particular reflect my own training, which emphasized the architectural traditions of North America and their relationship with those in Western Europe. I would argue that because certain authors—Vitruvius, Alberti, Laugier, Ruskin, and Le Corbusier among them—contributed to a model of the architect that has now attained global reach, their ideas are indispensable to a full understanding of the contemporary discipline. Apart from such key figures, however, each chapter-length theme could be explored just as effectively using buildings, architects, time periods, and locations entirely different from those included here. My hope is simply to provide a discussion that can serve as a foundation for far broader and richer ones that extend further than my own knowledge or this book's length permits. Ideally, these specific themes will also inspire an exploration of many others.

What Architecture Means has two goals: (1) to help everyone involved in architecture—as design professionals, collaborators, clients, consumers, and citizens—understand how buildings embody varying, often conflicting, sets of values; and (2) to help readers clarify their own beliefs about what "good" architecture is. What makes any building valuable is its ability to serve and express a complex matrix of needs, beliefs, and desires; some of these are clear, even quantifiable, whereas we may struggle to express others in any form of language. Accomplishing this is architecture's great challenge, and its glory. I hope this book will help you discern your own beliefs about what architecture should be, inspire you to look and learn more, and equip you to help make our built environment as good as it can be, for as many people as possible.

NOTES

1 In recent years, the architecture theory literature for introductory readers has been enriched by a number of excellent texts, including those by Fil Hearn, Krista Sykes, Colin Davies, and Rowan Moore (see bibliography).

2 Rem Koolhaas, lecture at Columbia University, 1989, cited by Shuman Basar, "The Poisonous Mixture," in A. Krista Sykes, ed., *The Architecture Reader: Essential Writings from Vitruvius to the Present* (New York: George Braziller, 2007), p. 317.

INTRODUCTION
WHAT IS "ARCHITECTURE"?

BEFORE INVESTIGATING WHAT ARCHITECTURE might mean in a broader sense, we should ask what we mean by "architecture" as a category. You probably have ideas about this already; consider what descriptive words or phrases come to mind, and write them down. How many would apply to the structure in Figure 0.1?

There are many reasons to call the Guggenheim art museum in Bilbao, Spain, "architecture": It is by a world-famous architect, Frank Gehry. Its design is distinctive and memorable. As a cultural institution, it serves a dignified public

FIGURE 0.1 Frank Gehry, Guggenheim Museum, Bilbao, Spain, 1997.

function. The building has also been influential: Locally, it anchored a decaying city's revitalization and made Bilbao a magnet for tourism. Globally, it inspired dozens of cities around the world to commission flamboyant new buildings from famous architects, hoping to mimic its success (the "Bilbao effect").

SELECTIVE DEFINITIONS OF ARCHITECTURE

Most of us would probably consider the Guggenheim Bilbao "architecture." We often use this word for buildings that are important or special. The twentieth-century architectural historian Nikolaus Pevsner started one of his books by declaring: "A bicycle shed is a building; Lincoln Cathedral is a piece of architecture."[1] His confident sentence sets up two categories: "building" and "architecture." Lincoln Cathedral is obviously a building, so Pevsner certainly does not mean that works of architecture are not buildings. Rather, he establishes a **hierarchy** between "mere" buildings and a subset of structures that are *better* than others—"architecture." Pevsner offers a **selective definition** of architecture.

Lincoln Cathedral suggests what this category's distinguishing qualities might be. Although Figure 0.2 shows many buildings, we can guess (correctly) that Lincoln Cathedral is the enormous one looming over smaller surrounding structures. Like Bilbao, Lincoln is large in scale—the biggest building in town—with tall

FIGURE 0.2   Lincoln Cathedral, Lincoln, England, 1185–1311.

towers and pointed triangular forms (spires) and richly carved surfaces. Its profile, window shapes, and steep roof pitch are different in **style** than the brick houses in the foreground. Its yellowish-gray color derives from another *material*, stone. All these set the cathedral apart from its **context**. All this implies that "real architecture" is visually distinctive: its scale, style, and material claim our attention and mark a building as special.

Large size implies cultural importance. When it was built from 1185 to 1311, Lincoln Cathedral could contain most of the city's people. Time also adds distinction: the cathedral took almost 130 years to build and has stood for over 700 years. If this church were lost, Britons would lose a connection to their past. Such an object is called a **monument**, a word derived from the Latin word for "memory." Age also provides **authenticity**. To enter Lincoln and touch its stone details connects us to the medieval craftsmen who carved them eight centuries ago. If the church were destroyed and a replica were built in its place, that link would be broken. Similarly, if it were carefully disassembled and rebuilt elsewhere, it would not be the same. Here, "authenticity" implies continuity of place and substance over time.

Pevsner used a building with impressive visual and cultural credentials to embody "architecture." His example begins a book on European architecture, but this category applies to works around the world, like the Taj Mahal (see Figure 0.3). Like Lincoln, the Taj is large, and its towers, domes, and arched niches give it a distinctive, recognizable appearance. Its marble exterior is adorned with colorful, intricately carved inlay. Here too, scale, style, and material all distinguish the building

FIGURE 0.3   Taj Mahal, Agra, India, 1632–1653.

from its context and mark it as special. Its cultural importance is also clear: travelers journey from around the globe to visit this centuries-old authentic monument. Now that it is a World Heritage Site, its loss would be mourned globally.

While the Taj Mahal and Lincoln Cathedral both fit Pevsner's definition of "architecture," they fulfill his criteria differently. The Taj is the focus of a coordinated complex of buildings and gardens, bordered by a river, enclosing walls and gateways that frame our view as we approach. In contrast, Lincoln stands within an irregular urban context. We can glimpse it through city streets, but the entire building is visible only up close, or from afar. Both also share garden settings; Lincoln Cathedral's yard has an irregularly shaped perimeter that is open to its urban context. Apart from the meandering river, however, the Taj Mahal's entire setting is perfectly symmetrical and geometric. The building is raised on a podium, and the towers at its corners define a "box" of space that sets it apart from its surroundings.

These are all *formal* features: qualities we can see. They suggest differences in *design history*. The Taj Mahal's consistency and discipline imply a coherent plan; in fact, the complex was built in about twenty years under one team of architects. Lincoln's irregularity reflects a gradual evolution over many phases and centuries as church and town adapted to each other over time.

Historic information clarifies what memories these "monuments" preserve. Lincoln was begun by a French-born bishop who imported a foreign style, now called "Gothic." However, local builders reinterpreted the French model in ways later celebrated as "English." Lincoln became an emblem of British cultural identity persisting against Continental influence. The Taj Mahal's style, reflecting the architecture of seventeenth-century Persia, was also imported. The project was commissioned by a Mughal shah, part of a Muslim dynasty from central Asia ruling a Hindu population. While the Taj is now a symbol of modern India, it is also a reminder of a centuries-old cultural division.

Lincoln Cathedral also preserves memories of religious schism. When it was built, all of Western Europe was Catholic, but during the sixteenth-century Protestant Reformation Britain became religiously divided and suffered decades of civil war. Originally a Catholic church, Lincoln Cathedral now belongs to the Protestant Church of England. It too carries memories of conflict and changes in religious identity.

If visually distinctive buildings that carry important cultural memories clearly fulfill Pevsner's definition, what about the opposite end of his spectrum? A selective definition means we must exclude certain buildings. So what disqualifies a building as "architecture"? A convenient stand-in for Pevsner's bicycle shed is the sort of garden tool shed sold at home improvement stores. Would that meet any of your own criteria for architecture? It could: these sheds enclose enough space to contain people. Many have symmetrical designs and even sport ornamental details.

Many sheds are also tiny and made of plastic—an industrial, cheap, everyday material. Hundreds, perhaps thousands, of identical copies are made each year. They are not special, unique, or hand-crafted buildings but mass-produced, factory-made consumer goods, like plastic soda bottles. Most lack visual distinction and serve a **utilitarian** instead of a culturally significant purpose. No shed is more authentic than any other, and—unless something truly newsworthy happens there—none is likely to become a monument. However perfect for stowing lawn mowers, tool sheds represent a different "class" of building than a Gothic cathedral.

But we might decide to splurge a bit. Fancier mass-produced tool sheds feature wood siding, more substantial roofs, and decorative details. Given the budget, skilled builders could create a tiny Taj Mahal for tools. How much extra dignity turns "non-architecture" into architecture? That would be very hard to decide. Although a selective definition reflects distinctions we make between noble and humble buildings, marking a boundary between these categories is harder than identifying extremes on a spectrum. We must either judge for ourselves or rely on a *critic* who sorts for us. Someone must draw the line separating "architecture" from regular buildings.

A "UNIVERSAL" DEFINITION

What if we want discussions about architecture to also include "non-special" buildings? One way is through a category called **vernacular architecture**. "Vernacular" describes everyday speech, versus official or specialized language. It defines a category of buildings that are not unique or special, but can certainly have an important impact. A suburban big-box store, however large, is no Taj Mahal. But measured in terms of cultural, economic, and environmental impact, it can represent a far more important form of architecture.

Another case is the Neolithic city of Çatal Hüyük in Turkey, over 8,000 years old. It had no big, distinctive buildings, but does this mean it had no architecture? We could say that the city as a whole, built like a honeycomb of similar cells, is itself architecturally significant. The absence of prominent structures is itself important evidence about Çatal Hüyük's culture. Every building is valuable and informative, although any 8,000-year-old human artifact is rare and thus important.

Figure 0.4 shows a **favela**, a neighborhood on the outskirts of Rio de Janeiro. These houses are not ancient but recent. They are not built by famous architects but usually constructed out of scavenged materials by the people who live there, usually illegally. Most are migrants from the countryside drawn to jobs in a city where housing is unavailable or unaffordable.

Are favelas "architecture"? They might prove far more interesting than cathedrals if we study how buildings can demonstrate human initiative, reflect

FIGURE 0.4   Favela outside Rio de Janeiro, Brazil.

changing demographic conditions, and enact social and economic transformation. Ironically, like the Guggenheim Bilbao, favelas have become major tourist attractions. Busloads of visitors come to see these areas, now famous for generating much of what makes Brazilian culture vibrant.

We could call favelas vernacular architecture, or we might find this distinction unnecessary. Why not simply call all buildings "architecture"—a **universalist definition**? How we define architecture reflects our perspective and priorities. A universalist view is natural for people who study connections between people and buildings, like archaeologists, sociologists, and economists. An all-inclusive view of architecture is also very democratic, because it considers whatever buildings might be important to each of us. A critic might not label my house "architecture," but its design structures my life more than any famous museum. Our homes, schools, neighborhoods, workplaces, and shopping and entertainment venues are usually the most influential architecture we experience.

BUILDINGS, OR NOT?

A universal definition directs attention to all buildings, but it also generates too much material to easily process. Whether we prefer the selective or universal approach, at least we can all agree that architecture is about buildings—physical structures and spaces that people can inhabit. Or is it? Does it have to exist physically? There are many "buildings" we know only from descriptions, drawings, or photos. Some used to exist physically, like the Seven Wonders of the Ancient World, of which only one survives (the Great Pyramids of Giza). But the design of another, the Lighthouse at Alexandria, has been reconstructed using images on coins and later lighthouses that probably imitated it. A work of architecture can survive in words, images, and copies long after the building vanishes.

Architectural images and documents also reflect how buildings are made. Many begin as an idea in someone's mind, which is translated into a graphic image. That initial idea is often developed and revised. The resulting building is usually executed by another group of people. It might then be adapted years later for new conditions: cathedrals can become offices or condominiums.

Drawings, photographs, verbal accounts, and models can document phases of development that help clarify how the final building came to be—like a medal showing one vision for St. Peter's basilica in Rome (see Figure 0.5). They can also show architecture that was never built in any form. Actual buildings require legal permission, money, and reliable construction methods; experimental mistakes are catastrophic. Developing new building ideas is usually much faster, easier, and cheaper in drawings and models. **Paper architecture** (whether on paper or not) often holds the most daring design experimentations of any period and can provide important insights into what real buildings are meant to achieve.

FIGURE 0.5   Medal depicting Bramante's design of St. Peter's, 1506.

Digital visualization tools blur the distinctions between real and imaginary architecture even further. Creators of films, video games, and other immersive media create ever-more convincingly simulated objects and environments that can seem almost as real as the spaces we inhabit physically. Architects use the same tools to create virtual architecture, which allows us to "see" buildings before any ground is broken. Can virtual architecture fulfill your criteria for architecture?

REAL NON-BUILDINGS

You may limit your definition of architecture to structures you can touch. But even tangible, constructed projects can be difficult to define. The Vietnam Veterans Memorial in Washington, DC (see Figure 0.6), is a physical, built work. It has become as significant a monument to many Americans as Lincoln Cathedral or the Taj Mahal. Like them, it is a site of pilgrimage that preserves the memory of conflict and a shift in a nation's cultural identity.

The memorial was designed by Maya Lin, who was still an architecture student at Yale when she won the competition. But it is not a building: it has no roof, or enclosure, just a pathway along a reflective granite surface carved with the names of the dead. The visitor walks alongside this stone wall, descending deeper into the earth, then gradually returns to ground level. While not a building, the memorial uses an architectural vocabulary of movement, surface, material, site, and form to build a commemorative experience through design. Lin's design and her later practice bridge multiple categories: landscape architecture, sculpture, and environmental art. But if architecture meets human needs and expresses cultural identity through construction, her memorial might qualify, building or not.

Architecture occupies an intersection of technology and culture. Like bridges and automobiles, it applies knowledge to meet human goals through design and construction. But those goals are often intangible; architecture at

FIGURE 0.6   Maya Lin, Vietnam Veterans Memorial, Washington, DC, 1981.

any scale can embody beliefs and ideals, express identity, or preserve and manage memories. This is why understanding it is such a complex task. What we observe in stone and metal, on paper or a digital screen, can reflect many things: faith, family, or community; one designer's vision and ideas about beauty and creativity; a particular culture's technological resources, its distribution of power, and views of justice. One work of architecture can be about any or all of these things at once.

Architecture is also a set of ideas about what makes buildings meaning-ful. Exploring these involves a wide range of other subjects—religion, sociology, art, science, history, and philosophy, to name a few. Our discussion will not be exhaustive (an impossible goal), but simply introduce several ways architecture's value can be, and has been, defined. Some may reflect your current ideas; some may be new. You may discover new support for your existing beliefs, or reasons to question them, or appealing ideas you never considered before. In my view, any of these outcomes would make your experience with this book a success.

Defining architecture and discerning our own beliefs about this phenom-enon requires conceptual work. This falls under the category of **theory**. We often use this to mean an explanation based on evidence, or an abstract form of knowl-edge (versus "practice"). A theory is also a "picture" from a distance that reveals how things relate overall. This comes closest to the term's original Greek meaning, as "an observed view." When we step back to make sense of complex informa-tion, ask big questions, and perceive the big picture, we do theory.

All three of these meanings are relevant as we explore architecture as an idea, using ideas as analytical tools. Your initial list of qualities is very important—not because it is right or wrong; this book, unlike Pevsner's book, will never declare what "real architecture" is or is not. It offers a starting point as you develop your own ideas about what architecture means.

VOCABULARY

authenticity, context, favela, hierarchy, monument, paper architecture, selective definition, style, theory, universalist definition, utilitarian, vernacular architecture.

STUDY AND REVIEW QUESTIONS

1. List three reasons why the Guggenheim Museum in Bilbao might be considered "architecture" instead of "just" a building.
2. How does Pevsner's distinction between Lincoln Cathedral and a bicycle shed construct a selective definition of architecture?

3. Describe three architectural similarities and differences between Lincoln Cathedral and the Taj Mahal.
4. Give two examples of "formal" characteristics in architecture.
5. What is the connection between an architectural "monument" and memory?
6. Using Pevsner's bicycle shed example, what might make a building *non-*architecture?
7. How does a selective definition of architecture create the role of critic or judge?
8. Why might some people prefer to categorize all buildings as architecture? Does that have any disadvantages?
9. Why might non-buildings—images, models, descriptions, or built environments—belong in conversations about architecture?
10. Describe the three different views of "theory," and how each might apply to architecture.

NOTE

1 Nikolaus Pevsner, *An Outline of European Architecture* (New York: C. Scribner's Sons, 1948), p. xvi.

FURTHER READING

Freire-Medeiros, Bianca. "The Favela and Its Touristic Transits." *Geoforum* 40, 4 (July 2009): 580–588.

Ling, Bettina. *Maya Lin.* Austin, TX: Raintree Steck-Vaughn, 1997.

Pevsner, Nikolaus. *An Outline of European Architecture.* New York: C. Scribner's Sons, 1948.

Rybczynski, Witold. "The Bilbao Effect." *Atlantic Monthly* (September 2002).

Verma, Som Prakash. *Taj Mahal.* Oxford: Oxford University Press, 2012.

PART I
WHERE IS ARCHITECTURE?
DIVINITY, DOMESTICITY, COMMUNITY

CHAPTER 1
SACRED SPACES

ARCHITECTURAL HISTORIAN NIKOLAUS PEVSNER deliberately illustrated his definition of "architecture" with a religious structure. The designs of many buildings created for spiritual purposes, including Pevsner's example, Lincoln Cathedral, announce their function as not just practical, but special: they are built to be sacred.

We often associate sacredness with faith, but it also exists outside religious contexts. The 2001 attack on the World Trade Center in New York that destroyed its two office towers also gave them new meaning. The loss of thousands of lives, obliteration of a city's tallest structures, and assault on a proud nation's confidence changed its site into a place of profound significance for millions of people. Such traumatic events can make a place sacred; if the trauma is collective, the sacredness becomes not just personal, but cultural.

The 9/11 Memorial by Michael Arad and Peter Walker was built to express that depth of meaning. It transformed the Twin Towers' footprints into two vast

FIGURE 1.1   Michael Arad and Peter Walker, *Reflecting Absence*, 9/11 Memorial, New York, NY, November 2004.

cubic voids. Water flows from quiet perimeter pools into cascades that crash down the cubes' sides before vanishing into an abyss. Like the Vietnam Veterans Memorial (see introduction), the design leads visitors through a garden, carves simple forms into the earth, uses somber black granite, and emphasizes the names of the lost.

Both memorials also use an abstract design vocabulary instead of one drawn from religious architecture. This reflects a more diverse, secular U.S. culture. We readily associate Lincoln Cathedral's Gothic style with Christianity, but our individual beliefs help determine whether we experience sacredness in that church. Because people of many faiths and no faith died at the World Trade Center, a memorial emphasizing any one religious tradition would not represent all the victims. Its design instead expresses death, loss, and memory through methods that begin in prehistory, and recur in multiple forms of religious architecture.

READING STONES: PREHISTORIC DESIGN

We express sacredness through many different things—foods, rituals, words, symbols, music. Architecture can declare that a place has special significance through constructions as elaborate as Lincoln Cathedral, or as simple as a single stone. Near Carnac, in northwestern France, an enormous, upright **megalith**—a large stone—rises almost 30 feet (9 meters) above the ground; its total weight is estimated at 150 tons (136,000 kilograms). This **menhir** is one of many vertical megaliths whose position was not caused by natural forces, but is the product of design and construction. The Kerloas menhir was erected by prehistoric humans, probably 5,000 to 8,000 years ago. It originally stood even higher (some height was lost to lightning); another fallen menhir nearby was twice as tall.

We naturally wonder how Neolithic people made a 150-ton stone stand up. Our next question is probably: why? Unlike Lincoln Cathedral or the Taj Mahal, no other explanatory evidence exists. But we can infer that this location was deeply significant to its builders. People invested enormous energy and ingenuity to ensure that this particular spot would be noticed for as long as this stone endures.

Some might not consider one standing stone (or many—some menhirs are arranged in groups) to be "architecture" because it does not enclose space. But other megalithic structures do: **dolmens**, in which upright stones support a horizontal one. A menhir occupies one spot, but a dolmen defines the volume around a spot; a person can occupy that special point.

Over 30,000 dolmens survive on the Korean peninsula. Unlike Kerloas, memories of their use survive. Most were shrines where families performed rites honoring their ancestors. This, along with a form which resembles a doorway, even a rudimentary house, suggests certain meanings: a gate dividing the living from

FIGURE 1.2   Ganghwa Dolmen, Bugeun-ri, Hajeom-myeon, South Korea, first millennium BCE.

the dead, or a home where an earthly family can meet relatives living on as memory and spirit.

The Poulnabroune dolmen in Ireland is similarly linked to death and memory. Over twenty sets of human remains were found there, which explains this site's sacredness: any place we bury someone's body becomes invested with their memory. Carbon dating shows that the remains belonged to multiple generations, and archaeological evidence shows the builders practiced agriculture. Farming cultures are naturally attached to the land that sustains them. When a community buries its dead in one location over many years, this further connects who they are to where they live. The Poulnabroune dolmen was originally an entry and burial chamber for a **barrow**, an artificial hill made by piling stones into an enormous, earth-covered mound. Such tombs were also visible landmarks that announced the people's ownership of the land, and gave them another reason to defend it.

STONEHENGE: GEOMETRY, ORIENTATION, AND MEANING

The British Isles' most famous megalithic structure is Stonehenge, the largest, most elaborate Neolithic monument still standing. Its megaliths are smaller than the Kerloas menhir. The largest of these sarsen stones is about 24 feet (7.3 meters) tall and weighs 50 tons (45,000 kilograms); the others average 25 tons (22,600 kilograms) each. Their geological source was 19 miles (30 kilometers) away. Eighty dolerite "bluestones" weighing up to 4 tons (3,600 kilograms) each were also transported over 150 miles (240 kilometers) from their source in Wales. Obtaining

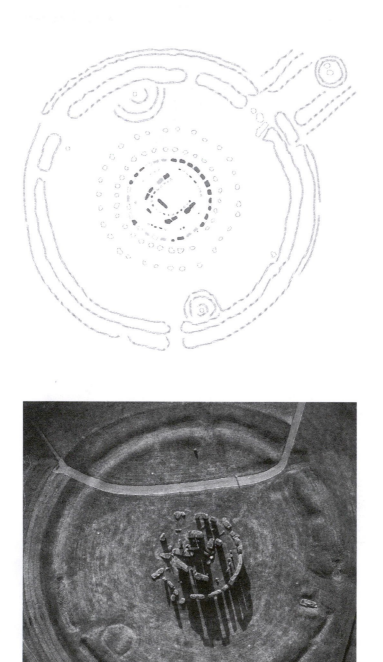

FIGURE 1.3   Stonehenge, Wiltshire, England, ca. 2600–1600 BCE.

these materials and coordinating the site's construction were enormous logistical and technological undertakings.

Although these megaliths appear irregular, they were shaped with tools. The vertical stones each have a small knob on top (a **tenon**) meant to slip into a corresponding hole (a **mortise**) in a lintel stone. The lintels were connected laterally with tongue-and-groove joints to form a continuous ring. Such interlocking details stabilized the construction, but demanded precision stonework along with heavy lifting.

Archaeological research has reconstructed much of the site's long, complex history. Stonehenge was built in three major phases over more than a thousand years. Its first phase consisted of wooden structures and a circular ditch with a gap toward the northeast, plus a series of small, chalk-filled holes just inside (called "Aubrey holes," after the first person to document them). Centuries later, builders added an inner circle of bluestones. Finally, a perimeter ring with a continuous lintel was built using the sarsen stones, and five **trilithons** (two vertical megaliths supporting a horizontal one) were arranged in a U-shape at the center. The bluestones were then rearranged into a circle and horseshoe that mirrored the sarsen forms.

These design phases were all concentric: their circular forms, including the U-shape's curve, all shared one center, just above the so-called "altar stone." But the U's straight sides also define a parallel line through that center: an **axis**. This axis aligns with the ditch's gap, a fallen stone inside the ditch (the so-called "slaughter stone"), and another farther out (the "heel stone").

During every phase, Stonehenge's geometry pointed in two directions: inward, toward the circle's center, and outward from that center along the axis. This line conveys movement—a path. Center and path combined suggest a procession, a ceremonial journey to and from this significant spot. The axis also points in two astronomically significant directions: the point on the horizon where the sun rises on the summer solstice, the longest day of the year and, viewed in reverse, the point of midwinter sunset. Both mark when the sun's annual cycle changes direction, as increasing darkness becomes increasing light, and back again. For agrarian people, knowing when to plant and harvest is crucial for survival, so accurate prediction of seasonal changes was vital information. Ancient farmers experienced celestial bodies and weather patterns as powerful forces, arbiters of life and death.

Stonehenge's link to death was reinforced when archaeologists discovered over 200 sets of human remains in the Aubrey holes. They were buried over a period of 500 years, mostly during the phase of sarsen stone construction. Nearby remains of a circular wooden settlement date to this same period, and probably housed Stonehenge's builders. The similar forms suggest they were "twin" cities, for the living and the dead. Taken together, Stonehenge's geometry, the monumental construction effort involved, the length of time it was used, and the functions it seems to accommodate—ritual, burial, and cosmically linked ones—all confirm that this site was deeply sacred to early Britons.

One question we cannot answer about Stonehenge is: why there? Whatever feature or event motivated a millennium of construction in that precise location is lost to us. Such questions are answerable only for *historic* cultures, those whose stories have survived in writings or oral traditions that help explain their beliefs. These can sometimes confirm the sacredness of certain structures and explain their use, choice of location, and design strategies.

THE ACROPOLIS: STORIES IN STONE

Ancient Greeks, like prehistoric Britons, marked sacred sites with elaborate stone architecture. The most famous is the *Acropolis* (meaning "high city" in Greek) in Athens. Prehistoric inhabitants had settled on this defensible hilltop for safety. Later, it housed and protected signs of the city's relationship with the divine.

The Acropolis is a **temenos**, a sanctuary surrounded by a wall. Stonehenge's circles define spatial boundaries, but the Acropolis' encircling wall creates a literal separation. Its main entrance is a monumental gateway, the Propylaea (Figure 1.4, photo; below, at center). Inside, several temples stand as free-standing objects. The most famous are the enormous Parthenon (at right in photo; see also Figure 4.2) and the smaller Erechtheion (left). Between them lie the foundations of another destroyed temple.

This site, like Stonehenge, was modified many times over many centuries. But Greek writings explain what made this hilltop sacred: here the city forged its special relationship with Athena, goddess of wisdom, through a divine contest. She and Poseidon, god of the sea, competed to be the city's patron. Each offered a gift: Poseidon a salt spring, Athena an olive tree. After the people preferred Athena's gift and named their city in her honor, the spring and the tree were preserved as relics of the gods' presence, holy sites on a holy mountain.

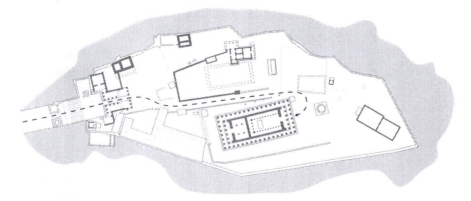

FIGURE 1.4   Acropolis, Athens, rebuilt fifth century BCE.

FIGURE 1.4 *(continued)*

The Erechtheion was built to honor those relics. It also replaced the temple of Athena Polias ("Athena of the City"), formerly the Acropolis' most sacred building, which housed a precious wooden image of Athena. In 480 BCE, the Persians destroyed this temple and its sacred image along with the entire Acropolis, a devastating loss to the city. When they rebuilt, the Athenians commemorated the Polias' destruction by *not* rebuilding it. Like the World Trade Center, its footprint became an empty, honored void.

The Acropolis was the destination of the Panathenaic ("across Athens") procession, an annual ritual to celebrate Athena's birthday. On that festival day, the public could enter the temenos through the Propylaea. Their processional route (dotted line on the plan in Figure 1.4) passed between the Polias Temple site and the Parthenon, and stopped outside the Parthenon's main door on its far side, facing east. The orientation (literally, "pointing east") is significant: Greek temples usually faced east toward the sunrise, the realm of the gods. Entering the Acropolis was a journey from the west, the mortal world, into the divine.

The Acropolis' temples were sacred spaces, but not public spaces; most Athenians never stepped inside. Public worship involved sacrificing and burning oxen on outdoor altars—a messy undertaking best conducted outdoors. But a Greek temple's inaccessibility, like controlled access to the Acropolis, contributed to its sacredness. Restricting who can enter a space makes it *exclusive*—significant because of who is excluded—and more special.

A Greek temple's exteriors, however, were designed for the public eye. Their decorative sculpture retold sacred stories. The Parthenon's western **pediment** (the triangular end of a gable roof) showed Poseidon and Athena's competition for the city, its eastern pediment Athena's birth. A sculpted **frieze** (horizontal strip of imagery) crowning on the inner wall under its porch depicted the Panathenaic procession, proudly immortalizing the citizens' own ritual on the sacred building.

The Parthenon's vast interior was not built for crowds, but it did contain something colossal: a 40-foot-tall statue of Athena. The temple was a house for the goddess, on a scale worthy of her power. The statue, covered in gold leaf and elephant ivory, cost more than the temple; both were extravagant proof of the city's devotion. On her birthday, Athenians could glimpse their glittering goddess through the doorway. The rest of the year, Athena's hilltop home was visible throughout the city, a constant reminder of her protection.

ARTIFICIAL MOUNTAINS: PYRAMIDS AND BARRIERS

Divine powers are often associated with the sky, humanity with the earth's surface. Stories about encounters between people and gods frequently take place on mountaintops, an intermediate realm. The association of elevation with sacredness even led some cultures in flat landscapes to construct artificial mountains. These include ancient Sumerian ziggurats in Babylon and Ur (modern Baghdad), and pyramids by the Mayans, Aztecs, and other Mesoamerican cultures. Like the Acropolis, they were temple platforms, meant to be climbed during religious ceremonies, with stairways built into their exterior surfaces.

Such artificial mountains include the Great Pyramids at Giza, whose height stands in dramatic contrast to the flat Nile river valley. Today they can be climbed because their outer layer of smooth white limestone was removed over the centuries (some remains at the peak of Khafre's pyramid). But ancient Egyptian pyramids had no exterior stairs and a pointed apex. They were not temple platforms but—like barrows—tombs for Egyptian kings, or pharaohs.

Monuments to powerful individuals, they were also spiritual instruments for the community. Ancient Egyptian religion taught that if a pharaoh's body was properly, permanently preserved through mummification and a secure tomb, he could join the gods in the afterlife and protect his people. Pyramids were investments in public welfare. Mummification involved multiple ritual phases in different settings, and royal tombs were architectural complexes with spaces for a sequence of sacred rites. Giza's mortuary temples were east of the pyramids, on the Nile's western banks, connected to them by pathways.

Pyramid-building stopped because all were robbed, so they failed to provide safety. Later, the tomb of Hatshepsut, a rare female pharaoh, was carved into an existing mountain, an elaborate mortuary temple built into its face. The Great Pyramids and Hatshepsut's tomb are a millennium apart, but both buried the royal body within a protective mountain, the culmination of an elaborate ritual and architectural journey into immortality.

They also share a spiritual understanding of geography. Ancient Egyptians saw the Nile River, their source of life, as a boundary separating the living and the dead. Its eastern bank was for earthly life, the western bank for the afterlife. A funereal journey west across the river, following the sun's path into the night, was a momentous "crossing over" from one realm to the other.

Architectural boundaries, including different vertical levels, walls, and gateways, can distinguish between the sacred and the profane—literally, "outside the temple." Temples to Egyptian gods marked their entrances with a **pylon**, a solid, trapezoidal wall covered with sacred imagery. Its imposing bulk makes crossing the threshold into the Temple of Amun at Karnak a momentous, dramatic act.

FIGURE 1.5   Temple of Amun, Karnak, Egypt, begun ca. 1550 BCE.

Behind the pylon is an enclosed open court containing another pylon at its far side. Beyond its gateway lies a forest of enormous stone **columns** (a **hypostyle hall**). This leads to another pylon, then another, and another (six pylons in all). Their multiple, axially aligned doorways lead to the temple's most sacred space, its innermost sanctuary—the most protected from the outside world. These accumulated barriers construct a journey deeper into the sacred. Every crossed threshold brings further separation from the everyday, and greater proximity to the divine. Each door also admitted fewer and fewer people, with the innermost sanctuary accessible only to the priestly elite. The more socially exclusive the space, the greater its spiritual importance.

Building designs manifest a culture's ideas about how reality should be ordered. The hieratic divisions in ancient Egyptian and Greek religious architecture mirror their powerful priesthoods. In both cultures, organized religious professionals controlled sacred spaces and managed the relationship between the people and the divine.

HINDUISM AND THE TEMPLE

In south Asia, religious architecture helped change religious practice, as belief systems that originally relied on human leaders became more focused on spiritually charged sites and spaces. One is Hinduism, among the world's oldest active religious traditions. This diverse family of faiths and practices all share sacred texts, the *vedas*, which are over 4,000 years old. The early "Vedic" period lasted until the first century BCE, when new practices emerged.

The earliest Hindu temples coincide with this shift. The Vedic priesthood that managed rituals at outdoor altars declined, and use of home shrines increased, as did temple construction and worship. Most forms of Hindu observance cultivate a relationship with a deity through personal devotion in both locations.

Like the Parthenon, a Hindu temple or **mandir** ("house" in Sanskrit) provided a home for a god. The mandir's site was chosen through divination, a ritual that analyzed a potential site's soil, geography, and the stars to ensure the god would feel welcome. The Kandariya Mahadeva at Khajuraho, like the Parthenon, is an imposing stone building with exterior sculpture narrating stories about its god. Its exterior form features a range of irregular peaks, culminating in one dominant, parabolic tower. Hindu gods dwell inside mountains, so such forms evoked the divinity's original home by design.

One peak rises significantly higher than the others: the **shikara**. It corresponds to the temple's most important space beneath, its most honored sanctuary. This contains a statue of the god, and its height, like the Parthenon's size, might accommodate a large interior volume. But the temple's name, which means "cave of Shiva" (one of Hinduism's four chief deities), hints at the sanctuary's character.

FIGURE 1.6   Kandariya Mahadeva Temple, Khajuraho, India, 1025–1050.

Like a cave, it is enclosed and small, protected by the shikara's bulk. The inner sanctum's importance is achieved through contrast with a soaring exterior form.

Like at Karnak, the Kandariya Mahadeva constructs a journey through a sequence of rooms, aligned along a single axis with the main door facing east. Upon arrival, visitors remove their shoes, bow, and touch the threshold to honor entry into the sacred precinct. Access to spaces is also limited by caste and gender, reflecting social hierarchies. Inside the innermost shrine, the devotee meditates, prays, circumambulates (walks around the sacred image, usually clockwise), recites scriptures, and offers the god flowers or food.

The floor plans of many Hindu temples feature overlapping square and circular forms. These refer to the **mandala**, a sacred composition of circles and squares that symbolize the (square) earth, with its four corners, elements, and cardinal directions, and (circular) heaven, perfect, balanced, and eternal. The mandala diagrams the cosmic order, constructing a spiritualized space where heaven and earth, human and divine, intersect—precisely what a temple is built to achieve.

BUDDHIST SHRINES: THE STUPA AND PAGODA

Several religions born in India, including Hinduism, believe the soul is eternal, but goes through repeated cycles of life, death, and rebirth. These include Buddhism, which redefined the meaning of earthly suffering and offers believers a way to escape the cycle.

Buddhism originated with one historic individual. Siddhartha Gautama, a sixth-century BCE prince, lived a privileged, sheltered, and complacent life until he saw his first glimpse of human misery. Its effect was transformative: he rejected all earthly comforts, moving from extreme luxury to self-deprivation. Years later, Siddhartha had a revelation while meditating beneath a tree in a walled garden: true wisdom is found in neither pleasure nor suffering, but through a "middle way" of balance and detachment from this world. Such enlightenment allows the spirit to let go of the earth, escape the cycles of life and death, and achieve nirvana, complete spiritual freedom. Siddhartha's disciples called him the "Buddha," meaning "enlightened one."

Early Buddhist practice did not require any specific architecture. After Siddhartha's death, however, his followers divided his ashes and buried them where key events in his life took place. One was Sanchi, in north-central India. A small brick commemorative mound built over his remains was protected by a **chatra**, a canopy and traditional sign of honor.

Centuries later, this shrine was enlarged by the Emperor Ashoka into a stone **stupa**. Its hemispherical form resembles Neolithic barrows; like Egyptian pyramids, it has regular geometry and solid stone construction. All mark significant burial sites with an artificial, sacred mountain. The stupa contains no chambers; it is a solid object providing a focus for worship, like a cult statue. Monks climb stairs to a path partway up the hemisphere, protected by a wall, and circumambulate, chant, and pray.

On top of the stupa are a **harmika**, a square fence symbolizing the enclosure where the Buddha received enlightenment, and a three-tiered **chatra**—both an honorific canopy, and the tree he sat beneath. Its vertical pole marks an axis connecting the Buddha's ashes at the hemisphere's center to heaven above and the earth below.

FIGURE 1.7   Great Stupa, Sanchi, India, 250 BCE–250 CE (photo with inset plan).

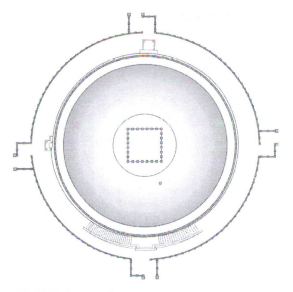

FIGURE 1.7   (continued)

A solid wall surrounds the stupa, with tall open gateways called **toranas** at its four entrances. In plan, the circles of the outer wall, hemisphere, chatra, and raised path dominate. But the harmika and the four toranas define squares with a common orientation, a few degrees off the cardinal directions (this angle remains unexplained, but perhaps had cosmic significance). While the Great Stupa's design is entirely different from a Hindu temple, both share inspiration in the mandala's sacred geometry. Buddhists use mandalas as a visual focus during meditation, and the stupa's geometry similarly defines a spiritual space entered through prayer.

Growing Buddhist communities eventually needed large interior spaces for group worship. These typically used a sculpted image of the Buddha as a focus for processions and meditation. While similar to the cult image in a Hindu temple's sanctum, or the Parthenon's Athena, the Buddha was not worshipped as a powerful divinity, but venerated, shown special respect for revealing the path to enlightenment.

Born in the Indian subcontinent, Buddhism spread most widely across China, Korea, and Japan, where its architectural vocabulary evolved. The Buddhist temple precinct in Hōryū-ji near Nara, Japan, looks quite different from Sanchi. At the center of its rectangular sanctuary are two buildings: a **kondo** ("golden hall") on the right, and a tall tower with multiple layered roofs: a **pagoda**. Its stacked roofs are a memory of the three-layered chatra, or umbrella-tree form. This small element crowning a larger structure became a building type.

The stupa's multiple functions—marking the location of sacred relics, recalling the sacred tree, and providing a focus for ritual and meditation—had evolved into separate structures. The kondo hall contains a Buddha, providing

FIGURE 1.8   Temple of Hōryū-ji, near Nara, Japan, 670–714.

a space and focus for prayer and worship. A pagoda, like the stupa, preserves holy relics or sacred texts. Unlike Sanchi, Ho¯ryu¯-ji's sanctuary walls are precisely oriented to the cardinal directions. The precinct's arrangement is not symmetrical, but achieves a harmonious, appropriately Buddhist balance.

JUDAISM: HOUSING ONE GOD AND HIS PEOPLE

Many ancient religious traditions were polytheistic, with multiple gods, as in Egypt or Greece. Hinduism has four primary deities, although they can be considered manifestations of a single divinity. Buddhism never defines God, but emphasizes wisdom and ethics. A few ancient Near Eastern religions are monotheistic, believing in one all-powerful God. Judaism, Christianity, and Islam—which, like Hinduism, share an emphasis on sacred texts—have very closely related beliefs, culture, and architecture.

The oldest of these is Judaism. Historians debate whether early figures such as Abraham existed, but monotheism was certainly practiced over 3,000 years ago in what is now Israel. While Greek gods had human forms, and ancient Egyptian and Hindu divinities combined human and animal attributes, Judaism insists that no image can express God's identity, or should try. He is known through his interventions in human history, and the laws he gave his people.

The earliest sacred Jewish structure was not a building, but the Ark of the Covenant, a portable box containing the tablets with the Ten Commandments and other sacred relics. Appropriate for a nomadic people, wherever they stopped it was protected by an honored tent, the tabernacle. But once settled, the Jews constructed a sacred building: the Temple in Jerusalem. As recounted in I Kings (among the oldest surviving passages about architecture), the people asked to build a temple for their God. The honor of constructing it went to King Solomon in the tenth century BCE.

The temple site was Mount Moriah, another holy mountain, where God tested Abraham's faith by asking him to sacrifice his only son, Isaac. Already sacred, this became the only location that Judaism considers intrinsically holy. The biblical description of the temple emphasizes its proportions and splendid ornamental materials. Two bronze columns stood at the entrance, the Holy of Holies was lined with gold, and decorations depicted angels, flowers, and plants—not God, but his creations.

This written description is invaluable, because the Temple was destroyed by the Babylonians in the sixth century BCE. Many features of its overall design can be reconstructed, however. Solomon's Temple, like Egyptian and Hindu temples, had a sequence of spaces with increasingly restricted access. Visitors climbed a flight of stairs to an entrance vestibule. Beyond was a large central room, with a flight of steps at the far end. This led to the Holy of Holies housing the Ark of the Covenant. The Temple's most sacred, elevated, and exclusive space, it could be entered only once a year by the High Priest. It was also the smallest: like the Hindu sacred cave, it provided an intimate space in which to meet the Almighty.

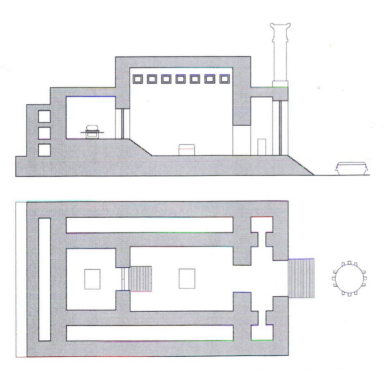

FIGURE 1.9   Temple of Solomon, Jerusalem, tenth century BCE (plan and section).

Rebuilt in the sixth century BCE, the Temple was the center of Jewish religious practice for centuries. Herod the Great remodeled it in the 20s BCE, but his aggrandized temple had the shortest life. In 6 CE, Judea became a province of the Roman Empire, which insisted all subjects worship its emperor as a god. Unlike polytheists, for Jews this was blasphemy. Out of respect for their ancient faith, Rome gave Judea a unique exemption from the imperial cult.

However, when the Jews revolted against Rome, the Empire responded harshly. After an uprising in 70 CE, the Romans destroyed the Temple in Jerusalem, leaving only part of its foundation (the Western Wall). In 135, after further rebellion, the emperor Hadrian erased Jerusalem as a Jewish city. He built a temple to Rome's three imperial gods on the Temple Mount and exiled Jews from Jerusalem. They were completely cut off from their religion's one sacred site for 500 years.

The traumatic loss of the Temple and their holy city profoundly altered Judaic religious practice. Ritual sacrifices could occur only at the Temple, which could only be in one inaccessible place. So the temple priesthood ended, and worship that emphasized study of scriptures, especially the Torah, the first five books of the Bible, became dominant. Communal study centers called **synagogues** ("houses of assembly" in Greek) were already widespread. They were used for public prayer led by a teacher, or rabbi. After the Temple's destruction, they became the primary form of Judaic religious architecture.

Synagogues were not restricted, exclusive spaces like the Temple, but admitted the entire community. The interior provides seating for communal study and prayer. It also has an elevated platform called a **bimah**, from which the rabbi reads and preaches, and a **torah ark**, a structure that protects and displays the holy scriptures. The torah ark is usually placed in the wall facing Jerusalem. This makes the synagogue a geographic and spiritual compass, pointing to Judaism's one sacred site.

CHRISTIANITY: CONGREGATION TO BUILDING

Exile produced the diaspora (Greek for "scattering"), and Judaism became a faith practiced by isolated communities in foreign lands. This also brought a new Jewish sect that believed Jesus of Nazareth was the Christ ("anointed one" in Greek), to cities throughout the Roman Empire. As Christianity distinguished itself from Judaism, it lost its exemption from imperial cult observance, becoming an illegal, underground faith. It grew exponentially during its first centuries, especially among the empire's large population of slaves. Christianity, like Buddhism, redefined the meaning of suffering, inverting the relationship between earthly and spiritual status. Instead of punishment for disobedience, or the whim of fickle gods, Jesus called misfortunes "blessings," modeled humility and suffering, and reportedly returned to life after his execution. This affirmed those without power or rights, and offered them hope for salvation and honor after death.

The young faith increasingly infiltrated Roman society until even an emperor's mother was a Christian. That emperor, Constantine, had a vision that marching under its symbol, the cross, before battle would bring victory. When his vision came true, Constantine legalized Christianity in the year 313. By 380, it was the Roman Empire's state religion.

Originally, a "church" was a group of people who worshipped wherever possible, usually in a member's house. Legalization raised an architectural question: what should a Christian house of worship look like? Like synagogues, they should accommodate communal worship, and have a **pulpit** or **ambo**, like the bimah, for reading and preaching. Unlike synagogues, churches needed an altar for the **Eucharist**, a ritual reenactment of Christ's Last Supper, when he declared bread and wine were his own sacrificial body and blood. The clergy also processed in and out of the sanctuary, carrying the scriptures.

The only "architectural" passage in Christian scriptures is in the Revelation of John, describing his vision of the "New Jerusalem" as an immense, glowing cube in the sky with twelve gates of precious stones—inspiring, but impractical. The Roman temple provided a possible model, but like Greek temples, their interiors were not usually public spaces. More importantly, they were symbolically objectionable because they represented "paganism," Christianity's spiritual enemy. A preferable building type was the **basilica**, a courthouse with a large, longitudinal interior space. It had a small half-cylindrical space at one or both ends, called an **apse**, containing an altar and statue of the (divine) emperor. But basilicas were more strongly associated with Roman law than religion, so the pagan association was minimal.

The first St. Peter's in Rome adapted the basilica for Christian worship. A flight of steps led to an entrance gate into a walled entry atrium. At its far end was a porch (narthex) protecting the doors into the sanctuary. Inside was a high, column-lined rectangular main space (nave), a longitudinal space in which an axis from the door to the main altar in an apse became an aisle for processions. High windows along the upper wall, a **clerestory**, brought daylight into the tall interior. Its resonant acoustics and clear lines of sight allowed a large congregation to see, hear, and participate.

Despite Christ's emphasis on humility, early church interiors were resplendent with gold mosaics and rich marble. They expressed triumph after centuries underground, and a devoted community offering its finest to glorify God. But early church exteriors usually appeared plain from without. This contrast mirrored the Christian view of the body as a humble, temporary shell for the glorious soul inside.

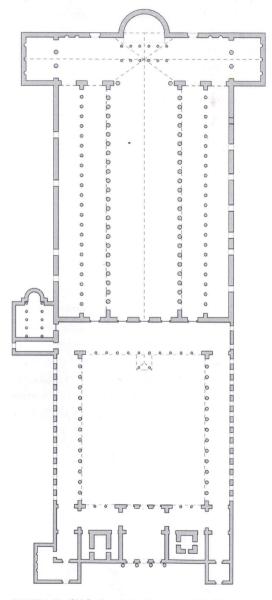

FIGURE 1.10   Old St. Peter's Basilica, Rome, 333–390.

CHURCH AS MIRACLE: HAGIA SOPHIA AND THE GOTHIC

Constantine's influential decisions included establishing a new imperial capital in the Greek city of Byzantium, at the crossroads between Europe and Asia,
renamed Constantinople in his honor. A century later the Roman Empire's western
half fell to invading tribes, but its eastern half persisted for another thousand years

as the Byzantine empire. Its liturgical practices and church architecture became Christianity's Eastern Orthodox tradition.

The most ambitious, influential Orthodox church is Hagia Sophia ("Holy Wisdom" in Greek) in Constantinople, now Istanbul. It was built in the early sixth century under the Byzantine emperor Justinian as a **cathedral**, a church where a bishop presides. Like a basilica, its plan had an enclosed atrium, entry narthex, and a longitudinal nave culminating in an apse. The sanctuary is not rectangular with rows of columns, however, but a square with irregular supports, or **piers**, at its corners, and two trapezoids at either end. The overall plan is a mandala-like square with a circle in the center.

That central circle is a dome. Described by one early visitor as "suspended from heaven," it appears to float on a ring of windows that flood the interior with light. Hagia Sophia shows two new ideas in church design: the dramatic dome pulls the eye upward into a form whose geometry and illumination suggest heaven. The soaring space beneath the dome also defines a strong vertical axis that balances the lateral view toward the altar. This transforms the basilica's **longitudinal plan** into a centralized one.

Hagia Sophia used daring engineering, soaring verticality, and heavenly light to produce an inspiring, miraculous-looking interior space. Here, Christian architecture invoked a transcendent sense of God's presence through design. One missing element today is the church's original covering of mosaics. Its interior, like most early Christian and Byzantine churches, was filled with representations of Christ, saints, biblical stories, and other images. Christians discontinued Judaism's prohibition against representing God because he took human form as Jesus, making himself visible. Like ancient Greek, Hindu, and Buddhist architecture, Christian churches used images to express their beliefs and aid worship.

FIGURE 1.11   Hagia Sophia, Istanbul, Turkey, 532–537.

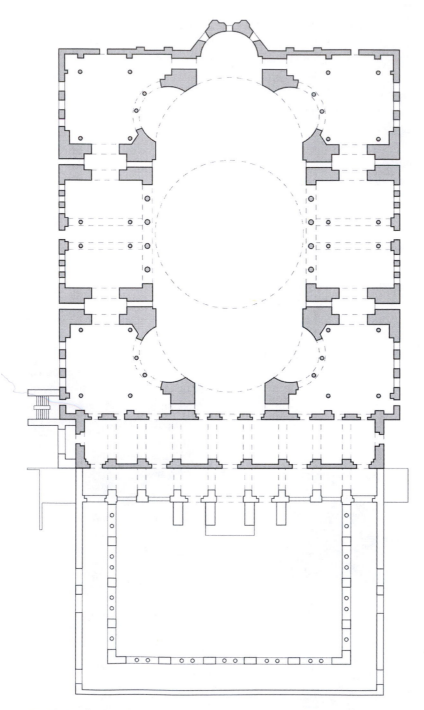

FIGURE 1.11 (continued)

Hagia Sophia's confident expression of a Christian empire was built as Western Europe entered a long period of warfare and upheaval that prevented major building. When this ended, Western builders developed their own way to use dramatic verticality, daring structure, and abundant art and light to construct an image of heaven on earth.

France was among the first regions to regain enough stability to support ambitious construction. By the 1100s, its builders had produced grander stone buildings than any seen in the West since the Romans. These skilled designers worked with Abbot Suger, head of the Abbey of St.-Denis, a Benedictine monastery outside Paris. Saint Denis was the patron of France, whose kings had been buried at this important abbey for 500 years.

Abbot Suger studied writings by an early Christian philosopher who described God as light. Suger and his builders tried to use architecture to express this idea when remodeling the area behind the abbey church's altar (the choir). They brought together several recent innovations. One was using pointed, not round, arches to support the roof. This more vertical and structurally stable form meant that a stone ceiling could be supported by slender columns instead of heavy piers and solid walls. Instead of a space divided into small, dark cells, the choir became open, taller, and brighter. More stability and height permitted larger windows to flood the choir with divine light.

St.-Denis' marriage of theology and technology gave birth to the "Gothic," the architectural vocabulary used at Lincoln Cathedral. Within decades, that experimental remodeling became a pan-European style producing spaces just as miraculous as Hagia Sophia. Instead of a floating dome, Gothic interiors soared higher than any

FIGURE 1.12   Cathedral of Notre-Dame, Amiens, France, 1220–1270 (view of nave).

yet built. Enormous stained glass windows, a new innovation, produced colorful, glowing spaces that echoed Saint John's vision of the New Jerusalem.

A Gothic cathedral was supposed to feel like heaven on earth, a vision of paradise for the faithful. Music, incense, and ceremony made worship a multimedia, multisensory experience exploiting every thirteenth-century technological capability. They also relied on religious imagery. Building exteriors, especially doorways, were covered with sculpted images of Christ, saints, biblical characters, and other spiritual themes. Inside, paintings and stained glass presented religious portraits and stories.

For an age when few could read and worship was conducted in an ancient language, church art helped people understand their faith's characters, stories, and principles. Glorious architecture convinced believers that the church was the stairway to heaven.

PROTESTANTISM: MEETING HOUSE TO MEGACHURCH

Eastern Orthodoxy and Roman Catholicism differ mainly in politics, not theology: the Orthodox do not accept the bishop of Rome as head of all Christianity (Catholics call him the Pope). But when a Catholic monk named Martin Luther protested dozens of church teachings in 1517, this began the Protestant Reformation, which permanently fragmented Western Christianity.

Some Protestant movements retained many Catholic beliefs and practices, like the Church of England. Lincoln Cathedral easily become a Protestant cathedral because Anglicans had bishops and used traditional liturgy. They also largely maintained the Catholic and Orthodox belief that Christ becomes present in bread and wine during the Eucharist. The belief that worship includes a uniquely sacred phenomenon supports church architecture that honors this as special and rightly separate from everyday reality.

Protestant traditions with different beliefs have different priorities for worship spaces. Many groups adopted the early church's humility, and saw elaborate architecture as a pompous distraction. One such group, the Society of Friends (Quakers), is famous for its commitment to simplicity and equality. They gather in "meeting houses" that feature little decoration. Seating is arranged so members face each other, often in a square instead of focusing on a prominent altar or pulpit. Quaker meetings are not led by clergy, but invite believers to share freely and equally.

Some groups considered the most Christian form of architecture to be no architecture, an idea expressed in the evangelical tradition of itinerant preachers and tent revivals. During the 1950s, one Southern California minister, Robert Schuller, observed that Los Angeles' many drive-in theaters were empty on Sunday mornings. He founded a drive-in church, and preached from the snack bar roof. When it outgrew the drive-in, Schuller wanted to keep the outdoor experience, so architect Richard Neutra designed a "walk-in, drive-in" church where the congregation could come inside or stay in their cars.

When the church expanded yet again, architect Philip Johnson proposed a very different solution. The Crystal Cathedral's transparent sanctuary walls maintain a visual connection to the outdoors, yet its soaring, light-filled interior also recalls the Gothic. Schuller's Reformed denomination has no bishops, so the term "cathedral" was strictly architectural. The sanctuary's design reflected Protestant priorities: the focus was a monumental pipe organ, choir, and pulpit, but it had no altar. The worship space was clearly designed for music and preaching rather than formal liturgy. Ironically, in 2012, the Crystal Cathedral, whose congregation experienced difficulties after Schuller's 2006 retirement, was purchased by the local Catholic diocese. After an interior remodeling, it will be rechristened Christ Cathedral—a cathedral in fact as well as in name and architectural spirit.

Architecturally, the Crystal Cathedral was unusual within a wider phenomenon it helped create: the evangelical **megachurch**, a Protestant congregation with thousands of members. The sanctuary of Lakewood Church in Houston, Texas, is more typical. Its 16,800-seat sanctuary is a windowless cocoon, hermetically sealed from the outside like a temple's inner sanctum. Such spaces rely on high-tech lighting, sound, and projection systems to support worship for an

FIGURE 1.13   Philip Johnson, Crystal Cathedral, Garden Grove, California, 1977.

enormous crowd. Architecturally, Lakewood is difficult to distinguish from a secular auditorium; in fact, its main building was originally a sports arena.

Some Protestant churches use symbolically neutral architecture deliberately, to attract those who might avoid a traditional-looking church. Yet many, like Lakewood, also use visual spectacle, audio technology, and overwhelming scale to make worship as dramatic as Byzantine and Gothic cathedrals. Whether through soaring domes and stained glass, or amplified music and digitally projected sermons, Christian architecture has long used every available technology to promote faith.

ISLAM: MONUMENTS, MOSQUES, AND MAUSOLEUMS

Like Buddhism and Christianity, the youngest major monotheistic faith, Islam, began with a charismatic individual. Muhammad lived in Mecca, on the Arabian peninsula in the late sixth and early seventh centuries. Its population included Christians, Jews, and polytheists. Like Judaism and Christianity, which he honored as ancestor faiths, Muhammad asserted the existence of only one God, Allah. His revelations were recorded in a sacred text, the Qur'an. Islam, meaning "submission" in Arabic, began when Muhammad and his followers left Mecca for Medina in 622 and his teachings became public.

Islam simplified monotheistic doctrine and practice. Judaism's ancient corpus of scriptures required ongoing study and reinterpretation. By the seventh century, Christianity had developed an intricate theology and an authoritative church hierarchy. In contrast, Islam could be summarized in its Five Pillars of the Faith: believe in one God and honor Muhammad as his prophet, pray five times a day, give to charity, fast during the month of Ramadan, and make a pilgrimage to Mecca. The most fundamental sacred space in Islam is the prayer rug, which transforms any environment into a temporary, individual sanctuary for the believer.

Islam spread quickly as early adherents conquered new territories. By the eighth century it stretched west across North Africa, north into southern France, and east to India and central Asia. Muslim armies captured Byzantine Jerusalem in 638, only six years after Muhammad's death. Jerusalem, where Jesus was crucified and resurrected, was also Christianity's holiest site. But it was also sacred to Islam, which holds that Muhammad ascended to heaven from the Temple Mount.

The Muslim shrine on this location inaugurated Islamic monumental architecture. The Dome of the Rock's gilded hemispherical dome crowns an octagonal base, both typical Byzantine forms. It also continues the Byzantine practice of elaborate, colorful decoration. Like Judaism, however, Islam taught that images of sacred figures were sacrilegious. Muslim ornament consists of intricate geometric and botanical patterns. Its one form of sacred decoration is

FIGURE 1.14   Dome of the Rock, Jerusalem, 687–691.

text: Qur'anic passages in sophisticated calligraphy write holy scripture onto the architecture itself.

The most widespread Islamic building type is the **mosque**. Its name comes from *masjid*, Arabic for a place where people bow, because Muslims pray bowing toward Mecca. It provides space for communal Friday prayers, when the faithful listen to the Qur'an and hear an imam (leader) teach. A mosque typically

FIGURE 1.15   Great Mosque of Uqba, Kairouan, Tunisia, 836–875.

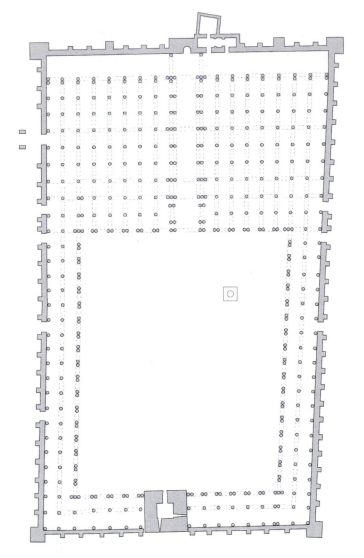

FIGURE 1.15 *(continued)*

includes elements seen at the Uqba or Great Mosque at Kairouan, Tunisia, begun in 670. Its most prominent feature is a tower called a **minaret,** the solid square form in the plan. A minaret is both a visible landmark and an instrument for sound; a singer (muezzin) sings the call to prayer from the top. Like a bell tower, height increases his voice's reach.

The Great Mosque's heavy perimeter wall frames an immense courtyard. At its southern end is a large prayer hall with a **minbar**, a raised pulpit. Its far wall contains the **mihrab**, a niche for the Qur'an, in a wall (the **qibla**) pointing toward Mecca. The scripture display and orientation toward a sacred

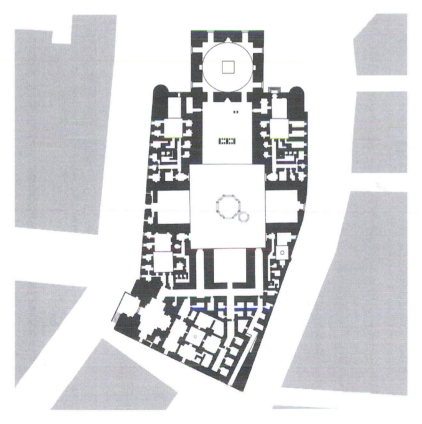

FIGURE 1.16   Sultan Hasan Mosque, Cairo, 1356–1363.

city both recall the torah ark. Like a church or synagogue, a mosque must also accommodate a large community. Kairouan's large prayer hall also has a dense grid of columns that support its roof, but obstruct views of the imam. That such hypostyle halls are found in many early mosques shows that listening was more important than observing.

The fourteenth-century Sultan Hassan Complex in Cairo, Egypt, houses a mosque and a school, hospital, guest quarters, and other functions. The complex's perimeter follows the city's irregular street pattern, but its largest, cross-shaped interior spaces have a different orientation: they are the mosque, and point toward Mecca. The central space, an unroofed courtyard, features a fountain at its center. Many faiths link water and spiritual purity—Hindus and the Ganges river; Christian baptism; the Jewish mikvah—and mosques provide water for ablutions before prayer.

The Sultan Hasan mosque is an entirely open-air space. Its main prayer hall is in a large, arched niche called an **iwan**, the largest of four surrounding the central court. From the city, the mosque's spaces are invisible. Its most dominant form is a solid, masonry cube with a smooth dome framed by two minarets. This is a **mausoleum**, a monumental tomb. Placed between the qibla and Mecca, it was built for the ruler who sponsored the mosque, although he was never buried there.

Islamic sacred architecture's common elements were expressed in a wide variety of architectural styles across three continents. An especially elegant, courtly version served the rulers of Persia's Safavid Empire, seen in the Shah (now Imam) Mosque complex at Isfahan. Among its striking features are subtly bulbous domes, sculpted iwan vaults, and surface ornamentation of intricately patterned glazed tiles dominated by a rich blue. This sophisticated style inspired the first Islamic building we discussed.

The Taj Mahal, built by a Muslim ruler in Northern India, gains further meaning when seen in relation to Islamic and sacred architecture (see Figure 0.3). It is a domed mausoleum like Sultan Hasan's, built for Mumtaz Mahal, wife of the Shah Jahan. The Taj's design features many familiar elements: its exterior niches are iwans, and the four towers recall minarets. Its free-standing, symmetrical masses echo the Dome of the Rock, and the dome and iwan contours mimic the nearly contemporary Isfahan. The delicate ornament is strictly geometrical and botanical, and the calligraphy framing its four entrances consists of Qur'anic passages describing Paradise (Persian for "walled garden"). Raised above the ground, the design centers on the burial spot of an honored individual, and the value of its marble and semiprecious stone intarsia demonstrate sacrificial devotion. The Taj Mahal deployed multiple strategies for designing sacred space to commemorate a beloved queen. Centuries later, the result still draws pilgrims.

CONTESTING SACRED SPACES

Sacred space and architectural design can produce consensus, or conflict. Jerusalem's holiness for Judaism, Christianity, and Islam has spawned centuries of violence. When the city came under Muslim control, Jews were allowed back, but could not rebuild their Temple because of the site's holiness to Muslims. Medieval armies from Western Europe tried to regain the holy city for Christianity by force during the Crusades. Israel's establishment as a Jewish state in 1948 inaugurated decades of renewed, unresolved conflict. Repeated proposals to make Jerusalem a shared sacred city have not resolved competing, mutually exclusive claims to the same holy site.

The Christian Church of the Holy Sepulchre shows how a single (fractured) religious tradition can also have intractable conflicts over a sacred space. Built under Constantine to house shrines marking the sites of Jesus' crucifixion, burial, and resurrection, the church has been Christianity's most sacred pilgrimage destination for centuries. But over time, parts of the interior have been claimed by competing groups (including Greek Orthodox, Coptics, and Franciscans). On Palm Sunday of 2008, several monks even had a fistfight over territorial boundaries.

In addition, some Protestant pilgrims have found the church, filled with gold-framed artwork and shrines, so aesthetically alien that they have rejected it as inauthentic. Today many prefer to revere a simpler first-century Jerusalem tomb (the "Garden Tomb") as the true site of Jesus' burial and resurrection. Apart from the question of historic accuracy, the two sites reflect divergent views of what Christianity's most sacred space should look like.

We often disagree most violently when the stakes are highest. Buildings that embody deeply held beliefs about the meaning of life, death, and the divine are meant to inspire attachment and special respect. Yet they are also manifestations of the most common type of architecture: the home. Whether glorious or humble, conceived as a house for a god, a community of faith, or the dead, architecture for the spirit, a reflection of our highest ideals, also relates directly to something more down to earth: how we shelter our families.

VOCABULARY

ambo/pulpit, apse, axis, barrow, basilica, bimah, cathedral, chatra, clerestory, column, dolmen, Eucharist, frieze, harmika, hypostyle hall, iwan, kondo, longitudinal plan, mandala, mandir, mausoleum, megachurch, megalith, menhir, mihrab, minaret, minbar, mortise and tenon, mosque, pagoda, pediment, pier, pylon, qibla, shikara, stupa, synagogue, temenos, torah ark, torana, trilithon.

STUDY AND REVIEW QUESTIONS

1. Describe how the World Trade Center Memorial design communicates its site's sacredness. Why are its methods so different from those at Lincoln Cathedral?

2. How can one stone announce that a location has special meaning? Do we need to know why?

3. What features of Stonehenge's design suggest it was a ceremonial, "sacred" monument? What other information supports this interpretation?

4. What did the Acropolis mean to Athenians? How did they experience the site, and what design features made it meaningful?

5. Compare Egyptian pyramids and a pharaoh's burial journey to menhirs, barrows, Stonehenge, and the Acropolis. Find one or two common features with each.

6. How can physical boundaries like hills, rivers, gateways, and walls mark an area as "sacred"? What methods can achieve this without physical boundaries?

7. How does the exterior of the Hindu temple at Khajuraho communicate its purpose? How does its exterior relate to its interior?

8. What does the Hōryū-ji sanctuary's design share with Sanchi, and how is its expression of Buddhism different?

9. Compare how sacredness is constructed at Solomon's Temple and a Jewish synagogue.

10. Which building type did Rome's Christians model their churches on, and why? What made the result "Christian"?

11. How did the cathedral of Hagia Sophia in Constantinople both continue and alter the techniques found at Old St. Peter's?

12. Describe the different ways Protestant Christianity could approach church design. Why did some groups accept Gothic-style architecture while others did not?

13. Name at least four design elements that are necessary for any Islamic mosque. Why are a map and a compass necessary to build one?

14. Compare design features that unite and distinguish synagogues, early Christian churches, and mosques.

APPLICATION AND DISCUSSION EXERCISES

1. Locate a space in or near your home that could qualify as a "sacred space" (whether secular or religious). Briefly explain the source of its special meaning, then describe three physical qualities that remind you of sacred design strategies.

2. Identify examples of religious or "sacred" structure not discussed in the chapter. Compare it to at least three of the examples discussed. Which of the design techniques discussed—separation, geometry, orientation, visual drama, art, community, etc.—do they have in common?

FURTHER READING

Barrie, Thomas. *Spiritual Path, Sacred Place: Myth, Ritual and Meaning in Architecture*. Boston: Shambhala, 1990.

Bharne, Vinyak and Krupali Krusche. *Rediscovering the Hindu Temple: The Sacred Architecture and Urbanism of India*. Newcastle upon Tyne: Cambridge Scholars Publishing, 2012.

Blair, Sheila and Jonathan Bloom. *The Art and Architecture of Islam, 1250–1800*. New Haven: Yale University Press, 1994.

Cannon, Jon. *The Secret Language of Sacred Spaces: Decoding Churches, Temples, Mosques and Other Places of Worship around the World*. London: Duncan Baird, 2013.

Ettinghausen, Richard, Oleg Grabar, and Marilyn Jenkins-Madina. *Islamic Art and Architecture 650–1250*. New Haven: Yale University Press, 2001.

Hurwitt, Jeffrey. *The Athenian Acropolis: History, Mythology and Archaeology from the Neolithic Era to the Present*. Cambridge: Cambridge University Press, 1999.

Jarzombek, Mark. *Architecture of First Societies: A Global Perspective*. Hoboken, NJ: John Wiley & Sons, 2013.

Kostof, Spiro. *A History of Architecture: Settings and Rituals*. New York: Oxford University Press, 1995.

Mitchell, George. *The Hindu Temple: An Introduction to Its Meaning and Forms*. Chicago and London: University of Chicago Press, 1977.

Müller, Hans. *Ancient Architecture*. Milan: Electa, 1980.

Roth, Leland. *Understanding Architecture: Its Elements, History and Meaning*. Third edition. Boulder: Westview Press, 2014.

Sebag, Paul. *The Great Mosque of Kairouan*. Trans. R. Howard. London: Collier-Macmillan, 1965.

Wharton, Annabel. *Selling Jerusalem: Relics, Replicas, Theme Parks*. Chicago: University of Chicago Press, 2006.

CHAPTER 2
THE HOUSE

FOR MANY OF US, THE WORD *HOUSE* conjures a free-standing structure in a well-tended garden, like that seen in Figure 2.1. This appears to be a **single-family home** for one group of closely related people, rather than many families or unrelated strangers. Yet this classic Colonial Revival is a "faux" house; no one has ever lived there. It is a set at Universal Studios in Los Angeles, one used in television shows from *Leave It to Beaver* (1957–1963) to *Desperate Housewives* (2004–2012), feature films, and even hip-hop videos. Hollywood designed it to resemble the typical North American house, then used it to perpetuate an architectural **archetype** or model.

We may identify with this sort of home, or not. While the North American media often present it as normal, the single-family home is only one of many domestic architectural types. In U.S. culture, however, it can have an almost sacred

FIGURE 2.1   Colonial Revival house set, Universal Studios, Los Angeles, California, 1949.

dimension. This is curious; after all, houses are commonplace compared to temples and cathedrals. Yet the two architectural forms are related: houses for the gods were aggrandized versions of human homes. Synagogues, churches, and mosques all housed faith families, and they also began as ancient Near Eastern houses, part of the single-family home's architectural and cultural genealogy.

THE GRECO-ROMAN COURTYARD HOUSE

An ancient house on the Greek island of Olynthos was very different from a Colonial Revival. The plan, reconstructed from foundations and objects, shows a home that was largely closed off from the world: only one of its four perimeter walls opens onto the city, with two doors to the street. Two sides are shared **party walls**, while the back wall borders a narrow alley.

The center door leads through a vestibule into a court open to the sky, with two piers at one end. Another room opening onto both street and courtyard was probably used as a shop or office; this house combined private residential and public commercial space. The room at lower right, through another vestibule, had a fine mosaic floor. This formal space was for dining and entertaining guests. Its name (**andron**, from "male" in ancient Greek) indicates the house was zoned by gender. The family's men received visitors in the house's front half, but respectable women led cloistered lives in the **gynaeceum**, the area behind the courtyard piers and an upper floor, where domestic work took place.

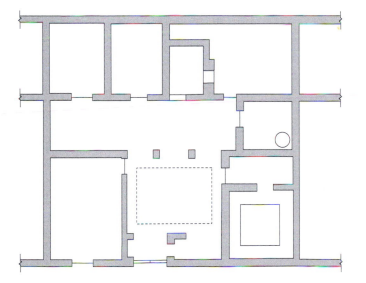

FIGURE 2.2   Plan, House vii.4, Olynthos, Greece, ca. 430–350 BCE.

The Olynthos house sits in a rectangular block of homes, all with roughly square perimeters. The pattern differs at Pompeii in Southern Italy, founded by Greek colonists but culturally Roman when buried in 79 CE. Its inward-facing houses also gain light and air from sky-lit courts, and include shops with street access. But most have irregular perimeters, like the House of Menander, which was gradually expanded as owners purchased adjacent spaces and connected them to the original home.

We know from the House of Menander's size that it housed a **patrician** (aristocratic) family. Romans called a grand townhouse a **domus**, the source of our word *domestic*. It had two types of courtyards: The first, off the main entrance, was an **atrium** whose sunken pool, an **impluvium**, collected rainwater. Beyond was a **peristyle** garden, ringed by a column-supported porch. Instead of a house in a garden, the domus frames its garden with a house.

The domus had zones defined less by gender—Roman women had more freedom than Greek ones—than by social class. The innermost area was restricted to intimates and invited guests, while the atrium and adjacent rooms were open to all during the morning "salutation," when the male head of the household received visitors. His family included several generations of relatives, paid staff, and slaves. He was also a **patron** to clients who came to pay their respects and ask favors. They were received in the **tablinum**, holding family records, visible across the atrium from the entrance.

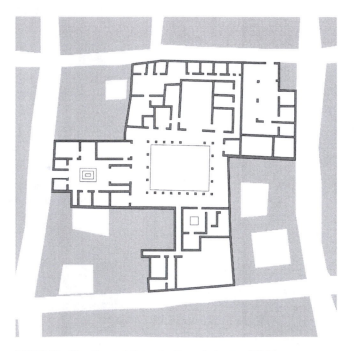

FIGURE 2.3   Plan, House of Menander, Pompeii, destroyed 79 CE.

The domus had a strong public dimension, but its size was invisible from the street. Apart from its main doorway, which might be large and ornate, a home's character was only revealed inside. The size of its atrium and garden, number of rooms, mosaic floors, and colorful wall frescoes declared the family's wealth and status. The House of Menander did have a few windows in rooms on street walls, but they were small, high, and protected with iron bars and shutters. The elegant domus also provided refuge from dangerous, filthy city streets.

TOWN AND COUNTRY: VILLA AND PALAZZO

Privileged ancient city-dwellers regularly quit their luxurious townhomes for country **villas**. Latin for "farmhouse," villas were originally complexes for agricultural production. Gradually, aristocrats turned the *villa rustica*, a rural family farm, into more luxurious retreats. Some aristocrats also built a *villa suburbana* closer to the city. While the domus carves internally focused interior voids within a solid urban block, the villa was a visible object set in and open to its landscape. Roman villas in preserved paintings feature wide-reaching wings and open colonnades. Generous windows, terraces, and porticoes provided platforms from which to enjoy fresh air and views of the countryside or sea.

Ancient Roman aristocrats described their villas as rejuvenating, inspirational places. Their pleasure depended on peasant and slave labor, and on the Roman army's defense of the empire's distant borders and many roads. A physically open country house may be scenic, but is also vulnerable. After the Roman Empire fell in the fifth century, isolated aristocratic residences in Europe became fortified complexes in defensible locations— castles, not leisurely retreats.

By the thirteenth and fourteenth centuries, increased stability revived Western European cities, where manufacturing and trade helped generate wealth. The central Italian city of Florence was dominated by powerful and competitive families who controlled their own neighborhoods. Each had a tall defensive tower for security when competition became violent. An open portico called a **loggia** provided a public stage for family ceremonies and business. These landmarks, plus the family crest, announced who owned certain districts.

The seat of family control was a multi-story urban home known as a **palazzo**. It was organized in vertical layers, with a public ground floor for business and residential spaces above, around an open courtyard called a **cortile**. Like the domus, it housed one powerful family's extended household of relatives, associates, and servants. The first floor above street level, the **piano nobile** ("noble floor"), held the largest, most prestigious rooms for important visitors. The level above had rooms for the family. Servants slept in the attic and worked in basement-level kitchens.

Also like the domus, a medieval palazzo's exterior was often indistinguishable from adjacent homes in its city block. But as many Florentine families became wealthier during the fourteenth and fifteenth centuries, they gave their private palaces impressive stone **façades**, distinct "faces" that made them recognizable from the street.

One upstart family in Florence, the Medici, made a fortune in international banking and began competing with the long-established families who controlled the city's ancient center. Instead of trying to squeeze into older, crowded neighborhoods, the Medici instead invested in a newly developing area on the city's edge, where they purchased property and sponsored projects at two major churches. On a prominent corner, visible from the cathedral, they claimed this neighborhood with a history-making urban house.

The Palazzo Medici follows the traditional pattern, with rooms arranged around a courtyard in vertical layers. But its lower-density neighborhood permitted a house of unprecedented size—about 40,000 square feet (3,700 square meters)—that dwarfed their competitors' homes. Unlike older, remodeled palaces, its brand-new construction featured a perfectly square cortile and orderly plan. This regularity is showcased through evenly spaced windows along the palazzo's costly stone façade, crowned by an enormous wooden **cornice**. A bench along the sidewalk provided seating for Medici clients waiting to see their patron, continuing the ancient Roman tradition.

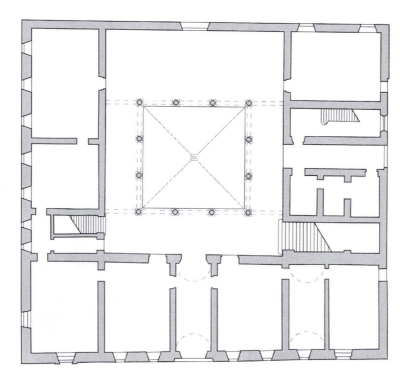

FIGURE 2.4   Michelozzo di Bartolomeo, Palazzo Medici, Florence, begun 1444.

The Medici built no tower, but at 80 feet high their palazzo was both secure and visible. Its ground-floor corner arches were originally open as a public loggia, but later enclosed. Soon the Medici were powerful enough to ignore local tradition. Although their huge palazzo on Florence's periphery was scandalously expensive—it cost several times their empire's annual profits—the investment paid off. Many families tried to keep up with the Medici by producing copycat palazzos, but none benefited the same way, and some went bankrupt.

The palazzo, like the domus, housed an extended family and accommodated its business and social interests. Our notion of individual privacy was nonexistent in antiquity, but the grandest new palaces also included a type of space designed for the owner's use alone. A small alcove, usually off the master's bedroom, was called a **studiolo**: a private study for one. A studiolo built for the duke of Gubbio, now in New York's Metropolitan Museum, was embellished with elaborate wooden intarsia paneling. Its inlaid images show book-filled cabinets and scientific objects that express the owner's erudition, deliberately conveying his personal—rather than family—identity.

As fifteenth-century Italians increasingly compared their lives to the ancient Romans—a cultural phenomenon known as the Renaissance—aristocrats wondered whether their farmsteads and castles could become what the ancients described as a "villa." The term was revived and soon applied to rural estates like the Medici farmhouse in Cafaggiolo. Its solid, high walls; few, tiny windows; and defensive towers were more typical of castles than an ancient country retreat.

As Florence became more powerful and secure, however, villa design changed. A later Medici villa at Poggio a Caiano features more, larger, and symmetrically arranged windows, as well as a colonnaded portico adorning its main entry. Such houses were conceived as objects for admiration, and as platforms for viewing the landscape from spaces like Poggio a Caiano's raised terrace. This structure was built to maximize access to a setting offering a range of environments: there were cultivated fields, a lawn, and planting beds inside a gated wall, and another walled garden with elaborate geometric plantings nearby was created to delight the senses and the mind.

The modern villa is an essay on human control over nature—not untamed, but rationalized and managed. Among the most famous examples is Andrea Palladio's Villa Rotunda near Vicenza, Italy. The villa dominates its surroundings, commanding a river valley from its hilltop site. This perfectly symmetrical house

FIGURE 2.5   Andrea Palladio, Villa Rotunda, Vicenza, Italy, 1567–1570.

is an idealized, perfected object, both a foil for the landscape and a platform from which to view it. Like Poggio a Caiano, the house's form includes spaces for viewing nature, here the colonnaded porches on its four identical sides. We can enjoy the landscape from the house, or the architecture from the garden, but the design keeps these two realms distinct.

Palladio's other villa designs blur the boundary between house and landscape. At his Villa Barbaro, long side wings extend into its garden as arched ground-floor porticoes and frame its intimate upper-level garden. These elements shape architecture and landscape at the same time. We can associate these different approaches with different uses: the Villa Rotunda was a Venetian cardinal's weekend social retreat, while the Villa Barbaro was also a working farm. Its lateral wings also housed practical agricultural functions.

VILLAS ABROAD: BRITAIN AND THE AMERICAN SOUTH

Palladio wrote a widely read book cataloging his designs. One fan was the eighteenth-century British aristocrat Richard Boyle, Earl of Burlington, who had an intense interest in architecture. Like most of his peers, Burlington's life was divided between a country estate that provided his wealth and a London town-house, where he participated in national politics and class-based social rituals. But Palladio's pleasure-villas inspired him to design a third residence, a middle ground between his Yorkshire manor and grand city palace: an elegant but small (relatively) villa suburbana.

Burlington's Chiswick House, adapted from the Villa Rotunda, was a retreat that housed his art collection, library, and an architectural studio. Burlington called it a "House of the Muses" after the mythical Greek women who inspired art and poetry. It was where he could pursue personal interests instead of public obligations. Although to us it appears sized for a family, Chiswick House expressed Burlington's individual interests and provided him with privacy—a villa-sized studiolo.

The homes of Old World aristocrats like Burlington were models for the estates of planters in the American South. Thomas Jefferson, the famous early American politician, was also an amateur architect who shared Burlington's respect for Palladio. Jefferson designed, built, and redesigned Monticello, his Virginia plantation over many decades. Like Burlington's villa, Monticello's main house looks to the Villa Rotunda as a design **precedent** or model: it shares its colonnaded portico, culminating dome, and dominant hilltop position. But if we view it from the west, its compact, one-story form does not seem terribly oversized for one person. This is deceptive, however: Jefferson's design camouflages a structure that housed over twenty relatives, guests, and employees. It extends up two floors above the

FIGURE 2.6   Thomas Jefferson, Monticello, west façade, near Charlottesville, Virginia, 1768–1809.

main level, and laterally with two L-shaped, basement-level wings half-buried in the hill. Their roof supports a balustrade-lined walkway for viewing the landscape.

Monticello's community also included slaves—usually over eighty. Unlike ancient Roman slavery, which was political, not ethnic, New World slaves were drawn almost exclusively from western Africa, and thus were racially distinct from their owners. While the domus housed a complex household behind one door, plantations like Monticello zoned occupants architecturally by status and race. The owner's family lived in a larger, more elegant house. Some house slaves dwelled in the main house's attic or basement, but symbolically its design was associated with the white occupants alone. Most of the slaves who produced the owner's wealth were housed in separate, rough cabins, like Monticello's Mulberry Row. Their visibly inferior housing reinforced the slaves' lower status, and distanced them from the owner's family symbolically.

This relationship was typical of Southern plantations. But Monticello's lower-level service wings, which contained stables, kitchens, laundry, food storage, and quarters for house slaves, were unusual elements. They gave architectural expression for the world of slave labor as both a separate, inferior zone and a support for the main house. The way Monticello's composite form constructs a hierarchy of separate, connected, interdependent, and unequal zones acknowledges how fully the home's gracious (white) lifestyle above depended on a world of (black) labor below.

Monticello, like a domus or palazzo, was a public stage for Jefferson's duties as patriarch of a complex household and a political figure. But this house for dozens was always *his* home, as owner and architect. The private study adjacent to his bedroom holds devices he invented to mechanize tasks usually requiring human assistants, although they did not quench Jefferson's thirst for solitude, which inspired his later retreat at Poplar Forest. We see in Monticello's design tensions between community and individuality—both a house of many, and a house for one.

DEMOCRACY, HEALTH, AND THE URBAN TENEMENT

While Jefferson's house carefully safeguarded his own privacy, he believed that domestic architecture was not a private concern, but essential to the young Republic. He argued that only economically independent voters can vote their conscience, because if employed we naturally consider our employer's interests too. Democracy thus required a nation of **yeoman farmers** who supported themselves from their own land—like he did. That Jefferson's "independence" relied on enslaved people was one of the many contradictions in his character, along with his phrase "all men are created equal." Architecturally, his ideas added momentum to a widespread notion: that Americans should dwell in a free-standing house surrounded by nature, source of health, freedom, and virtue.

This ideal reflected early American demographics: in 1820, a majority were farmers, and over 90 percent lived in communities of 2,500 people or fewer. Political and economic power, however, concentrated in the nation's rapidly growing cities. From 1820 to 1870, the number of U.S. cities with over 25,000 people increased from five to forty-five. New York City, the nation's largest, grew from 150,000 in 1820 to 1 million by 1870.

The assumption that the country was safer and healthier than the city was justifiable. As New York received thousands of impoverished European immigrants, its living environments became overcrowded. Former middle-class houses were subdivided, squeezing many families into spaces designed for one. Others were replaced with new **tenements**, multi-story multi-family housing with small rental apartments.

The city's narrow, deep lots had insufficient width for a central court. Early tenements had one large, narrow building facing the street, a smaller one off the alley, and an open yard between. This provided facing rooms with light and ventilation, but also held outdoor privies and heaps of garbage. Even worse, the inner rooms along party walls lacked windows, and had no daylight or air at all. The later "railroad" tenement cleverly eliminated the smelly yard and made an entire site rentable. Its solid block also meant nearly all rooms had no windows—just stifling stench and darkness.

An 1879 law humanely required all apartment rooms to have windows, and all buildings indoor plumbing. The resulting "dumbbell tenement" fulfilled this with two flush toilets per floor, and replaced solid party walls with pencil-thin courtyards. These inaccessible light courts soon filled with garbage, however, making ventilation unpleasant. No matter the design, tenement overcrowding persisted

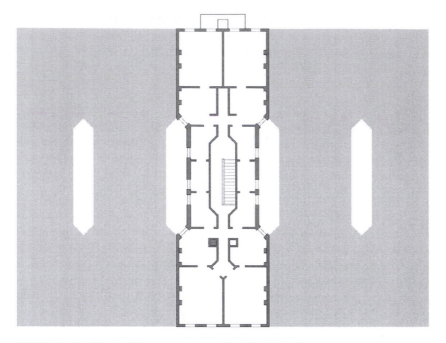

FIGURE 2.7   Plan, "Dumbbell" tenement plan, New York City, 1879–1900.

in New York because demand outstripped supply, rent stayed high, and families sublet rooms in their tiny apartments to survive.

Prosperous inhabitants moved north toward Central Park, built after 1850 to provide a healthy dose of nature to counteract the city's vice and disease. But the discovery of microorganisms soon showed that objects, including the many tenement-manufactured consumer goods, could spread disease anywhere. Increasing concerns with public health reinforced the notion that the healthiest homes were outside the city.

THE RIGHT KIND OF HOUSE

Rich, poor, or middle class, most nineteenth-century Americans believed a house in a garden provided the safest, happiest life possible. This "American Dream" also borrowed from a recent English trend. Britain's empire produced wider prosperity for those in manufacturing, trade, and professions. Its rising but largely urban middle class aspired to formerly aristocratic pleasures, such as regular escapes to country homes in a garden setting.

A new housing type developed to meet this demand: the bourgeois compact villa (**bourgeois** described a well-off urban professional). Such homes were more modest than Burlington's "solo" retreat, but ample for a middle-class family and its servants. Architect Peter Robinson's book of villa designs offered readers a menu of twelve house styles, shown with trees, lawns, shrubs, and hills, confirming the intended garden setting. Less individual than Chiswick or Monticello, choice provided a compromise between custom-designed homes and a uniform repeated type, like the attached row house. The final product still expresses the owner's taste and individuality.

Such British suburban villas were usually weekend retreats; in America, they became an idealized form of dwelling. Books like Robinson's inspired Andrew Jackson Downing, a landscape designer from New York state, to offer modified villas for full-time family life. His book *The Architecture of Country Houses* (1850) presents a range of home sizes and styles to fit the owner's station in life. Downing specifies that it is the male head of household whose identity is expressed through the design, but sees the house's wider social role in almost religious terms. He writes that a nation of "smiling lawns and tasteful cottages" provides order and refinement, and "preserves the moral purity of the nation."[1]

For Downing, what fundamentally defines a good house is its setting in an orderly, healthful pocket of nature. His sample designs all feature attached covered porches, often with enormous verandas, to increase the beneficial connection to the landscape. His arguments reinforced and simplified Jefferson's message: "real" Americans live in a house with a garden.

WOMAN'S WORLD AND SUBURBAN DREAMSCAPES

Ironically, given Downing's emphasis on the house's male owner, the nineteenth-century American home was increasingly defined as a feminine realm. Victorian-era gender beliefs held that men were physically stronger, but morally weaker than women. Men belonged to the brutal worlds of industry, money, and politics in dangerous cities. A "Cult of True Womanhood" insisted that women—supposedly delicate, spiritual creatures—should provide a sheltered sanctuary for children that also renews men immersed in the filth of urban capitalism. True Womanhood's natural sphere was the house, where she presides as a domestic priestess guarding the nation's physical, moral, and spiritual health.

The Victorian era's iconic homes show its greater emphasis on bodily privacy, even within a family. Late nineteenth-century "Queen Anne"-style houses feature irregular clusters of turrets, bay windows, dormers, and gables that announce a complex division of interior spaces into multiple enclosed bedrooms, parlors, and studies. These made it possible to separate genders and generations according to prevailing standards of propriety. Significantly, these also convey a family of distinct individuals, not merely a collective under one head.

FIGURE 2.8   Queen Anne house, Fairfield, Iowa, 1896.

America's many poor women, who have always worked to support their families, could not easily fulfill this prescribed role. Regardless, all were inundated with the same cultural message: urban multi-family homes represented poverty and the danger of immorality, while detached single-family homes meant prosperity and respectability. During the nineteenth century, new streetcars and railroads allowed more families to live in such "best-possible" environments. Suburban development allowed men to commute daily to city jobs, while women and children stayed in adjacent enclaves of garden-ringed houses.

Development followed transit lines, and large-scale migration to suburban areas began soon after the Civil War (1861–1865). The most prosperous led the way, but suburban houses were also built for urban workers of modest means. **Streetcar buildouts** around a city's perimeter were within reach of factory jobs, but far enough from their smokestacks. Densely sited single-family homes with small yards made transit stops accessible by foot to as many people as possible. The houses were small and often identical for affordability, and more efficient row houses would made them even more economical. But symbolically, row house residents remained urban workers, while owners of detached suburban houses joined the middle class. No party walls and a tiny garden made buyers heirs to the Jeffersonian ideal, full participants in the American Dream.

Further out on the streetcar line were neighborhoods with more trees and fewer, larger houses. Low-density developments with curvilinear street patters and generous lots were called *picturesque enclaves*. Unlike city blocks where an entire complex neighborhood mingled in the street, or dense inner-ring suburbs where neighbors could overhear each other's conversations, residences in such areas were islands floating in tranquil gardens, with permanently occupied family villas.

Most were economically exclusive, with expensive lots and rules requiring that only large, dignified houses be built. While most homes had individualized designs, the overall image was that of uniformly luxurious homes for well-off residents. Many elite suburban developments were also ethnically exclusive through **restrictive covenants**, rules prohibiting residency by certain groups. African-Americans were most commonly excluded; northeastern U.S. cities might also prohibit Jews or Italians; in California, they might bar Mexicans and Asians. Elite picturesque enclaves provided their residents with an illusion of consistent, monochrome prosperity, a stark contrast with the late nineteenth century's complex reality of increasing poverty and ethnic diversity.

HOUSE AND MARKET

Along with many other cultural roles, the American house was also a commercial product, part of a private market of property owners and builders with only limited government involvement. During the late nineteenth and early twentieth centuries, houses could even be ordered by mail through Sears and Roebuck, the Chicago department store. A kit arrived by train with everything from pre-cut lumber to hardware and light fixtures, ready for a local builder to assemble on the foundation (not included). Like Downing, Sears offered options for every taste and budget, from spare cottages to plantation-worthy manors.

If choosing a house is a very private decision, housing is also a communal concern. How owners manage their property affects a community's health and safety, and what homes are available shapes a neighborhood's socioeconomic composition. In the U.S., the private housing market has consistently produced ample middle- and upper-class housing. But as New York's overcrowded, unsafe tenements show, private-market housing for the poor is often makeshift and inadequate.

Given this, the government might be expected to provide low-income homes. But U.S. property, construction, and banking interests have consistently resisted government ownership of housing. They see it as unfair competition, arguing that public provision of decent, affordable apartments would reduce tenants' incentive to save and enter the private housing market, source of their profits. The issue long received little attention, in part because Americans believed anyone who worked hard would find success and escape the slums. In theory, poverty was either a temporary, motivating condition, or proof of laziness.

This ideology came into question during the Great Depression. Economic collapse after the stock market crash of 1929 created a nationwide crisis and widespread doubt in the private market. Shared pain helped increase support for an expanded government role in ensuring everyone had a safe, healthy place to live. Housing advocate Catherine Bauer, whose 1934 book *Modern Housing* argued that the private housing market was inadequate, also criticized Americans' preference for detached single-family homes. She supported multi-family structures or row houses, whose greater efficiencies in land use and construction materials could shelter more families for less money.

Bauer co-authored the 1937 Housing Act, which offered cities federal subsidies to construct low-income housing. But World War II brought more direct government involvement. A federally coordinated economy built factories in strategic, often undeveloped locations. New housing for thousands of workers was crucial to the war effort, along with childcare and prepared meals that allowed more women to work outside their "natural" sphere in defense jobs, while the men fought.

POSTWAR EXPANSION AND LIMITS

Federally managed housing and family support were seen as strictly temporary measures for the war effort. Wartime advertisements reminded the public that a "normal" future of single-family homes and traditional gender roles would return. Housing construction quickly returned to the private market. After years of war-motivated efficiencies in construction, builders like Eli Kaufmann in California and William Levitt in the northeast would mass produce single-family homes on a scale Sears never could. Developers built on cheaper agricultural land further away from mass transit, assuming every family would own an automobile. Their acres of houses usually repeated the same small, simple design to keep costs down. But many included nonessential details, like gable roofs, shutters, and chimneys, that symbolically evoked the idealized country cottage.

The demand was overwhelming, in part because government intervention allowed more people than ever to buy suburban houses. Before 1937, banks required most home buyers to pay half up front, and repay the balance in three to five years—impossible terms for working families. The Housing Act established government guarantees for certain mortgages, meaning the bank would be repaid if a borrower defaulted. This instituted much easier 20-percent-down payments and twenty-year repayment periods. The Federal Housing Authority expanded the program in 1949, and began issuing mortgages in 1955. Veterans could purchase homes with no down payment at all.

This expanded and democratized home ownership, but only for certain Americans. Although racial covenants were declared unconstitutional in 1948,

FIGURE 2.9   Aerial view of Levittown, New York (*Life* magazine, 1949).

many developments, including Levittowns, remained restricted to white residents. Levitt insisted this was not racism but "good business," because white buyers, a majority of potential customers, preferred all-white neighborhoods. Federal policy supported him. The FHA charted racially diverse neighborhoods, called **redlining**, and refused to underwrite loans for homes there. Identical finances did not provide equal housing access: a white family had the FHA supporting suburban home ownership, and a widening rage of new houses to purchase. A black family could buy in few neighborhoods, with no FHA mortgage subsidies.

The 1968 Fair Housing Act criminalized discrimination in home lending, sales, and rental, but informal segregation persisted. This influenced America's racial inequality because houses create wealth and directly shape a family's financial security. Limiting any group's participation in the housing market limits their economic power over multiple generations, and keeps opportunity uneven.

DREAM HOUSES

The predominance of private housing is also why U.S. house designs tend to be conservative, like the Universal Studios' Colonial Revival house. While a domus or palazzo usually housed a family for many generations, most contemporary U.S. families relocate frequently (every seven years on average), following jobs or changing houses as family size and wealth evolve. Much of a house's value depends on its appeal to future buyers; market-tested styles and familiar spatial arrangements make a home easier to sell when needed, and proliferate accordingly.

But American suburban houses have undoubtedly evolved, particularly in size. An average new home in 1950 was under 1,000 square feet (93 square meters), but over 2,500 square feet (232 square meters) in 2013. Developers started producing homes that are more aristocratic manor than country cottage. **McMansions**, a late-twentieth-century innovation, are mass-market homes with elite pretentions. At 3,000 to 5,000 square feet (278 to 464 square meters), they are more aristocratic villas than country cottages.

McMansions have proliferated despite the declining average size of the U.S. household (2.6 people in 2010). They were born of both profligate lending practices during the 1990s and early 2000s, and an enduring faith in houses as ever-safe investments. This proved to be yet another myth surrounding the single-family home when the resulting bubble burst in 2008. The devastating effects of the resulting market collapse validated Jefferson and Downing's belief that the single-family home shapes national well-being, if not quite the way they imagined.

The crisis also motivated a healthy critique of how well the U.S. housing market provides the homes Americans need, or want. Does the archetypal "house-and-lawn" model still match the lives most Americans live, or want to? In any form—sprawling courtyard home, urban townhouse, mobile home, or high-rise apartment—houses shape our lives intimately and universally. This most private of building types is the only architecture most people ever own. Given how directly decisions about houses affect us, we do well to question received myths about a "good house," and carefully consider how different types construct different visions of family, work, individuality, privacy, gender roles, domestic versus public work, social class, and relationships with nature.

America's iconic single-family home embodies one clear truth: any house's character depends critically on its environment as much as its architecture. Villas and their suburban descendants respond to the perceived shortcomings of urban environments, but cannot be fully understood apart from the cities that generated them.

VOCABULARY

andron, archetype, atrium, bourgeois, cornice, cortile, domus, façade, gynaeceum, impluvium, loggia, McMansion, palazzo, party wall, patrician, patron, peristyle, piano nobile, precedent, redlining, restrictive covenants, single-family home, streetcar buildout, studiolo, tablinum, tenement, villa, yeoman farmer.

STUDY AND REVIEW QUESTIONS

1. Compare the ancient houses on Olynthos and in Pompeii: how were their designs similar and different, and how do both compare to the Universal Studios "house"?
2. What defined an ancient Roman domus and a villa? What made a country retreat a viable option, and when did that change?
3. How did the palazzo demonstrate a Florentine family's control over its neighborhood? What did the Medici's new palazzo do differently?
4. How does the Villa Rotunda's design affect how it relates to its surrounding landscape?
5. Explain how Monticello's architecture is both typical and unique for a Southern plantation house.
6. What was considered the most "American" type of home after Independence, and why? What did A. J. Downing believe such homes accomplished?
7. How did nineteenth-century attitudes about women and propriety affect ideas about the house?
8. How did various U.S. suburbs differ in design and socioeconomic terms?
9. Explain the wider effects of commercially produced houses in a private market on their availability and design.
10. What led to the explosion of suburban homes in the U.S. after World War II? Who was able to benefit, and who was excluded?

APPLICATION AND DISCUSSION EXERCISES

1. Investigate some of the many different housing traditions in your area, or in a chosen location around the world. Describe the houses' typical size, forms, spatial arrangements, and inhabitants, and decide which of the housing types in this chapter provides the most interesting comparison.
2. Compare where kitchens, dining rooms, spaces for socializing, and sleeping are located in the different houses discussed. What do different arrangements suggest about differences in family life?
3. What qualities do you believe define a "good house"? Do you believe the homes in your area meet these needs? Should there be different options, and what might they be like?

NOTE

1 Andrew Jackson Downing, "The Architecture of Country Houses," in H. F. Mallgrave, ed., *Architectural Theory Vol. I: An Anthology from Vitruvius to 1870* (Malden, MA: Blackwell, 2006), p. 464.

FURTHER READING

Ackerman, James. *The Villa: Form and Ideology of Country Houses*. Princeton, NJ: Princeton University Press, 1990.

Archer, John. *Architecture and Suburbia*. Minneapolis: University of Minnesota Press, 2005.

Bauer Wurster, Catherine. *Modern Housing*. New York: Houghton Mifflin, 1934.

Colomina, Beatriz, ed. *Sexuality and Space*. New York: Princeton Architectural Press, 1992.

Costanzo, Denise. "The Medici McMansion?" in D. Medina Lasansky, ed., *The Renaissance: Revised, Unexpurgated, Expanded*. Pittsburgh: Periscope Press, 2014.

Downing, Andrew Jackson. *The Architecture of Country Houses*. Reprint edition. New York: Da Capo Press, 1968 (1850).

Harris, Dianne. *Little White Houses: How the Postwar Home Constructed Race in America*. Minneapolis: University of Minnesota Press, 2013.

Nevett, Lisa. *Domestic Space in Classical Antiquity*. Cambridge: Cambridge University Press. 2012.

_____. *House and Society in the Ancient Greek World*. Cambridge: Cambridge University Press, 1999.

Wallace-Hadrill, Andrew. *Houses and Society in Pompeii and Herculaneum*. Princeton, NJ: Princeton University Press, 1994.

Wright, Gwendolyn. *Building the Dream: A Social History of Housing in America*. New York: Pantheon Books, 1981.

CHAPTER 3
THE CITY

THE HOUSE PROVIDES REFUGE from a more public, collective realm: the city. Since 2010, over half the world's people have lived in cities. Many have grown exponentially into megacities of over 10 million; today's largest, Shanghai, has nearly 18 million. Cities grow because they generate economic opportunity, which also supports cultural development. Because of this, cities have longstanding associations with social order and refinement that have shaped our vocabulary. *Urbane*, *civilization*, *citizen*, *polite*, *politics*, *police*, *cosmopolitan*—all derive from Latin and Greek words for "city" (*civitas, polis*). Taken as a group, these words suggest people have long believed that urban environments promote a controlled, cultured, and communally engaged form of life.

FIGURE 3.1   Model of Shanghai as projected in 2020, Urban Planning Exhibition Center.

SAFETY, SPACE, AND THE GRID

While cities contrast with agrarian living, the two are closely related; urban development cannot happen without a reliable, productive agricultural system to support larger communities. Traditionally, most cities developed where good farmland, water, and transportation were easily available, such as along a river. Because suitable locations would be attractive to competing groups of people, ancient cities also required defense. A hilltop or island might protect a small settlement, but larger ones needed defensive walls. Protective walls increase security, but also impose fixed boundaries; as more people want the city's safety, it becomes densely populated. The built physical structure of solid buildings, streets, and open spaces behind an early city's walls—its **urban fabric**—is typically dense as well.

As seen in chapter 1, ancient Athens began as a mountaintop **citadel**— the Acropolis. Later, the growing community moved below, behind a larger wall. The Panathenaic Way, the path for Athena's birthday procession, linked these lower and upper cities. Before culminating on the Acropolis, it crossed the **agora**, an open space in the dense city. This was framed by several **stoas**, long, free-standing porticos for commerce and social life distributed around the agora's perimeter (the "Stoic" philosophers met in one). One corner of the otherwise square-shaped void was occupied by a large council chamber for the 500 representatives who governed the city. Overall, Athens' agora had a permeable, geometrically irregular boundary defined by streets and scattered buildings.

Open spaces are crucial to city life, providing places where residents can gather for celebrations, business, or politics. Other structures supported "civilized" life in Greek cities, including those where boys received education and athletic training (the *gymnasium* and *stadium*) and theaters where the public was entertained by drama, poetry, and music. These amenities were the result of a concentrated population, which allows division of labor and specialization. When people's basic needs are met more efficiently, this leaves extra resources to support economic, educational, and artistic development.

Intellectual life would influence Greek cities in return. In the early fifth century BCE, the destroyed city of Miletus asked Hippodamos, a local philosopher, to create a rebuilding plan. He arranged streets and blocks in a grid, which maximizes occupancy and organizes access to a city's valuable space. Temples, an agora, and a theater were grouped near the city center. Located on a peninsula, Hippodamos aligned the grid with its length and adjusted its proportions in response to the irregular shape. Even with water protecting three sides, a wall encircled Miletus' entire perimeter. The design addressed the three fundamental urban functions: defense, order, and public life.

Hippodamos is the earliest named person given credit for designing an entire city. But the gridiron layout was not new; the Indus Valley holds examples

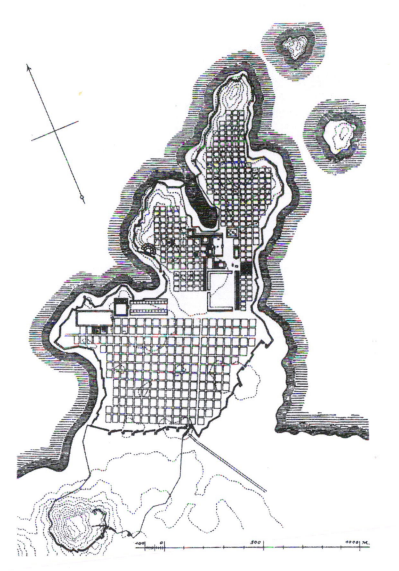

FIGURE 3.2   Hippodamos' plan for Miletus, fifth century BCE.

that are nearly 2,000 years older than Miletus. Around the same time as the Miletus plan, the *Kao Gong Ji*, a fifth-century-BCE Chinese encyclopedia, describes a gridded city layout in detail. Its square, walled city is carefully aligned with the cardinal directions. Three gates on each wall connect to six wide intersecting streets. Two open plazas are adjacent to the ruler's palace, which sits at the center behind another wall. The nobles, tradesmen, and craftsmen each had designated neighborhoods, but peasants were excluded entirely. The city's physical layout established a social configuration focused on the ruler at center.

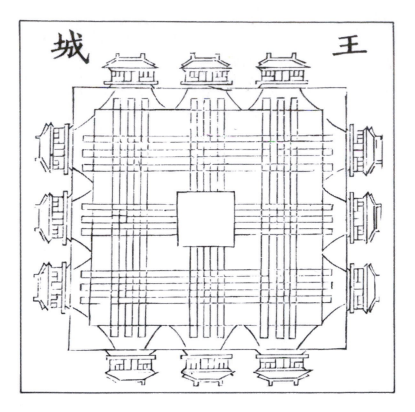

FIGURE 3.3   Plan for the "Ruler's City" based on description in the *Kao Gong Ji*, ca. fifth century BCE.

This abstract scheme, probably centuries older than the book, is manifest in real capital cities built by centuries of Chinese emperors. Xi'an, a square, walled city begun less than a century after the *Kao Gong Ji*, also had three gates per wall and a north-oriented orthogonal street grid. The palace—not at center, but at the city's northern end—remained its focus. Like at Miletus, the grid is used flexibly; varied block sizes and street widths create a hierarchy of neighborhoods and streets. Zhouli principles were still followed centuries later when the Yuan dynasty built its new capital, now Beijing.

The grid makes cities simple to plan and navigate, which led another Greek philosopher to argue against Hippodamos' approach. Aristotle observed that an irregular layout disorients strangers and gives residents a defensive advantage.[1] After the catapult was invented in 399 BCE, round towers and walls proved most resistant to projectiles, so these were incorporated into Greek ideas about the most effective city layouts. Military developments shaped urban design; cities were survival machines to sustain the civilized life within.

THE CASTRUM PLAN

The ancient Romans also approached city-building from a rational, military perspective, but disregarded recent Greek recommendations when building new cities. Most began when an occupying Roman army built a **castrum**, a fort with a square perimeter wall containing a grid of tents. This layout was used in Roman cities from Spain to Syria, North Africa to Britain. A castrum was roughly oriented in the cardinal directions. Each side of the wall had a gate leading to one of two intersecting main streets: the **cardo** (north–south) and **decumanus** (east–west). Temples, theaters, and other public spaces clustered near their intersection at the city's center.

The Romans retained the more vulnerable grid and square corners because their vast empire's security relied less on defensible cities than a mobile army and good roads—a Roman specialty. Cities were central to cultural life, however, and offered the ancient world's best infrastructure. Aqueducts provided fresh water, public baths promoted hygiene, and sewers handled waste from public latrines, drastically reducing (if hardly eliminating) stench and disease, unfortunate by-products of concentrated, "civilized" living.

A Roman city's chief open space was the **forum**. Rome's pre-Imperial Forum Romanum had an irregular-shaped plan and free-standing buildings, like an agora. Later emperors, however, built new forums as orderly, rectangular spaces framed by a continuous colonnaded portico like a stoa around the perimeter. An arched entry gateway was aligned with a temple opposite. The forum's controlled space expressed imperial power and administrative order, and became a symbol of Rome. Even after its Western empire collapsed, this urban pattern endured. Dozens of Roman cities retained their castrum layout into the Middle Ages and beyond.

DISORDER, DIAGRAMS, AND THE IDEAL CITY

Grid patterns reveal a rational, intentionally planned layout. But many cities have erratic, **organic** street patterns and perimeter walls. Such haphazard plans respond gradually to topographic and property conditions. Organic cities also need open spaces for markets and public gatherings, but they occur opportunistically and are often irregularly shaped. In medieval Italy, an opening in the urban fabric was called a **piazza**. These voids in the solid city, usually found in front of churches or civic buildings, provided spatial relief from tiny homes and narrow, winding streets—outdoor living rooms.

The organic city's geometric irregularity is a flexible response to practical conditions. But the hope that a rational configuration will produce a more orderly, harmonious community resurged during the Renaissance, when English author

FIGURE 3.4   Piazza Santissima Annunziata, Florence, Italy, 1419–1516.

Thomas More invented the word **utopia**. It can mean either "good place" or "non-place"; an abstract ideal. A 1460s book by architect Antonio di Averlino, known as Filarete, outlined an **ideal city** ("Sforzinda"). His scheme's double wall combines a circle and an eight-pointed star, with defensive towers where they connect. Eight radial streets intersect at the center, site of the main piazza, cathedral, palace, and markets: another vision of security, public life, and organization.

Fifteenth-century Italy, already quite urbanized, offered few opportunities to build such schemes. But they fed a growing appetite for urban order that occasionally altered existing cities. In the 1420s, a new orphanage in Florence framed one side of an irregular piazza with a long, arched portico. Thirty years later, the adjacent church added a new façade. Instead of dominating the piazza as expected, its scale and style mimicked the portico next door. Sixty years after that, the building across from the orphanage added its own matching arcaded portico.

These projects transformed the Piazza Santissima Annunziata into a visually unified urban space. Its three coherent sides make the space appear (deceptively) like a perfect rectangle, recalling a Roman forum. It took nearly a century to produce this pocket of harmony because it involved modifying many properties with multiple owners. Either all parties agree to the changes, or they must be imposed by force. Realizing a new urban vision in an existing city requires either great patience, or great power—often both.

REMAKING ROME

If anyone had enough power to restructure an Italian Renaissance city, it was the Pope. The most important city for the papacy was Rome, from which it ruled

Western Christendom and much of central Italy. But Rome's urban structure was nothing like a castrum. The city grew organically around hills by the Tiber river. Later emperors imposed islands of order, such as the imperial forums, but Rome's overall layout remained chaotic.

Many Romans did not welcome papal rule, and the city's labyrinthine structure made it dangerous for popes to travel across hostile neighborhoods with narrow, winding streets. The ideal of an orderly city thus had strategic political value: wide, straight roads and regular urban spaces would permit more secure, impressive religious processions, and assert papal authority over *urbis et orbis* (city and world).

Popes seldom ruled long, however, so most change happened incrementally. Modern Rome's first straight street was built by Pope Alexander VI in 1500. Ten years later, Pope Julius II's via Giulia created an upscale neighborhood across the Tiber for wealthy Florentine supporters. By the 1580s, Rome had many wide, straight streets and newly developed areas. Yet its chaotic core remained an impediment for the papacy, and the thousands of religious pilgrims visiting each year who supported the city's economy.

One pope who reigned for only five years, Sixtus V (1585–1590), left the greatest mark on Rome's structure. His advisers proposed a network of intersecting straight streets that linked major sites, providing clear navigation routes through the maze. At **nodes** where these streets converged, **obelisks** (tall granite

FIGURE 3.5   Gianlorenzo Bernini, Piazza San Pietro, Rome, Italy, 1667.

Egyptian monoliths imported by the ancient Romans) were erected as landmarks. Pedestrians could see them from afar and find their way to important monuments.

Sixtus V's pathways through Rome's chaos produced a more manageable and orderly city. Major nodes became important symbolic spaces. The disordered square in front of the new St. Peter's basilica, one of Rome's biggest attractions, was dramatically regularized in the seventeenth century. Two framing colonnades created an elliptical forum, now one of the world's most recognizable urban spaces. Rome became known as a city of grand piazzas, and made a world-class city synonymous with straight streets and harmonious open spaces.

Italian Renaissance urbanism's emphasis on urban organization also gave birth to the **ghetto**. The city of Venice's Jewish community had been invited to come in the fifteenth century. But in 1516 the city forced all Jews, viewed suspiciously as outsiders, to move onto a tiny, formerly industrial island (*ghetto* derives from Venetian for "iron foundry"). The ghetto was rebuilt as a walled enclosure with gates, locked at sunset and unlocked at sunrise—a de facto prison for the entire community.

Authorities saw enforced separateness as a rational solution for "outsiders" in their city. The idea later spread: in 1555, Rome created a ghetto for its ancient Jewish community; Florence created another in 1571. Ghetto residents were not necessarily poor, but a growing population within a fixed boundary resulted in inadequate, overcrowded conditions. "Ghetto" eventually came to mean any substandard neighborhood housing a marginalized population.

A "NEW" LONDON?

Although order, grand spaces, and regularity came to be associated with the "modern" city, most European cities were ancient. London, originally a castrum city, was destroyed in late antiquity. An organic city grew within the restored Roman walls—now London's financial district. The wall's southeastern intersection with the Thames river was defended by the Tower of London.

During the seventeenth century, the city expanded outside its walls: docks and warehouses were built to the east; to the west appeared elegant residential districts with London's first planned, regular squares. The area within the ancient wall remained an overcrowded warren of narrow, increasingly impassable streets. These conditions contributed to an outbreak of bubonic plague in 1665 that killed almost 100,000 Londoners. A year later, the Great London Fire destroyed 80 percent of the city, including the 500-year-old St. Paul's cathedral. This disaster also provided a unique opportunity: to restructure a major European city according to modern ideas.

Dozens of people proposed ideas for a new, better-functioning London with improved circulation and orderly open spaces. Some, like Richard Newcourt,

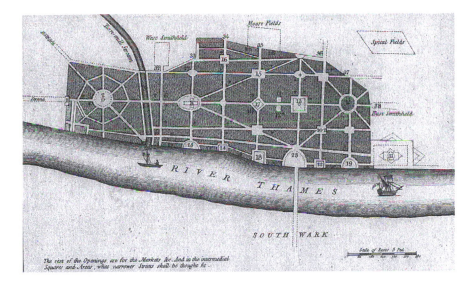

FIGURE 3.6   Plans for rebuilding London by Richard Newcourt and Sir John Evelyn, ca. 1667.

resurrected the city's former grid pattern. Newcourt's plan features a rectilinear city of rectangular blocks with a small church at each center, with the largest of five major squares at its geometric center. His layout retained no trace of the old London. A proposal by Sir John Evelyn approximates London's former perimeter and preserves the location of St. Paul's, but introduces an orthogonal grid of large blocks overlaid with diagonal avenues. At major nodes, Evelyn shows plazas of various regular shapes. A similar plan by Christopher Wren used smaller blocks closer in scale to the old city.

None of these rational, modern plans were built, however. Imposing any new layout involved obliterating city-wide property ownership patterns, which proved politically and economically impossible in Britain's parliamentary democracy. Even in a burnt-out city, it required absolute power to sweep aside private citizens' objections and impose an ideal plan.

Old London was rebuilt to improve traffic, sanitary conditions, and safety. Streets followed their former pattern but were widened; all property owners sacrificed a little frontage for better access. New building codes required fireproof construction and set maximum building heights. Today, London's ancient core contains both a 1,000-year-old street pattern and an adapted vision of modern urban order. Rational schemes were more easily built elsewhere, such as the New World.

IDEAL CITIES IN AMERICA

One city across the Atlantic is strikingly similar to Newcourt's London plan: Philadelphia. There too, two main streets converge on a central square that breaks the overall rectangular grid. Now the site of City Hall, it was intended to be an open space surrounded by a Quaker meeting house, government assembly halls, a market, and school—all the city's communal functions, like Miletus or Sforzinda. One of the plan's creators, William Penn, was in London after the fire, and carried Newcourt's urban vision to America.

The grid that structures much of the American landscape was promoted by Thomas Jefferson. When the young Republic annexed the Ohio valley in 1812, nearly doubling its total territory, Jefferson proposed the land be surveyed and divided into a grid of 6-mile squares (**townships**) subdivided into thirty-six **sections** of 1 square mile each. Township and section boundaries would be applied across the expanding U.S., and determined the location of railroads, political boundaries, farms, and roads. Unlike ancient grid cities, bounded by protective walls, this system was infinitely extensible. Instead of a contrast between the city's built order and disordered nature, wilderness was redefined as "property," ready to be claimed by a nation increasingly convinced that it was destined to occupy an entire continent. The uniform grid was also appropriately egalitarian. On paper, each square appears equal, like each vote.

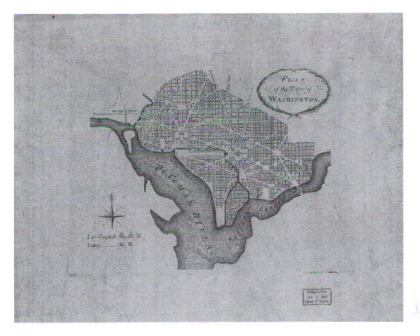

FIGURE 3.7   Pierre Charles L'Enfant, Plan of Washington, DC, 1792.

But even democracy includes hierarchies. Washington, DC, was built as a symbolic capital, a city set apart from a system of competing states to represent the nation as a whole. Its plan was designed by French planner Pierre Charles L'Enfant, familiar with Rome-inspired axial networks, in consultation with Jefferson, proponent of the grid. Like Evelyn's London plan, Washington employs both systems: a background grid is overlaid by a network of diagonal streets, with nodes for major national institutions.

The President's ("White") House and the Capitol both sit at nodes with five intersecting streets on opposite ends of diagonal Pennsylvania Avenues. The White House faces south, and the Capitol, elevated on an artificially constructed hill for commanding height, looks west toward an enormous park, the Mall. Both face a third structure, the Washington Monument. Its colossal obelisk form appropriately serves the same urban function as it would in Rome: a landmark in a city of monuments.

HAUSSMANN'S PARIS: THE POWER OF ELEGANCE

Despite the many difficulties involved in modifying existing cities, European powers fought to make their old, dense capitals work for modern life and political reality during the nineteenth century. Urban disorder in Paris, for example, directly affected French national stability. Narrow streets allowed neighborhoods to isolate themselves by constructing barricades, behind which they could hold off the French army. After the French Revolution of 1789, civic uprisings contributed to a cycle of nationwide revolutions; controlling Paris was key to controlling France.

Like London, Paris began as a castrum city, then became a dense organic city. Its first open space, the Place Royale (now the Place des Vosges, 1605–1612) began when France's Florentine queen, Catherine de' Medici, had a royal palace destroyed. Her son rebuilt it as an idealized version of SS. Annunziata: a perfect square ringed by uniform elegant houses. Napoleon Bonaparte attempted to remake Paris in the early nineteenth century, which proved harder than conquering Europe. When his great-nephew came to power in 1848 as Napoleon III, he resolved to make Paris a more orderly and navigable city.

The executor of Napoleon III's plan was Georges-Eugène Haussmann, given vast authority as "Prefect of the Seine." Early in his rule, Napoleon III decided where he wanted new streets and boulevards carved into the city. Haussmann was empowered to purchase, seize, and demolish private property. Within a few decades, a network of wide boulevards cut through formerly dense neighborhoods—especially those with a history of uprisings.

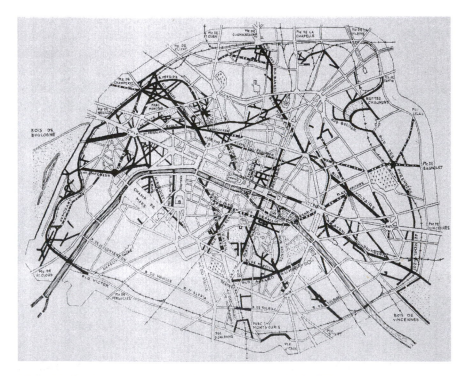

FIGURE 3.8   Plan for the transformation of Paris under Napoleon III, 1853–1870.

Enlarged, straight streets eased movement of both merchandise and troops, promoting order and commerce. This helped the government, as well as business owners and professionals—the *bourgeoisie*. Haussmann also modernized the city's infrastructure. New sewers, paved streets and sidewalks with street lights, benches, and trees made Paris cleaner and healthier. New building codes dictated that façades along the new boulevards follow a fixed pattern. Uniform height and aligned rows of windows gave the Place Royale's coherent, orderly elegance to entire "Haussmannized" neighborhoods.

Another revolt ended Napoleon III's reign in 1870. But his urban changes were too far along to halt. Once complete, they proved effective: Parisian uprisings would not threaten the national government again until 1968. Napoleon III rebuilt central Paris into a refined-looking modern city for wealthier residents, a process we now call **gentrification**. But the original inhabitants of its newly dignified districts could no longer afford them and had to move elsewhere. Haussmann's interventions ejected over 300,000 poor Parisians from the city center. Most ended in peripheral shantytowns—proto-favelas.

CERDÀ: CITIES FOR ALL

In Barcelona, Europe's most densely populated city in 1850, a heavy city wall and exploding urban population also led to uprisings. The city sent architect and engineer Idelfonso Cerdà to Paris for two years to study its modernization. Cerdà returned both impressed and critical. Haussmann's Paris was undoubtedly healthier and more beautiful. But he considered pushing the poor out of the city to be a mistaken and inadequate strategy.

Cerdà proposed a comprehensive philosophy of city development in his 1867 *General Theory of Urbanization*. He views cities not as fixed structures, but living organisms with interdependent systems. The wealthy depend on products and services produced by the poor, so no exclusively upper-class city can remain healthy. Any sustainable long-term urban plan must accommodate all necessary groups, and be adaptable over time.

Because urban fortifications had become militarily obsolete, Cerdà had Barcelona's confining wall demolished in 1858, and enlarged its area by ten times. Despite his organic metaphor, he did not propose an "organic" plan, but a grid overlain by two crossing diagonal boulevards, with a plaza at their intersection. If Haussmann's Paris elaborated Rome's network, Cerdà's Barcelona simplified Washington, DC.

The plan enacts Cerdà's progressive logic by establishing a flexible framework that could be developed freely to accommodate functions as needed. The square blocks' corners were also chamfered (cut off), creating a mini-plaza for

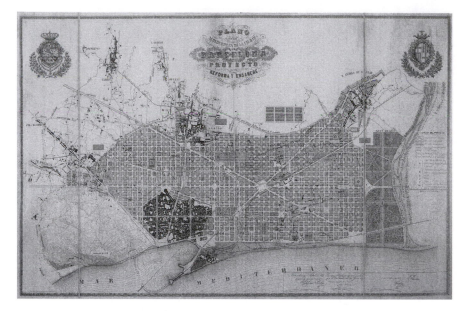

FIGURE 3.9   Idelfonso Cerdà, Plan for Barcelona, 1859.

public life at every intersection. Cerdà's plan shaped modern Barcelona and other cities. More fundamentally, he argued that cities should support a healthy life for all residents into an unpredictable future.

URBAN ORDER VS. URBAN PLEASURE: SITTE

Vienna's past was similar to Paris and London: born as a Roman fort, later a walled organic city. But its medieval Altstadt ("old city") was surrounded by fortification walls and a **glacis**, or open buffer zone. Lower-density development surrounded this empty ring of space. Vienna's 1857 modernization neither reshaped its organic core, like Paris, nor stretched into unbuilt landscape, like Barcelona. Planners instead exploited the open zone between the Altstadt and the outer city. A 2-mile-long beltway road, the Ringstrasse, anchored a grand, spacious district with a new national parliament, city hall, museums, opera house, and university.

Yet one Viennese observer was unimpressed with the elegant, orderly Ringstrasse. Camillo Sitte, an art historian and educator, preferred the narrow, crooked streets, intimate plazas, and unpredictable structure of the organic Altstadt. Long, wide, straight boulevards and widely spaced monuments are practical and imposing, but for pedestrians diagrammatic purity can become boring. Sitte's *City Planning According to Its Artistic Principles* (1889) contradicted four centuries of expert thinking about the city. His interest in the city's "artistic" qualities contrasts with a more typical emphasis on rational order and spaciousness. Sitte asked: what makes us enjoy a city? He believed designers should learn from how organic cities create interesting, delightful places, a view few shared until his writings became popular decades later.

DIAGRAMMATIC NON-CITIES: HOWARD, CIAM, AND THE SUBURB

Other critics believed large cities had become unworkable and unnecessary. Trains and factories were incompatible with historic fabric built for pedestrians and cart traffic. Walls no longer offered security, so the ancient cause of density no longer applied. Rather than conduct major surgery on cities built for another age, new communities should be designed for modern life. Ebenezer Howard of Britain's proposed Garden City (1898) promoted a decentralized model of "urban" living that integrates residents with nature. Inspired by elite U.S. suburbs, he envisioned a cluster of six small towns of 32,000 inhabitants in single-family homes. They would surround a central, larger town of 58,000 to produce a total population of 250,000—a region of "slumless, smokeless cities" rather than one metropolis.

Howard's ideal city diagram separates built-up zones with greenbelts of open space and binds them with modern transportation: railroads, canals, and roads link separate but interdependent communities. All necessary support functions are distributed across the towns and the landscape: agriculture, hospitals, schools, factories, even an insane asylum and a "home for inebriates" (alcoholics)—each has a place in his scheme.

Like the ideal city plans in the *Kao Gong Ji* and Filarete's Sforzinda, Howard assumes that a good city results from naming all its necessary components and arranging them into a logical diagram. This approach to city design would become widespread in the twentieth century. In 1933, the International Congress of Modern Architects (CIAM) asked design professionals from around the world to draft principles for modern urban design. The result, published by participant Le Corbusier in 1943 as the "Athens Charter," shaped cities for decades.

CIAM asserted that cities exist to accommodate four basic functions: dwelling, working, recreation, and transportation. Like Howard, it held that a good city clusters these activities into separate, well-connected zones, so that people reside in one district and work in another part of the city. Unlike the Garden City, the CIAM approach said that with enough open space and efficient transportation, people could live together in a modern city of millions. Many CIAM-affiliated urban schemes concentrated people into large, widely spaced buildings to maximize open space, and separated vehicular and pedestrian traffic on different levels for safety.

A number of schemes by modernist architects Ludwig Hilbersheimer and Le Corbusier illustrate CIAM's modern urbanism of low-density, widely spaced buildings in separate districts zoned by function. Although their stark tower blocks in space looked quite radical, the CIAM planning formula was already found in U.S. suburbs; most carefully separated dwelling from industrial and commercial districts, and provided generously scaled parks and roads for recreation and transportation. Both the huge city of towers and the picturesque suburb also inverted traditional urban fabric: instead of a solid city with carved-out streets and plazas, they consisted of wide-open voids punctuated by scattered object-buildings.

URBANIZING THE AUTOMOTIVE CITY

The U.S. government shaped urban structure through interventions in the mortgage market (see chapter 2) and through federal transportation policy. After World War II, federal support shifted from public transit and railroads to freeway construction. In 1956, the Interstate and Defense Highways Act made constructing a national system of limited-access freeways a coordinated, federally funded endeavor. This reflected influence from the automobile industry and another military development: the nuclear age. World War II demonstrated dense cities' vulnerability to aerial bombing. A population distributed over a large area, with roads allowing people to drive themselves out of danger, was considered safer.

After World War II, the growth of American's cities no longer followed streetcar and train lines, but freeways. Access ramps determined the locations of new development by linking distant fields of isolated houses to jobs. Low-density suburban sprawl was possible because of proliferating freeways and cars. The postwar frontier of vast suburbs dominated by single-family homes and roadside commercial strips posed urban problems, however. Dividing functions into detached, widely spaced buildings only accessible by private motorized travel could produce great social isolation. American critic Lewis Mumford believed CIAM's four functions missed the city's most necessary "fifth function": space for civic life, like the agora, forum, or piazza.

In the 1950s, two new building types tried to compensate for the U.S. suburb's decentralization. One was the **civic center** with enclosed spaces for scheduled community events. Victor Gruen, an architect who moved to the U.S. from Vienna in the 1930s, believed the necessity of shopping could draw people into a space that promoted more spontaneous social encounters. If protected from the weather, it could also improve on the traditional street by being comfortable year round. Add parking, and the alienation of the automobile city is solved.

Gruen's solution was the enclosed *shopping center* or *shopping mall*, now a familiar feature of cities around the world. However, unlike city streets, most are privately owned facilities whose space is not truly public; if you hold a political protest in one expect to be escorted outside by guards immediately.

Malls are private spaces that are public in scale, but not control. Civic centers and malls, like the suburban house, are also objects in a spatial void. They provide some of urban life's amenities, but not an urban experience—something many U.S. suburban dwellers sought in cities like New York, itself undergoing dramatic change.

A NEW NEW YORK

Robert Moses led New York City's modernization from the 1930s through the 1960s. A "Haussmann" of sorts, Moses' legacy includes dozens of bridges and expressways, public parks, and pools that reshaped the twentieth-century city. One especially prestigious project was Lincoln Center, a fine arts campus for New York's opera, symphony, ballet, theater, and conservatory. Its performances provide cultural experiences seldom available in the suburbs, and its design provides the city with a coherent, elegant urban piazza.

Clustering performing arts venues into one district is classic diagrammatic planning. But it is not necessarily "rational": the institutions are administratively independent, and people typically attend only one performance an evening. Lincoln Center's campus was meant to showcase New York's cultural sophistication and promote the performing arts, and the collective image of the ensemble was considered more powerful than scattered facilities.

FIGURE 3.10　Lincoln Center for the Performing Arts, New York City, 1955–1969 (photo by Matthew G. Bisanz).

The complex was also developed to gentrify a West Side district. The same federal program subsidizing suburban mortgages after World War II also provided funds for cities to demolish **slums** with substandard housing, often dominated by crumbling and unlivable tenements, and build new projects. This process was called **urban renewal**. Lincoln Center's campus displaced about 7,000 area residents, largely African-American dock workers. The original project plan included new housing units for 4,400 people, but far fewer were completed. The priority was removing what city leaders considered "blight" that occupied valuable property and gave an image of poverty. Like Haussmann's Paris, the goal was a magnetic, pleasurable city of prestige and prosperity.

With most suburbs racially restricted, minority residents displaced by urban renewal had fewer options than the Parisian working class. Federal subsidies also supported new low-income housing, often built as degraded versions of CIAM's vision of residential towers in open gardens. Because of inadequate maintenance and isolation from jobs, among other reasons, many failed—none more dramatically than the award-winning Pruitt-Igoe in St. Louis, dynamited in 1972. In the U.S., "inner city" and "housing projects" came to signify modern ghettos, unlocked but still confining.

JACOBS: THEORY, REALITY, AND ACTIVISM

Rationally diagrammed urban solutions did not deliver utopia. Architectural journalist Jane Jacobs observed how many expensively "renewed" areas that followed the CIAM formula—separation of functions, plenty of green space between buildings—were often run-down only a few years later. Jacobs also studied healthy urban neighborhoods that attracted residents and visitors. They were usually densely structured, with a mix of functions and building types that produced activity and safety, breaking all the CIAM rules.

In 1961, Jacobs offered an alternative route to the good city in *The Death and Life of Great American Cities*. She reminded readers that history has demonstrated that many widely accepted, "scientific" theories, like medical bloodletting, can be wrong. If planning dogmas such as single-use zoning do not reliably produce better cities, she asks, why should they be followed? Her solution: learn from reality, and temper abstract theories and seductively logical diagrams with common sense. Jacobs, who successfully battled Moses' plan to divide her New York neighborhood with a freeway, also advocated local activism against authority and experts. Hers became one of many voices in the 1960s insisting that a city should serve its people, not its rulers.

Cities reflect the complexities of an entire culture: physical resources, security concerns, social organization, distribution of power, ideals of order (or disorder), and patterns of life. But Jacobs' frustration with city planners in her day is a reminder that urban environments also result from decisions by authoritative individuals and groups. Those who design and construct buildings and cities bring specific priorities and visions to the process. Who are they?

VOCABULARY

agora, cardo and decumanus, castrum, citadel, forum, gentrification, ghetto, glacis, ideal city, node, obelisks, organic, piazza, section and township, slum, stoa, urban fabric, urban renewal, utopia.

STUDY AND REVIEW QUESTIONS

1. What allows cities to exist and persist, and how can they provide people with a better life? Describe some of the amenities that made Greek cities like Athens seem "civilized" places.
2. Compare two different versions of the ancient grid city. What are the advantages and disadvantages in each case?
3. What causes organic cities to develop, and what sorts of structure and urban spaces do they usually have?
4. What sort of ideas about "ideal" urban organization and spaces emerged in the Italian Renaissance? Why were they limited in scope, and slow in implementation?
5. Why is the ghetto a "logical" product of Italian Renaissance urbanism?
6. How did proposals to rebuild London after the 1666 fire plan to make it an impressive, well-organized city? Why was London rebuilt the way it was? Is that good, or tragic?
7. What made the grid appropriate for organizing the American landscape? Why was it only part of the layout for Washington, DC?
8. What motivated the determination to make Paris an organized, modern city? What were Haussmann's changes like, and what effects did they have?
9. Compare Cerdà's plan for Barcelona with Haussmann's Paris; Washington, DC; Sixtus V's Rome; and the ancient walled city. What was new about Cerdà's philosophy of city planning?
10. Compare Camillo Sitte's idea of a good city with those of Ebenezer Howard and CIAM. What are the strengths and limits of a diagrammatic approach to urban planning?

11. How has an abundance of highways and automobiles shaped post–World War II American cities and suburbs? Do you agree with Lewis Mumford about their missing "fifth function"?

12. How do Lincoln Center's and Jane Jacobs' critiques of professional planners embody "top-down" and "grassroots" views of the city? Should one carry more weight than the other?

APPLICATION AND DISCUSSION EXERCISES

1. Using maps or satellite images, investigate the urban structure of your own neighborhood. How would you describe its structure and degree of density? How does this structure affect inhabitants?

2. Compare two different urban environments you have experienced: street patterns, building height and density, traffic, and types of activities. What are the benefits and weakness of each?

3. How would you design an "ideal city"? What would you most want it to achieve?

NOTE

1 Aristotle, *Politics*, Trans. H. Rackham (Cambridge, MA: Harvard University Press, 1944): VII.x.4–5.

FURTHER READING

Cerdà, Idelfonso. *The Five Bases of the General Theory of Urbanization*. Madrid: Electa, 1999.

Choay, Françoise. *The Modern City: Planning in the 19th Century*. New York: Braziller, 1970.

Collins, George R. *Camillo Sitte: The Birth of Modern City Planning*. New York: Rizzoli, 1986.

Jacobs, Jane. *The Death and Life of Great American Cities*. New York: Random House, 1961.

Le Corbusier. *The City of To-Morrow and Its Planning*. Trans. F. Etchells. New York: Dover, 1987.

_____. *The Athens Charter*. Trans. A. Eardley. New York: Grossman Publishers, 1973.

Lynch, Kevin. *Image of the City*. Cambridge, MA: MIT Press, 1960.

Morris, A. E. J. *History of Urban Form before the Industrial Revolutions*. Harlow, England: Pearson, Ltd., 1994.

Mumford, Eric. *The CIAM Discourse on Urbanism, 1928–1960*. Cambridge, MA: MIT Press, 2000.

Mumford, Lewis. *The City in History: Its Origins and Transformations, and Its Prospects.* New York: Harcourt and Brace, 1961.

Sitte, Camillo. *City Planning According to Its Artistic Principles.* Trans. G. R. and C. C. Collins. New York: Random House, 1965.

Steinhardt, Nancy Shatzman. *Chinese Imperial City Planning.* Honolulu: University of Hawaii Press. 1990.

Van Zanten, David. *Building Paris: Architectural Institutions and the Transformation of the French Capital, 1830–1870.* Cambridge: Cambridge University Press, 1994.

PART II
WHO MAKES ARCHITECTURE?
BUILDERS, PROFESSIONALS, ARTISTS

CHAPTER 4
THE ARCHITECT

ARCHITECTS MAKE UP LESS THAN 0.1 percent of the U.S. population, yet they appear quite frequently as lead characters in films. Other professions are even more over-represented (assassins, surely), but the architect's visibility appears especially exaggerated when compared to a closely related field like engineering. America has five times as many engineers as architects, yet Hollywood rarely presents them as dramatic protagonists.[1]

This may reflect very different stereotypes about architecture and engineering. We often assume that architects combine independent creativity and confident professionalism, in effect a hybrid of artist and attorney. We might instead imagine engineering to be about mathematics, technical solutions, and precision more than creativity. Yet architects and engineers are both inventive problem solvers who use design to meet human needs. In fact, for most of history, these two disciplines were one.

ARCHITECTURE'S OLDEST SIGNATURE: IMHOTEP

The design of Stonehenge was conceived and modified in several phases over many centuries by multiple human imaginations. But the idea that a building has one "author" is as old as the site's first circular ditch (see Figure 1.3). Over 4,600 years ago, during ancient Egypt's Old Kingdom, the pharaoh Djoser had a chief adviser named Imhotep, a high priest. A commoner, his priestly education let him advance into the kingdom's elite. He was also a healer, for which he was deified (declared a god) after his death—the ultimate honor.

Imhotep is also the earliest known person to receive individual credit for a building design. He rethought the traditional royal tomb, originally an underground chamber covered by a flat-topped platform with slanting sides—a **mastaba**. Imhotep proposed stacking a series of mastabas of diminishing size on top of the first. The result, a "stepped pyramid" that rose almost 200 feet, led to Giza's first Great Pyramid a century later. Imhotep's new idea offered Djoser a more impressive monument, and also guaranteed his own legacy. He was given the honor of being depicted in portraits and buried in his own tomb. Today he is considered the father of three professions: architecture, engineering, and medicine. Deification aside, his name lived forever.

Simply imagining a new form could not secure Imhotep's immortality; his idea had to be achievable through construction. Traditional mud-brick mastabas would have crumbled under a taller monument's weight. But Imhotep saw untapped potential in Egypt's natural abundance of high-quality stone, only quarried in limited amounts at the time, and in its skilled masons. His project initiated an era of vastly expanded stone extraction for large-scale construction. It also took knowledge of material, technical, and social resources for his vision of an artificial honorific mountain to become reality.

Imhotep was literate, knew mathematics, and understood enough about building to propose workable solutions and exercise authority over a project. But it is unlikely that he ever carved a block of stone. A great social distance divided the manual labor of lower-class craftsmen from the creative, conceptual endeavors suitable for Egypt's highest elite. Imhotep used a combination of abstract imagination and practical knowledge to turn a building project into a source of eternal glory, both the pharaoh's and his own.

THE GREEK ARCHITECT: NAME, MYTH, AND BUILDER

"Architect" comes from an ancient Greek word, *architekton* (αρχιτεκτον), which means "chief builder." "Archi"—as in "archangel" and "archenemy"—means "main" or "primary." "Tekton" is related to "tectonics" and "texture" (both about physical structure), and means "maker" or craftsman. Greek architects managed

FIGURE 4.1   Imhotep, Stepped Pyramid of Djoser, Saqquara, Egypt, 2681–2662 BCE.

any complex construction project—buildings, bridges, roads, canals, machinery, or ships—encompassing both architecture and engineering in today's terms.

According to the Greeks, the first architect was the mythical figure Daedalus, a clever inventor. While working for King Minos of Crete, one of Daedalus' devices secretly helped the queen have an affair with a bull. Her betrayal was revealed when she bore the Minotaur (which means, ironically, "Bull of Minos"), a creature with a bull's head and a human body. To hide this embarrassing and dangerous creature, the king had Daedalus design an inescapable prison: the Labyrinth. When Minos learned that his trusted adviser had helped the queen betray him, Daedalus and his son Icarus were imprisoned in the labyrinth. Daedalus invented wings with wax "feathers" to escape, and both flew out. Icarus, however, ignored his father's warning not to fly too close to the sun, and fell to his death when the wax melted. Significantly, "Daedalus" means "skillful one" or "cunning worker"; the designer's imagination is a powerful, and potentially threatening, commodity.

Surviving Greek writings also name the architects of known buildings. The Parthenon had two: Kallikrates, and Iktinos, who wrote a book (now lost) describing the project. This shows that Greek architects were literate, and important enough to be discussed by other authors. A later list of ancient Greece's "seven greatest architects" includes five historically documented builders (Iktinos among them), the mythical Daedalus, and the mathematician Archimedes, who invented machines that helped defend his city. However, unlike Imhotep, architects in Greek city-states were supervising craftsmen, not part of a ruling elite.

FIGURE 4.2   Iktinos and Kallikrates, Parthenon, Athens, 447–438 BCE.

ARCHITECTURE'S OLDEST BOOK: VITRUVIUS

The earliest surviving book by any architect comes from a Roman named Vitruvius, who lived from around 80 to 10 BCE. He is our chief source of information on Greek architectural writings.

Vitruvius built one basilica in the city of Fano (no trace survives), but spent most of his career designing and building weapons for Julius Caesar's army during his campaigns in Gaul (France). These included **ballistae**, torsion-powered catapults that shoot darts, and a smaller lighter version called the **scorpio**. This work earned Vitruvius a life-changing benefit: a pension that freed him from his military career. He used his secure income and free time to write *The Ten Books* ("Scrolls") *on Architecture* between 30 and 22 BCE.

Vitruvius addresses his book to "Caesar," but this is not the Julius Caesar he had served under, who was assassinated in 44 BCE. After that Caesar's death, his young great-nephew and adopted son Octavian cleverly outmaneuvered more seasoned opponents to seize control of Rome. Four years after defeating Mark Antony and Cleopatra at the Battle of Actium in 31 BCE, Octavian Caesar was honored with the title "Augustus" ("exalted one"). Augustus Caesar ruled for forty-five years, establishing a new, stable, and authoritative era—the Roman Empire. It is this Caesar, his world's most powerful ruler, to whom Vitruvius respectfully dedicates his work.

Existing books by architects mostly described specific projects or a particular style of building. Vitruvius instead offered a thorough treatment of architecture as a subject (ten was the number of completeness), something he claims had never been attempted. He also wrote in Rome's native language, Latin, instead of Greek, the language of intellectual writing and most of the books he used as references. This made his book accessible to people managing Roman construction, and also part of a wider Augustan-era promotion of cultural pride through Latin literature. Vitruvius promises Augustus that the book will ensure his monuments will "be worthy to go down to posterity by the side of your other achievements."[2] Excellent architecture, he argued, would further add to Rome's glory, and Augustus' own.

BALANCED AND WELL-ROUNDED: THE VITRUVIAN ARCHITECT

Vitruvius believed that great architecture comes from knowledgeable architects, and his book provides the earliest known description of an architect's education and skills. He considers whether architecture is primarily based on intellectual study, or craft experience. Vitruvius writes that the architect's knowledge "is the child of practice and theory": it is both.[3] An architect must apply educated, abstract reasoning to physical problems. Either entirely manual or strictly theoretical training will limit his (always "his" in Vitruvius' day) ability to excel and succeed.

Vitruvius names fifteen subjects an architect must study. Seven of these, often called the "liberal arts," marked a person as educated, and also provided architects with useful skills. *Grammar*, *rhetoric*, and *logic* are arts of communication and persuasion: proper verbal expression and an ability to make convincing arguments were crucial to professional success. *Arithmetic*, *geometry*, *astronomy*, and *music theory* were effectively branches of mathematics. Arithmetic and geometry clearly serve both business and design. Although astronomy and music theory may not seem relevant, they are relevant to design through ideas of proportion (see Chapter 5).

The list also includes *drawing* and *art*, which teach graphic representation, and *optics*, to ensure spaces have sufficient natural light. Vitruvius also requires *history*, *philosophy*, *law*, and *medicine*. He explains that history helps architects make correct associations as they tell stories through building form. For Vitruvius, philosophy includes both *ethics*, the principles of action and virtue that will earn architects trust and respect; and physics, the study of materials and structure. We might wonder about medicine and law; must architects be doctors and lawyers too? Vitruvius says no; the architect just needs to know enough to ensure that his structures do not make inhabitants ill, and to manage property boundaries, building codes, and contracts.

Vitruvius does not expect the architect to be an expert in every subject, but understand how each one affects building. His architect is a generalist who synthesizes many types of knowledge to solve complex problems. This education develops judgment that is sound, informed, practical, and responsible. The architect's knowledge of building is gained through apprenticeship with experienced craftsmen. Aspiring artisans were apprenticed as boys, while their aristocratic counterparts studied grammar and philosophy. Vitruvius knew Greek and received a liberal education, and probably gained his building skills later.

Vitruvius was not a professional scholar, but took up writing after years of field experience; he even apologizes to Augustus for his book's unrefined style. Yet his approach was intellectually ambitious. He took a practical subject and made it the object of the most advanced scientific method known at that time. Following Aristotle, it uses analysis, a literal "division" of something into its constituent parts, to reveal its underlying nature. After revealing everything that makes up an architect's knowledge, Vitruvius examines architecture the same way.

SIX ELEMENTS, THREE DEPARTMENTS, ONE TRIAD, AND INGENIUM

Vitruvius analyzes architecture by dividing it three times, in three different ways. His "Elements of Architecture" present six qualities that explain how architects approach design: *economy*, *propriety*, *order*, *eurythmy*, *symmetry*, and *arrangement*.

Economy ("household management" in Greek) is the efficient use of resources. Architects should make the best use of the materials, site, and budget they have available. Propriety ensures that a building's form and style are appropriate for its purpose. He explains, it is improper to build a puny temple for a great god, or a grand house for a humble owner.

Symmetry, order, and eurythmy have connected meanings. Today "symmetry" describes a form that is rotated or mirrored along a point or axis. For the ancients, it meant that all measurements are multiples of one module. Order and eurythmy describe the harmonious visual effects of a "symmetrical" or proportionally designed object. Arrangement, the organization of a building's parts into a coherent, convenient whole, is closest to the modern meaning of "design." Vitruvius says arrangement is the result of "reflection" and "invention." It demands both rationality and an ability to envision creative new possibilities.

He then describes three drawing types with Greek names: *ichnographia* or "foot-drawing" means footprint—a **plan**, representing a structure as if sliced horizontally and viewed from above. *Orthographia*, usually translated **elevation** (*ortho* means "straight"; *graphein* means "to write"), shows all features on vertical surfaces. Today, any scale drawing with exact dimensions is called an **orthographic projection**. The third type, *scaenographia*, derives from theater backdrops, and gave a visual sense of three-dimensional forms. Often translated **"perspective,"** surviving Greek and Roman art shows how convincingly their artists could depict objects in space. All three of these drawing types are still used in design practice.

Vitruvius then states that architecture has three "Departments": *buildings*, *timepieces*, and *machinery*. Buildings are obvious, and machinery reflects both Greek tradition and Vitruvius' career. Timepieces, the most surprising of the three, included sundials, another application of astronomy. Vitruvius' last, shortest and most general definition of architecture is also his most famous. His three "principles" of good design, often called the **Vitruvian triad**, are *firmitas*, *utilitas*, and *venustas*. **Firmitas** means solidity and durability; architecture must stand up and endure. **Utilitas** is utility or usefulness; architecture must perform some practical job. **Venustas** comes from Venus, the Roman goddess of beauty. Architecture is not only solid and useful, but pleasing to the eye.

Does a machine's appearance matter? Vitruvius apparently believed so; his architect designs and builds anything useful, and any good design has strength, practicality, and beauty. Two of his ten books present machinery, and roads, bridges, and aqueducts, so these were not tangential subjects. Romans were masters of infrastructure, and it is appropriate that *engineer* derives from Latin. *Ingenium* can mean a personal skill or talent, or a clever, almost animated mechanical device. *Engine*, *engineer*, and *ingenious* all share this root. While *architect* comes from a supervising craftsman's job title, *engineer* celebrates design creativity.

Distinctions were occasionally made between areas of design, however. A book on aqueducts by Frontinus, a first-century Roman aristocrat who administered

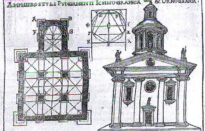

FIGURE 4.3 Page from Vitruvius, *The Ten Books of Architecture*, Book III, with ichnographia (plan) and orthographia (elevation) drawings; Cesariano edition of 1521, Como (courtesy American Academy in Rome Library).

Rome's water supply, proclaimed these "indispensable structures" were more valuable than celebrated architectural masterpieces like the ("idle") Great Pyramids and ("useless") Greek temples, because fresh water was crucial to health and survival. Frontinus' preference for infrastructure over cultural building anticipates our modern distinction between "practical" engineering and "artistic" architecture.

CITIES AND THE VITRUVIAN LEGACY

While never part of his definitions, Vitruvius expected architects to design cities. He describes a circular ideal city with eight radial streets rotated off-axis from the cardinal directions. This layout reflected the knowledge of his day; ancient people believed that temperature, humidity, and winds affected health. The Greeks identified eight separate winds originating from different compass directions. It was considered unhealthy to have any of the winds blow directly on people, so the streets were shifted to avoid them.

Although Vitruvius' urban ideas reflect recent Greek debate on the subject, he never mentions the Roman castrum. He was less interested in documenting contemporary practice than in presenting knowledge from books, supplemented by his own experience, into a comprehensive resource that would elevate and improve Roman architecture. Most of Vitruvius' source material is now lost, so the *Ten Books* provide a priceless portrait of ancient Greek architectural thinking and practice. But he could not explain the future of Roman architecture under Augustus' successors that unfolded over the next four centuries.

Vitruvius' portrait of the architect presents his own training as an ideal. We do not know whether typical architects of his day also knew philosophy, rhetoric, stonecutting, and weapons design, as he prescribes. The *Ten Books* did become a fundamental resource on architecture as a subject, and perhaps propagated Vitruvius' professional model. The Roman Empire's extensive built legacy certainly required the sort of educated, creative, and practical problem solvers he advocates. But, while a few achieved individual fame, most worked within an imperial bureaucracy for the glory of the emperor.

Vitruvius probably hoped his book would lead Augustus to appoint him his architectural adviser, but no evidence about his career survives outside the *Ten Books*. Architecture was certainly one of many ways Augustus cleverly orchestrated support for his rule. He proudly proclaimed that he found Rome a city of brick and left it a city of marble, making his capital as monumental and glorious as Greek cities.[4] We cannot know whether Vitruvius' words influenced Augustus' strategy, but he did transform architecture into a field of study and put a practical discipline on the bookshelf. Whether or not he joined Augustus' inner circle, Vitruvius' book earned him immortality, and has influenced architecture ever since.

MEDIEVAL MASTER BUILDERS

Vitruvius' book survived because medieval monasteries preserved and copied it. His definition of the architect, however, did not mirror medieval building's social organization. Ancient Roman building trades each had a *collegium* or organization; these evolved into medieval carpenters' and masons' guilds. Within a guild workshop, skilled craftsmen could rise to become master builders who designed and supervised construction.

By the twelfth century, Western Europe's medieval master builders had produced ambitious structures that demanded first-rate engineering, logistical coordination, and a sophisticated artistic vision. Such works demonstrate their intelligence and expertise, and we know they were literate, had sophisticated drawing skills, and knew geometry. But building was a "mechanical art" or craft, socially inferior to intellectual fields learned exclusively through religious education. This prevented the balanced formation Vitruvius promoted for architects. When the educated, elite cleric Abbot Suger wrote his account of the origin and the meaning of the new Gothic style in 1149, he did not bother to name the master builders who made it happen.

Gothic architects found other ways to celebrate their successes. The cathedral of Reims, France, contains a stone slab with an incised portrait of a man holding a model of the church in his arms. The inscription reads: "Here lies Hugh Libergier, who began this church in the year 1229 and died in the year 1267."

FIGURE 4.4   Tomb of Hugh Libergier, Cathedral of Reims, France, 1267.

Here, a named individual is credited with starting a church. Hugh's clothes mark him as a layman, not clergy. He is surrounded by a compass, a right angle, and a long measuring staff. All were drawing and construction instruments for the study of geometry and its application in building—emblems of a learned builder. Hugh was the first of a series of architects who directed Reims' construction. Four other masters are named in a labyrinth on the church floor, an emblem used in many cathedrals as a deliberate reference to Daedalus. Gothic architects wrote their professional pride and ancient professional heritage in stone.

TOWERS, DOMES, AND TUSCAN CRAFTSMAN BUILDERS

Many Gothic builders had international careers, spreading the new style as far as Britain, Poland, Spain, and Italy. Late medieval Florence, however, entrusted construction of a new cathedral bell tower to a curious person: Giotto di Bondone. Giotto was a trained craftsman, but not in masonry or carpentry, like most master builders. He was a painter, a specialist in surface appearances, not statics.

Other major building projects in Florence were managed by sculptors, whose mastery of wood and stone carving is closer to a builder's skills. Sculptor Arnolfo di Cambio built the Palazzo Vecchio, Florence's city hall, and designed a replacement for the city's fifth-century cathedral in 1294. Arnolfo's church featured a dome over its central crossing, like the cathedrals of Florence's biggest local rivals, Pisa and Siena. The church design was later expanded to include a vastly enlarged dome. Construction continued into the early 1400s, but completion became a problem. Florence's architectural ambition had exceeded its reach.

The base for the enlarged, octagonal dome rose 170 feet (52 meters), and its diameter was over 140 feet (42.7 meters). In other words, the largest dome attempted since antiquity would start at an elevation higher than the tallest Gothic vaults ever built. Masonry arches and domes were usually constructed on wooden frameworks called **centering**, which held blocks in position until an arch or horizontal ring was complete and stable. The cost for enough wood to center a dome that size would have exceeded the cost of the dome itself. Florence's giant new cathedral sat unfinished, a source of civic embarrassment instead of pride.

The solution came from another craftsman outside the building trades. Florentine Filippo Brunelleschi was educated for law and business during the late fourteenth century. He instead pursued the lower-status crafts, becoming a goldsmith and sculptor. He won a 1418 competition to build the dome with a scheme that, he insisted, could be built without centering. The dome's exterior design was already mostly established; Brunelleschi's design innovations were found in its interior framework of ribs supporting two separate shells. His innovative solutions to dozens of construction issues—hanging scaffolding, laying bricks, hoisting tons of raw materials hundreds of feet in the air—eliminated the need for centering.

Sixteen years later, Florence had its dome. Brunelleschi officially shared the project supervision with others, but later received individual credit for bringing the dome to completion through his own inventiveness. We may wonder how a goldsmith could resolve such a great building challenge. One factor was Brunelleschi's trip to Rome to study ancient sculpture in 1401. There he became increasingly interested in ancient Roman architecture. The Pantheon, the city's best-preserved ancient building, proved the Romans had built a dome nearly as big as the one Florence needed (see Figure 4.5). Its existence undoubtedly convinced Brunelleschi to persist.

FIGURE 4.5   Brunelleschi, Dome of Florence cathedral, 1420–1436.

His stay in Rome began Brunelleschi's transformation into a professional building designer—an architect. His educated, synthetic creativity and ambivalent social position reflects Vitruvius more than the Gothic master mason. It was Brunelleschi's orphanage on the Piazza SS. Annunziata that set the pattern for Florence's first regular urban space (see Figure 3.4). That project and others helped inaugurate *all'antica* or "ancient style" architecture, modern buildings emulating ancient Roman design. This was not easy; over a thousand years of history divided Renaissance Italians from the ancient Romans. A few ancient buildings like the Pantheon stood as instructive examples, but excavating fragments, reassembling them, and understanding them architecturally would take centuries, and still continues.

ALBERTI: ANCIENT ARCHITECTURE, MODERN MISSION

One of the Renaissance's great thinkers, Leon Battista Alberti, convinced people to attempt the difficult task of recovering and studying ancient buildings. Alberti held a doctorate in canon law from the University of Bologna and was an ordained clergyman. He worked in the Curia, the papal bureaucracy, writing documents in Latin, the language of Church business and educated discourse. Alberti also published dozens of works in both Latin and Italian on a vast range of subjects. He was a *humanist*, part of a circle of intellectuals fascinated by ancient culture. The medieval scholars who preserved Greek and Roman writings revered their wisdom, but gave Christian writings ultimate authority. Humanists read ancient literature differently, as a model for the best possible style of writing. They wondered whether modern people could equal ancient authors' eloquence, or the artistic achievements they described.

In 1434, the thirty-year-old Alberti was part of the Pope's entourage when he left a dangerously restive Rome for Florence, where he had more support. There they found Brunelleschi's dome, only two years from completion. Alberti was astounded by this mighty work, "wide enough to cast its shadow all over the Tuscan people, made as it is without any beam or abundance of wooden supports." He was certain that "nothing of the kind was ever to have been seen in antiquity."[5] Here was a modern achievement that not only rivaled, but even surpassed antiquity: a dome that enclosed more volume than the Pantheon, began over a hundred feet higher, and soared over twice as high, reaching 300 feet (91.4 meters).

Brunelleschi was only one among many revolutionary Florentine artisans; the city's painters, sculptors, and ceramicists were producing new art that (to many) equaled that of the ancients. Alberti became fascinated by this world. He visited artists' workshops, learning enough to cast his own bronze self-portrait.

Alberti had no intention of becoming a craftsman who made objects for a living; besides being too old to start, this was a lower-status career than his own position as a cleric and intellectual. But he did use his skills as a writer to advance these artistic movements. Alberti wrote two books on painting and sculpture, the first ever devoted to either subject. They combined information found in ancient writings with new descriptions of modern techniques used in Florentine workshops.

When one of Alberti's colleagues brought an unusually complete copy of Vitruvius to Italy, this presented him with a promising opportunity. He could study Vitruvius' eyewitness account of ancient architecture and use his wisdom to enrich the modern design revolution. Despite his scholarly knowledge of ancient writing, however, Alberti found the *Ten Books* very difficult to interpret because of its obsolete terminology and cryptic descriptions. Fourteen hundred years after Vitruvius wrote his book, the only surviving ancient text on architecture thwarted even an expert reader. This led to Alberti's most ambitious intellectual project: his own book about architecture.

FIGURE 4.6   Alberti, bronze medallion with self-portrait, 1435, National Gallery of Art, Washington, DC.

NEW AND BETTER: ALBERTI'S *DE RE AEDIFICATORIA*

Alberti's *De re aedificatoria libri decem* ("On the Art of Building in Ten Books," ca. 1450) was shaped by Vitruvius' example, and even repeats many of his passages and ideas. Its division into ten books communicates Alberti's similar intention to produce a complete reference to the subject. He also vents his frustration with Vitruvius, who "might just as well not have written at all, rather than write something we cannot understand."[6] Alberti needed clarifications about many things that Vitruvius could assume his readers knew. Even his few original diagrams did not survive after a thousand years. Alberti, a professional author, also had writing standards which the retired army engineer did not meet.

If Vitruvius' organizational structure can appear haphazard, Alberti's is perfectly clear. He admired Vitruvius' triad of architectural principles, and adopted them as an organizational scheme. Book one systematically defines all his terms, something Vitruvius never did. The next two discuss structure and materials (firmitas). The two following present building types serving varied purposes (utilitas). Another four books explain venustas, how to make a building beautiful through ornament and proportion. The last book covers a topic Vitruvius did not need: restoring ancient buildings.

Like Vitruvius, Alberti wrote in Latin, but this meant something different in his day. Vitruvius used Latin to make his book as accessible as possible. Alberti's sophisticated, precise Latin was accessible only to highly educated people, like the rulers and their intellectual (often humanist) advisers who decided what would be built. His book promoted another ancient language, that of Roman building. Alberti studied this language by reading Vitruvius, but did not stop there. After the papacy returned to Rome, he, like Brunelleschi, began exploring, measuring, surveying, and contemplating the city's ancient ruins. Alberti's book synthesizes his study of many ancient authors, firsthand observation, and his own reasoned meditations on a practical but, in his view, fundamental subject.

Alberti's introduction explains why architecture is worthy of such study, using arguments similar to Vitruvius'. Good buildings keep people safe, provide comfort, and support community. Well-designed buildings can also provide pleasure, pride, and lasting glory for their creators. Much as Vitruvius addressed Augustus, Alberti appeals to his own world's leaders: good architecture can produce happier, less rebellious subjects, and make future generations honor your name.

Alberti's definition of the architect deemphasizes balance in favor of authority. He values professional builders' ability to produce solid, useful structures. However, he writes that "the carpenter [builder] is but an instrument in the hand of the architect."[7] He distinguishes between those who construct, and those who decide what is to be constructed. For Alberti, an architect produces special buildings that demonstrate greatness. This demands a creative visionary, with just enough practicality to ensure designs can be built—more Imhotep than Iktinos.

Alberti's architect is less an educated craftsman than an active scholar who applies his intellect and imagination to building. He thinks abstractly about the principles of good design—theory—and how to embody them through construction. Alberti believed that ancient architecture demonstrated these principles; an architect should "speak" the language of ancient design as fluently as he wrote in Latin. Like Vitruvius, Alberti's architect is a self-portrait, but in his case we know it was prophetic. His expertise on ancient architecture led to a second career as a design consultant, advising rulers and their master builders about how to build all'antica buildings. His designs were conveyed in drawings and models, and he advised projects throughout construction. By his own definition, and later ones, Alberti was an architect.

BOOKS, PICTURES, AND ARCHITECTS

Alberti's book could have been ignored. A technological revolution during the 1440s, however, amplified the impact of all books, including Alberti's: Johannes Gutenberg's movable-type printing press. Until then, printing required carving a negative of an entire page; writing copies of a book by hand was faster. Manuscript (handwritten) books were rare, precious items for the wealthy, representing hundreds of hours of manual labor. Tiny letter blocks allowed a new page of text to be formatted quickly, and made hundreds of copies as easy to produce as one.

Gutenberg's first mechanically printed book, a Bible (ca. 1454), led to dozens of others. As printed books became more inexpensive and widespread, this created an intellectual, cultural and religious revolution in Europe as published ideas reached a wider population. Alberti's *De re*, circulated in manuscript editions during his lifetime, became architecture's first printed book in 1485; Vitruvius followed in 1486. Scholars published more accessible editions: one with illustrations in 1511, and another in Italian ten years later (see Figure 4.3). Reading Vitruvius became easier, and more people wanted to.

Alberti remained a definitive source for intellectuals, but Vitruvius was more popular, particularly among professional builders. It became the architect's "Bible," an authentic ancient reference. Even Vitruvius' less polished authorship made his writing relatable for a readership of educated artisans. But as more Renaissance artisan builders consumed books and wrote their own, they approached (if seldom achieved) Alberti's picture of the scholar-architect.

Sebastiano Serlio, a sixteenth-century painter-architect, inherited a treatise draft from Baldassare Peruzzi, then finished and published it in stages. Serlio's book was written in Italian and heavily illustrated with woodcut images. With less verbiage on design philosophy than Alberti, it was a more practical design guide for builders. Another painter-architect, Giacomo da Vignola, generously illustrated his 1560s book with dimensioned engravings and very little text; it would remain a standard reference into the early twentieth century.

But the most successful Renaissance architecture book was by Andrea Palladio, who began as a stonemason. A humanist employer, perceiving his potential, sponsored his education. Palladio traveled to Rome, illustrated a new edition of Vitruvius, and published his *Four Books on Architecture* (1570) after decades of practice. It presents abstract ideas, but mostly demonstrates good design through examples. Palladio illustrates ancient buildings, plus over two dozen of his own projects, with brief, practical descriptions of each—site, clients, and uses. Palladio's book carried his work around the globe and showed that writing, as much as building, could perpetuate both an architect's name and his vision (see chapter 2).

NEW WEAPONS, NEW CITIES: FORTIFICATION DESIGN

Renaissance architects were also expected to design cities and their defensive walls, still shaped by the 1,800-year-old catapult: tall walls to keep out projectiles, and rounded forms for impact resistance. But in 1453, Ottoman armies captured Constantinople, ending the thousand-year-old Byzantine empire. They also introduced Europe to gunpowder and cannons that could pierce high, thin stone walls, making existing defenses obsolete. Filarete's star-in-circle urban plan was his response to the new threat (see Chapter 3), and Alberti advocated a related "sawtooth" geometry for city walls. A designer from the next generation, Francesco di Giorgio Martini (1439–1502), would devise new, more effective ways for cities to deal with cannons.

Di Giorgio had special expertise in machine design, and was also a painter, sculptor, architect, and hydraulic engineer. His *Treatise on Architecture, Engineering, and Military Design* (1495) shows defensive structures with heavy battered (slanted) walls that absorb impact and deflect shot better than perpendicular ones. Pointed bastions extending from the city perimeter allowed defenders' cannons to cover more area. Over time these became a system in which star-shaped perimeter walls with multiple **bastions**, surrounded by moats and angled earthworks, defended cities from modern artillery. Architect Vincenzo Scamozzi's published ideal city plans reflected these developments, and were realized at Palmanova, a rare, brand-new Renaissance city built east of Venice in 1593 as an outpost against the Ottomans.

Renaissance architects applied design expertise to bridges, machinery, or churches as needed. But fortification design became more complex and more strategic in the sixteenth century, so this skill set gained special value. The expense of modernizing urban defenses dwarfed inserting new piazzas and straight streets into a city. This new design science developed in Italy, but few of the peninsula's small city-states could afford to implement it fully. Italian fortification experts found a promising job market in Europe's large continental empires such as Austria-Hungary. Vienna's bull's-eye plan (see Chapter 3) was born after the imperial capital

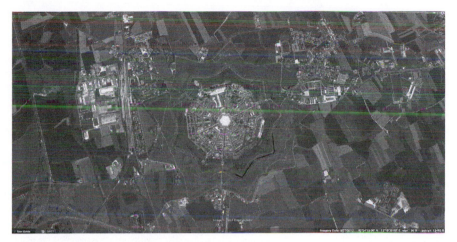

FIGURE 4.7   Vincenzo Scamozzi, Palmanova, Italy, begun 1593.

nearly fell to Ottoman armies in 1529. The emperor spent heavily to replace its medieval wall with pointed bastions surrounded by an open glacis, future home to the Ringstrasse. This enormous investment paid off in 1683, over 150 years later, when Vienna held out against another Ottoman siege. The defensive walls that confined nineteenth-century Barcelona were built after a 1697 attack by Europe's biggest, most aggressive power: France.

FRANCE: ARMY ENGINEERS AND BUILDING BUREAUCRACIES

King Louis XIV ruled France from 1643 to 1715, the longest reign in European history at seventy-two years (he became king at age 4). Although the Palace of Versailles famously expresses the Sun King's appetite for glory, his greatest priority was war. Louis XIV spent 75 percent of his kingdom's budget on military campaigns. One unusual expense was maintaining a full-time staff of military engineers, the Corps de Génie (from *ingenium*), an Army Corps of Engineers, which numbered 275 by 1691. This corps played a strategic role in the king's military ambitions, and also transformed this design specialization into a professional career.

The Corps of Engineers and the profession were shaped by an aristocrat who served under Louis XIV named Sébastien Le Prestre, Marquis de Vauban. Vauban received an elite education in mathematics and science, but when his privileged family lost its fortune he had to work for a living, and joined Louis XIV's army as officer. After Louis XIV began personal rule in 1663, he decided to retake contested territory along French borders and expand them where possible. Vauban was adept at breaching urban defenses and building new, impenetrable ones. He captured every city he placed under siege, and never surrendered one he defended—a perfect record that undoubtedly pleased his king.

His defenses, today known as "Vauban fortifications," had minimal design innovations over the star-shaped, bastioned *trace italienne* ("Italian perimeter"). They earned a label because of sheer volume: Vauban built thirty-seven brand-new cities, including a series of *villes de guerre* ("war cities") along France's flat, vulnerable northeast border. Dozens of others were rebuilt, often in record time. When the French recaptured Lille on the Belgian border in 1668, a brand-new, star-shaped citadel was in place two years later, compared to almost twenty years to rebuild Vienna's defenses.

This quantity, speed, and reliability resulted from a revolution in administration. Under Vauban, the Corps' full-time professionals turned battlefield experience into reliable strategies and fixed procedures. This coordinated bureaucracy was one of three that managed national construction. Besides military building, another office (Bâtiments du Roi) was set up to administer the "The King's Buildings," like the royal palaces. In 1716, after Louis XIV's death, an office of Ponts et Chaussées (Bridges and Roads) was established to manage civilian infrastructure projects—"civil engineering."

These offices had distinct professional cultures with different priorities and problem-solving approaches. Those working at each office also needed specific qualifications, creating demand for particular forms of education. Military and infrastructure building required designers to solve problems through rational, quantifiable, and repeatable methods. The design success of a royal palace or cathedral, instead, was judged in both technological and cultural terms. Another royal bureaucratic system established under Louis XIV categorized such projects in a way that separated "architecture" from the scientific realm of "engineering."

ACADEMIES, SCHOOLS, AND THE VALUE OF DESIGN

The French Academy system waged a different war for Louis XIV. The king wanted his realm to be Europe's best, militarily and culturally; French literature, science, and art should be second to none. The French minister of culture established separate **academies**, committees of experts for each discipline, to define a general doctrine of excellence and reserve royal approval for work that met their standards. The Academy of Architecture, the last one established in 1671, pushed French architects building for the king into the Albertian realm of the intellect, of theory.

Academies also operated affiliated schools, teaching each discipline's sanctioned methods and producing "properly" trained practitioners. An early-nineteenth-century reorganization combined the academies of architecture, painting, and sculpture into one academy. Its affiliated school, the École des Beaux-Arts (School of Fine Arts), provided the world's most influential architectural training, particularly after it began admitting international students in the 1830s. The École administered admissions exams; provided lectures in history, theory, science, and construction; and issued and judged design competitions, through which students earned greater standing. But a Beaux-Arts education mostly occurred outside the school itself in an **atelier**, or studio. Students rented space where a professional architect, sometimes an École professor, occasionally came to review their work. Students learned design and drawing in the atelier, mostly from each other.

The Beaux-Arts heavily emphasized schematic planning: every project started with a simple diagram called a **parti** (meaning "point of departure"). For top competitions, students created their parti, then turned it in to the jury. The completed project submitted weeks later either manifested that initial diagram, or it was disqualified. Beaux-Arts plans are clearly arranged, and hierarchically and axially organized. Students presented projects in elaborately composed and richly rendered drawings. Their color washes, decorative detail, and cast shadows vividly illustrated the envisioned building.

The Beaux-Arts awarded designs that spoke the language of ancient architecture as Alberti advocated by using approved historic styles. Its highest honor was the *Prix de Rome* (Rome Prize), a multi-year, government-sponsored fellowship in the Eternal City. There architects would learn how to glorify France through

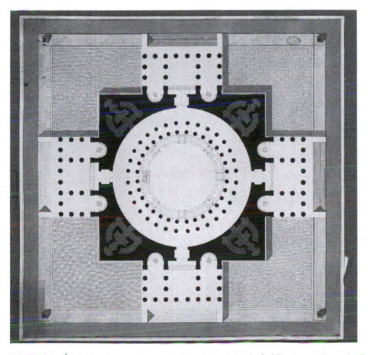

FIGURE 4.8 École des Beaux-Arts renderings; Joseph-Louis-Achille Joyau, "Imperial Residence in the city of Nice," student drawing from École des Beaux-Arts, 1860.

monumental, symbolic public buildings: palaces, churches, memorials. Although the Beaux-Arts taught structures and materials, the emphasis was not on practicality or economy, but the sort of artistically grand buildings Frontinus found overrated.

He would have preferred the École des Ponts et Chausées (Bridges and Roads), founded in 1756 to train civil engineers, and the École Polytechnique for military engineers, established in 1794 to replace its royalist predecessor (and still administered by France's Ministry of Defense). Both schools taught mathematics, physical sciences, mechanics, and structural analysis. Design and building construction instruction emphasized rationality and efficiency.

The value of France's engineering graduates was obvious to other countries, including the young United States. Its first engineering school was at West Point, a defensive fort on New York's Hudson River and site of the nation's first military academy. West Point's engineering program, in place by 1817, was modeled on the French polytechnic system; early cadets studied French to use textbooks from Paris. Cooperating public and private entities employed engineers to build a rapidly expanding nation's transportation infrastructure. More engineering programs began in the 1830s, and the 1862 Land Grant Act supported higher education in engineering and agriculture because they directly benefit economic development; architects' value was harder to quantify.

AMERICAN ARCHITECTS

Skilled builders from Europe had long found ample work in the New World. Early American architects were usually professional craftsman-builders; a few were full-time designers who learned drawing and design through office apprenticeship. The first American to receive a formal architectural education was Richard Morris Hunt, who began to attend the École des Beaux-Arts in 1846. He later worked for Parisian architects, then returned to New York in 1855 with world-class credentials. Hunt helped introduce French Beaux-Arts design to an American audience.

Hunt's elite design expertise appealed to wealthy families like the Vanderbilts that had amassed enormous personal fortunes through industry. They hired him to create architecture expressing their success in railroads, building lavish Vanderbilt homes in New York City; the resort town of Newport, Rhode Island; and their Biltmore estate in North Carolina. They and other elite families of the Gilded Age also practiced public philanthropy by sponsoring cultural institutions like the New York's Metropolitan Museum of Art and Public Library. Hunt's architectural expertise from Paris assured wealthy, cosmopolitan clients that the buildings they sponsored would live up to European standards.

Hunt's New York office became a *de facto* design school, a Beaux-Arts-style atelier where he trained apprentices using French methods. Other aspiring U.S. architects also studied in Paris or at American architecture programs established in universities, beginning with the Massachusetts Institute of Technology in 1868. Most followed the Beaux-Arts model, and several hired French design professors. A professional organization, the American Institute of Architects, defined architecture as a specific, largely elite subset within U.S. building practice. Architects usually managed projects where artistic design qualities were valued, while engineers provided efficient, practical solutions. Yet this seemingly neat nineteenth-century division belied an increasingly complicated relationship between architecture and engineering.

INDUSTRIAL MATERIALS AND THE BUILDING REVOLUTION

The Industrial Revolution transformed access to construction materials like iron, which had long been used in building, but only sparingly because it was handcrafted and costly. In eighteenth-century Britain, coke smelting and mass-production of iron greatly reduced its cost and increased its availability, revolution-izing building over the next century. During the nineteenth century, the French engineer and entrepreneur Gustave Eiffel (1832–1923) founded a company that specialized in trussed iron railroad bridges. These spanned formerly impossible distances while withstanding a train's weight and vibration, allowing level tracks that followed direct, efficient routes. In 1884, two of his designers wondered not how far, but how high such trusses could go. They calculated that a wrought-iron tower could rise 300 meters (980 feet). Modern materials could easily surpass

FIGURE 4.9   Office of Richard Morris Hunt, New York, 1859.

the 139-meter (455-foot) Great Pyramid of Khufu, the world's tallest building for almost 4,000 years, and the record holder, the 169-meter (555-foot) Washington Monument (with 12 percent of its mass).

Eiffel's world-famous tower, built for the 1889 World's Fair in Paris, remained the world's tallest structure until New York's Chrysler Building in 1930. Intended to be temporary, it instead became a symbol of Paris, French industry, and modern engineering. For many, the Eiffel Tower was a thrilling spectacle whose observation decks offered a new, exciting view of the world. Others found it a hideous, gargantuan alien defacing Haussmann's elegantly beautified city. For architects, it raised a difficult question: what did such construction mean for them? A profession grounded in tradition had to assess its relationship with a fast-changing culture.

LE CORBUSIER: ARCHITECTS AND ENGINEERING METHODS

Many new nineteenth-century building types, including train stations, department stores, and covered markets, combined historically conceived façades offering traditional "architectural" dignity with high-tech "engineered" iron and glass roofs that provided wide spans and natural light. They separated these elements in a way that other projects could not, including Thomas U. Walter's enormous new dome

FIGURE 4.10   Gustave Eiffel et Cie., Garabit Viaduct, near Ruynes-en-Margerides, France, 1880–1884.

for an expanded U.S. Capitol building in Washington, DC. That dome had to visually dominate a city of vast distances while meeting Congress's frugal budget. Modern engineering could meet these restraints, but propriety demanded a traditional, "architectural" appearance. The solution was three domes: two visible shells, one exterior, another interior, whose suitably dignified, historically inspired forms hide a trussed wrought-iron dome beneath. Neither of these design approaches— either separating industrial building systems from "architecture," or hiding them beneath a historic skin—would remain a satisfactory solution. Architects either held modernity at arm's length, or pretended it was absent.

FIGURE 4.11   Thomas U. Walter, U.S. Capital dome, 1850–1863.

FIGURE 4.11 *(continued)*

During the late nineteenth and early twentieth centuries, critics increasingly accused architects of living in denial, and challenged them to reconsider their professional model. The most influential was Swiss architect Charles-Édouard Jeanneret, who adopted the name "Le Corbusier" (1887–1965). His 1923 book *Towards a New Architecture* was a **polemic** designed to shake architects out of complacency and drag his discipline into the modern age. One of Le Corbusier's most provocative chapters argued that engineers were better architects than architects. His colleagues were "disenchanted and idle, boastful or morose," while engineers were "healthy and virile, active, and useful."[8]

Like the most influential Renaissance treatises, he argues using both words and images. One photomontage places icons of French architecture before a looming silhouette of a vast ocean liner. The illustration asks: which is more impressive? For Le Corbusier, it is obviously the ocean liner, one of many examples that suggest engineers produce better design than architects. Instead of imposing a preconceived, history-bound range of solutions, engineers' forms reflect the structurally efficient use of material and form. They embrace modernity, instead of hiding a revolution under nostalgia. Le Corbusier praised engineers to attack architects' pride; he wanted to goad them into escaping an ingrained emphasis on tradition, into embracing the modern world's potential.

Towards an Architecture's most famous page sets Greek temples and automobiles side by side. This pairing argues that ancient temples and modern cars are both great design, because they were each the result of "well-stated problems": What does each need to do? What is its essence? What are the constraints? Once these questions are answered in a workable model, design can refine it over

TOWARDS A NEW ARCHITECTURE

AUTOMOBILES

PARSTUM, 600-550 B.C.

When once a standard is established, competition comes at once and violently into play. It is a fight; in order to win you must do better than your rival *in every minute point*, in

THE PARTHENON, 447-434 B.C.

the run of the whole thing and in all the details. Thus we get the study of minute points pushed to its limits. Progress.
A standard is necessary for order in human effort.

HUMBER, 1907

DELAGE, "GRAND-SPORT," 1921

FIGURE 4.12   Doric temples and automobiles, Le Corbusier, *Towards a New Architecture*, 1923.

time into something more elegant, progressing toward and perhaps even—in the case of the Parthenon—achieving "perfection."

Importantly, Le Corbusier had no desire to eliminate architects. He considered engineers' design successes to be accidental, and limited. He wanted architects with their aesthetic sensibilities to adopt the engineer's rational method so they could produce even greater design. Le Corbusier pushed for escape from the creative confines of a Beaux-Arts architectural education, raising another question: what does a modern architect need to know?

ACADEMY OF THE MODERN: THE BAUHAUS

While Le Corbusier wrote in Paris, a new art school in Germany was revolutionizing design education for modernity. The Bauhaus (1919–1933) aimed at breaking down distinctions between "fine" and "applied" arts (crafts). Architecture was only taught late in its history, but Bauhaus ideology and faculty would transform architectural education around the world. They held that any designer should understand all available materials and methods, from welding to weaving. They approached design through abstract compositional principles—color, form, contrast—and intended objects to be mass-produced in factories. The Bauhaus wanted students to respond freely to modern culture, envision new forms, and explore the potential of new resources, not be bound to a historic vocabulary. Although design exploration emphasized craft, not mathematics, the goal was creativity liberated from traditional forms, like the engineer's.

The Gateway Arch in St. Louis was one modern architect's response to the Eiffel Tower. Finnish-American architect Eero Saarinen won a 1948 competition to commemorate Jefferson's Louisiana Purchase by proposing a colossal arch, 630 feet (192 m) high and wide at the base. While only two-thirds the Eiffel Tower's height, its radical simplicity appeared revolutionary. The sleek catenary form of stainless steel–clad, reinforced concrete suggested both the mathematics of projectile trajectories and arches from architecture's history. The blending of a triangular cross-section and three-dimensional curvature shows what Le Corbusier called "plastic imagination." It conveyed both rationality and poetry.

It also required close cooperation with structural engineers. During the scheme's development, Saarinen struggled with the catenary's profile. The geometry of pure efficiency did not quite meet his goal for an arch that would "soar" visually. His engineering partners figured out the mathematical adjustments to the curve that generated the sort of form he wanted; the design result is the product of professional collaboration. Modern design usually involves complex teams, yet the architect often receives individual credit for authorship, as Saarinen frequently does for the St. Louis monument. The image of the architect

FIGURE 4.13   Eero Saarinen, with F. Severud and H. Bandel, Gateway Arch, St. Louis, Missouri, 1947–1965.

as an individual creator of buildings, as old as Saqquara, remains a powerful cultural myth. Hollywood loves architects because they have a cultural mystique, an aura of personal creative power. Like most myths, they reflect what people want to believe more than reality.

Le Corbusier challenged architects to learn from engineers, but he also argued that architecture should go beyond efficient solutions to quantifiable problems. Architects must consider how humans respond to objects and spaces. The motivation for absorbing engineering's rational, exemplary methods of design is to achieve a goal that has defined the architect's special expertise: beauty. But what is beauty, and who can guarantee the ability to produce it? How could Vitruvius make venustas essential to good architecture?

VOCABULARY

academy, atelier, ballista, bastions, centering, elevation, firmitas, mastaba, orthographic projection, parti, perspective, plan, polemic, scorpio, utilitas, venustas, Vitruvian triad.

STUDY AND REVIEW QUESTIONS

1. Compare and contrast the significance of Imhotep and Daedalus as "first architect." How do they suggest different personal qualities and social roles for the architect?
2. Who was Vitruvius? What makes his book unique and important, and how did he define the architect's knowledge and cultural value?
3. Compare the origin and significance of the words *architect* and *engineer*, and discuss how well they relate to modern stereotypes about these two professions.
4. Who built Gothic cathedrals? Do they deserve to be called "architects"? How did their training and status compare to counterparts in ancient Egypt, Greece, and Rome?
5. What made Giotto, Arnolfo di Cambio, and Brunelleschi unusual leaders of major construction projects? How does this fit with Brunelleschi's record on the dome of Florence Cathedral?
6. Who was Alberti? How did he become involved in art and architecture, and what made his perspective unique?
7. What was Alberti's view of Vitruvius, and how do their books compare? Why did books have greater influence on architecture during the Renaissance?
8. What new weapons technology changed the way Renaissance city walls were designed ? How did this affect how design skills were valued?
9. What sort of countries were able to take advantage of the new Italian fortification design? How did Vauban influence the development of engineering as a profession?
10. What were the goals of the French Academy system? How was architecture taught at the École des Beaux-Arts in Paris?
11. Compare the professional market for trained engineers and architects during the nineteenth century. What sort of needs did each field best serve?
12. How and why did Le Corbusier compare architects to engineers? What were his opinions about their different approaches to design?
13. What does the Gateway Arch suggest about the relationship between modern architects and engineers?

APPLICATION AND DISCUSSION EXERCISES

1. Find a film featuring an architect or engineer as a main character. How does it portray their professional identity? How does this affect the story, and is it believable?
2. Compare the knowledge, professional role, and social position of three architects from the chapter. Which model do you consider best?
3. Investigate an architect or engineer from a place or period not covered in this chapter, and compare their training and professional role to one of the examples discussed.

NOTES

1 Films featuring engineers as compelling central characters include *Flight of the Phoenix* (1965) and *The Wind Rises* (2013).
2 Vitruvius, *Ten Books on Architecture*, trans. M. H. Morgan (Cambridge: Harvard University Press, 1914), p. 4.
3 Ibid., p. 5.
4 C. Suetonius Tranquillis, *The Divine Augustus*, trans. E. S. Shuckburgh (Cambridge: Cambridge University Press, 1896), 28.3.
5 Leon Battista Alberti, *On Painting: A New Translation and Critical Edition*, trans. R. Sinisgalli (Cambridge: Cambridge University Press, 2011), p. 18.
6 Leon Battista Alberti, *On the Art of Building in Ten Books*, trans. Joseph Rykwert and John Tavernor (Cambridge, MA: MIT Press, 1988), p. 154.
7 Ibid., p. 3.
8 Le Corbusier, *Toward an Architecture*, trans. J. Goodman (Los Angeles: Getty Research Institute, 2007), p. 94.

FURTHER READING

Alberti, Leon Battista. *On Painting: A New Translation and Critical Edition*. Trans. R. Sinisgalli. Cambridge: Cambridge University Press, 2011.
_____. *On the Art of Building in Ten Books*. Trans. J. Rykwert and J. Tavernor. Cambridge, MA: MIT Press, 1988.
Cuff, Dana. *Architecture: The Story of Practice*. Cambridge, MA: MIT Press, 1991.
Drexler, Arthur, ed. *The Architecture of the École des Beaux-Arts*. New York: Museum of Modern Art, 1977.
Frontinus, Sextus Julius. *The Two Books on the Water Supply of the City of Rome*. Trans. C. Herschel. Boston: Dana Estates, 1899.
Grafton, Anthony. *Leon Battista Alberti: Master Builder of the Italian Renaissance*. Cambridge, MA: Harvard University Press, 2000.

Hart, Vaughan. *Paper Palaces: The Rise of the Renaissance Architectural Treatise*. New Haven: Yale University Press, 1998.

Kostof, Spiro, ed. *The Architect: Chapters in the History of the Profession*. Oxford: Oxford University Press, 1977.

Le Corbusier. *Toward an Architecture*. Trans. J. Goodman. Los Angeles: Getty Research Institute, 2007.

Martini, Francesco di Giorgio. *Francesco di Giorgio architetto*. Milano: Electa, 1993.

Middleton, Robin, ed. *The Beaux-Arts and Nineteenth-Century French Architecture*. Cambridge, MA: MIT Press, 1982.

Ockman, Joan, ed. *Architecture School: Three Centuries of Educating Architects in North America*. Cambridge, MA: MIT Press, 2012.

Parcell, Stephen. *Four Historical Definitions of Architecture*. Montreal: McGill-Queen's University Press, 2012.

Saint, Andrew. *The Image of the Architect*. New Haven and London: Yale University Press, 1983.

_____. *Architect and Engineer: A Study in Sibling Rivalry*. New Haven and London: Yale University Press, 2007.

Vitruvius. *The Ten Books on Architecture*. Trans. I. Rowland. Cambridge: Cambridge University Press, 1999.

_____. *The Ten Books on Architecture*. Trans. M. H. Morgan. Cambridge: Harvard University Press, 1914.

Woods, Mary N. *From Craft to Profession: The Practice of Architecture in Nineteenth-Century America*. Berkeley: University of California Press, 1999.

Zanker, Paul. *The Power of Images in the Age of Augustus*. Trans. Alan Shapiro. Ann Arbor: University of Michigan Press, 1988.

CHAPTER 5
AESTHETICS

OUR DISCUSSION OF THE TAJ MAHAL so far has mentioned its craftsmanship, size, age, geometry, site, cultural importance, and its relation to Islamic sacred architecture (see Figure 0.3, Introduction, Chapter 1). But visitors travel far to see this building in person because of something else: its beauty. *Venustas* is the most powerful and elusive leg of Vitruvius' triad. It transforms solid, useful construction into something more. In recent centuries, expertise in beauty has most distinguished architects from other building professionals.

Is the Taj Mahal beautiful? Millions believe so—but what do they mean? Perhaps they admire its perfectly symmetrical design, with forms distributed around a central, vertical axis. This gives balance, order, and predictability: we can assume (correctly) that its invisible sides look like those we see. Its repeated rounded domes and iwans at different scales provide both rhythm and unity. The plinth and minarets frame the mausoleum's central form, setting it apart as separate and special. The design conveys great dignity, stability, and harmony. Its composition explains the building at a glance, but still offers much for our eye to enjoy.

In 2007, a very different-looking building, the Institute of Contemporary Art (ICA) in Boston by Diller, Scofidio + Renfro, was voted Boston's "most beautiful" by the city government and the Boston Society of Architects. The ICA lifts an enormous prism overhead and supports it at only one end. This precariously hanging **cantilever** creates the opposite of balanced repose. Its design relies entirely on box-shaped forms except for an angled "eyeball" hanging below the hovering volume. Its plain, unornamented exterior is clad in corrugated metal, glass, and wood. Typical of the warehouses that used to dominate its South Boston waterfront location, these industrial materials are used here for an art museum.

Whether we prefer the Taj Mahal or the ICA, or admire both equally, they embody very different notions of beauty. Ever since Vitruvius declared venustas an architectural necessity, architects have had to consider what those notions might be.

FIGURE 5.1   Diller, Scofidio + Renfro, Institute of Fine Arts, Boston, 2007.

GREEK STANDARDS, ROMAN CONQUERORS, AND THE ORDERS

During Vitruvius' lifetime, Rome had conquered a Greek world famous for its sophistication. Early Romans viewed themselves as simple, patriotic farmer-soldiers; many saw Greek cultural refinement as weakness. But Rome's armies also seized Greek sculpture, paintings, even building columns, and used these spoils to adorn their own cities. Ruling the Greek world and its centuries-old artistic traditions would change Roman civilization.

For instance, Greek sculptors usually depicted young, "perfect" and generic human figures, but Roman portraits traditionally emphasized individuality and character. Images of an aristocratic family's elderly, wrinkled, battle-scarred ancestors were displayed in its domus to show a legacy of virtuous, sacrificial service to Rome. Later imperial art became a compromise between Roman symbolic priorities and Greek artistic standards. Augustus and each successive emperor had a "signature" image for official portraits that never changed. Even coins and statues of Augustus made in his old age show him as an attractive, youthful leader—recognizable, but idealized.

Vitruvius wrote during this transformation's beginnings. Two of his ten books discuss a building type Romans seldom used: the **peripteral** temple, surrounded by free-standing columns on all sides like the Parthenon (Figure 4.2). Vitruvius discusses many Greek building types—houses, theaters, libraries, and athletic facilities. But he gives the temple far more emphasis than its frequency might suggest, because these houses for the gods had the highest cultural and architectural significance. Vitruvius never defines *venustas* directly, but his discussions of proper temple design showed how architects could achieve beauty in practice.

Peripteral temples had many variations, which Vitruvius names in meticulous detail. But his most famous categorization presents three distinct styles, a word appropriately derived from the Greek word for "column," *stylos*. These types, **Doric**, **Ionic**, and **Corinthian**, are recognized by their distinctive column designs, specifically the wider element at the column top called a **capital**. The Doric capital is the simplest, the Ionic significantly more elaborate, and the Corinthian capital is the largest and most complex. Column shafts are tapered upward with a narrower diameter at the top, and a slight bulge roughly one-third up called the **entasis**. Columns support a horizontal beam called an **entablature**. The triangular space at each end of the gable roof is a pediment. The Doric, Ionic and Corinthian are all variations on a common kit of parts, each a system with its own standardized moldings and details.

One clue to the different styles' origin is their names: two are ethnic and regional labels. The Dorians lived in Western Greece, while the Ionians lived in Eastern Greece, along the coast of Asia Minor. Doric and Ionic are varied treatments of structurally similar temples developed in different regions. "Corinthian" is also geographical, from the city of Corinth, but that order has a different history.

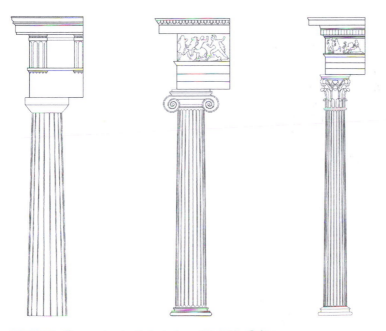

FIGURE 5.2   Diagram showing Doric, Ionic, and Corinthian Orders.

DORIC: SIMPLICITY AND EVOLUTION

Among the Greek orders, the Doric is the most austere. Figure 5.3 shows three different Doric temples built over the course of a century, which illustrate its development over time. One visible variation is the column's relationship with the capital. The capital at Hera I resembles a shallow inverted bowl; its curved underside extends out far from the column neck beneath. In contrast, the Parthenon

FIGURE 5.3   The temples of Hera I (ca. 550 BCE) and Hera II (ca. 470 BCE), Paestum, Italy, and the Parthenon, Athens (447–438 BCE).

FIGURE 5.3   *(continued)*

capitals are only slightly wider than the neck. At Hera I the column's curved profile is obvious, especially just below the neck, while the Parthenon columns' subtle bulge is harder to see.

The temples with surviving pediments also show a changing relationship between the columns and the roof they support. The earlier Hera II appears short and heavy, the later Parthenon taller and lighter. A smaller roof structure relative to column height creates that effect: Hera II's superstructure is nearly as high as its columns, while the Parthenon's is closer to three-quarters its column height. At 34 feet (10.4 meters), its columns are also far taller than those at Hera I, only 22 feet (6.7 meters).

Le Corbusier's comparison of Doric temples to automobiles emphasizes refinement over time. He believed the Parthenon's "perfection" demonstrates how greater beauty is achieved through gradual evolution in details. But these changes reflect factors besides appearance. The relationships between the column neck, capital, **abacus** (the square block above the capital), and entablature also reflect builders' growing structural confidence. While Hera I's entablature spans very little space between abacus blocks, that distance becomes wider than the abacus itself at the Parthenon. Over time, thinner, taller, and more widely spaced columns lift smaller roofs higher above the ground. Lightness and verticality reflect a growing structural confidence that allowed hefty, top-heavy temples to progressively soar toward the sky. Changing construction may have altered what people liked; or perhaps changing ideas of beauty pushed builders to be more daring.

IONIC AND CORINTHIAN: DELICATE AND ORNATE

Even at the Parthenon, the Doric appears heavier than the Ionic, which has slenderer columns and more ornate details. Carved column bases, capitals with spiraling **volutes**, and a sculpted *frieze* (a horizontal band along the entablature) give the Ionic a more intricate visual texture. Many surviving examples of the Ionic not only appeared taller, but were. The fourth-century-BCE Temple of Artemis in Sardis had Ionic columns (there are parts of one now at New York's Metropolitan Museum) that were 56 feet (17 meters) high, about 75 percent taller than the Parthenon. After the fifth century BCE, the Doric was used little; preferences changed, and Ionic remained the Greek order of choice until Vitruvius' day. He discusses the Ionic order most, no doubt reflecting his reliance on materials describing Greek practice during those centuries.

The third Greek style, the Corinthian, is similar to the Ionic, but has a larger, more ornate capital. It has small volutes at all four corners, and is covered with a **foliate** (leafy) pattern. Vitruvius tells a story about its origin: after a young girl in Corinth died, her nurse left a basket with her belongings on her grave, weighing it down with a flat tile. It sat on the root of an **acanthus**, a Mediterranean plant. As it grew, its leaves wrapped around the basket, and tendrils curled beneath the tile. A passing sculptor named Kallimachus admired the leaf-covered basket and copied it.

This story makes the Corinthian an artistic, not a building, innovation. Originally, Greeks did not use this order for whole buildings, but as a unique, special element. The Romans, following later, Hellenistic practice, used the Corinthian for

FIGURE 5.4   Ionic portico and Maiden Porch at Erechtheion, Athens, 421–406 BCE.

FIGURE 5.5   Maison Carrée, Nîmes, France, ca. 15 BCE or second-century-CE rebuilding.

entire buildings. A Roman temple in southern France, called the Maison Carrée, has a colonnaded porch and steps only at the front instead of all around. The rear eight columns on each side are half-cylinders attached to the wall (**engaged columns**). At the Maison Carrée, Romans blended a Greek style with their own temple traditions.

Vitruvius briefly discusses a fourth style used by the Etruscans, an ancient central Italian people. Etruscan ("Tuscan") temples also supported a gable roof with walls and round columns. But they are raised on a much higher platform, the **podium**. Their portico is at the front with a narrow set of steps, not all the way around, and enclosed rooms lie at the rear instead of the center. Vitruvius considers Tuscan temples, built of wood, mud brick, and terra cotta, primitive compared to Doric or Ionic. The Maison Carrée's layout is Tuscan, not peripteral, but its stone construction and Corinthian order give it a Greek flavor—a creative compromise, like emperors' portraits.

BEAUTY AND BODIES: THE ANTHROPOMORPHIC ANALOGY

Vitruvius' expectation that Roman architects use the Greek orders could be seen as obedience to a foreign artistic standard. But Vitruvius did not simply tell his proud countrymen they should bow to Greek cultural authority. He argued that the orders are a universally legitimate, beautiful architectural vocabulary—the best path to venustas—because they are "natural."

To Vitruvius, the orders are counterparts to their human builders: an **anthropomorphic** ("in human form") **analogy**. The Erechtheion's maiden porch on the Acropolis, where human figures become columns, makes this idea literal (Figure 5.4). Each has one knee bent, expressing the effort of supporting a heavy burden. A column's entasis also mimics the body's elastic response to load. Vitruvius makes another link to humans by assigning each order a gender, which architects must consider because temples express a god's identity. Each divinity's earthly house must reflect their nature—including gender—to fulfill "propriety."

Vitruvius says the Doric, the heaviest and least ornamental order, represents a man's body, while Ionic and Corinthian are both female. Yet all three Doric temples in Figure 5.3 are dedicated to the goddesses Hera and Athena. For Athena, an unmarried warrior-goddess, the Doric might be excused, but not for Hera, an emblem of wives and traditional femininity. Because Vitruvius was describing 600-year-old styles when he wrote, he may have conveyed a wide-spread but imperfect view, or his own mistaken interpretation. But the association is visually consistent with the "feminine" orders' ornateness, which supposedly derives from women's costumes (fluting resembles drapery, for instance), hair-styles, and jewelry. He associates the Ionic, slightly heavier and more sedate, with older, married women ("matrons"), and the more slender, delicate Corinthian with young maidens, like the one buried beneath the acanthus-covered basket.

The orders' anthropomorphism and gendering are also reflected in their proportions. Vitruvius claims the Doric and Ionic's diameter and height initially reflected the ratio between the human foot and height, typically 1:6 for adult men and 1:8 for women. This makes the correspondence between Greek orders and human bodies intentional and explanatory. It also suggests we find the orders beautiful because we see our ideal selves in them; this system mirrors us, and our idea of human beauty.

THE VITRUVIAN MAN: BODY, GEOMETRY, AND PROPORTION

Vitruvius presents the column diameter as both a memory of the human foot and a basic design module. Every architectural element should be either a multiple or a ratio of this module. Its exact size was irrelevant, so long as it provided a consistent reference for everything from a building's overall length to the width of tiny moldings.

Three of Vitruvius' six "elements" of architecture—symmetry, order, and eurythmy—concern proportion (see chapter 4). For him, "symmetry" ("shared measure" in Greek) means all design features are based on one module. This is another connection between architecture, the human body and nature. Vitruvius notes that our height is also an even multiple of the length of our head and our foot. Our arm and hand are multiples of the length of our index finger. He then connects the body to basic geometric forms:

For if a person is imagined lying back with outstretched arms and feet within a circle whose center is at the navel, the fingers and toes will trace the circumference of this circle as they move about. But to whatever extent a circular scheme may be present in the body, a square design may also be discerned there. For if we measure from the soles of the feet to the crown of the head, and this measurement is compared with that of the outstretched arms, one discovers that the breadth equals the height.[1]

Over 1,500 years later, Leonardo da Vinci famously illustrated this passage with a man standing with arms straight out inscribed in a perfect square. Spread-eagled, his limbs create a circle; the center of both shapes is at his navel. Vitruvius'

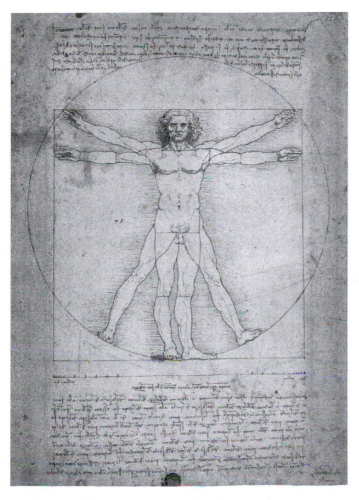

FIGURE 5.6   Leonardo Da Vinci, *Vitruvian Man*, ca. 1500.

logic is clear: if nature designs with ratios, proportions, and basic geometric forms, architects should too. Although the difference between 23.79 and 24.0 diameters may seem invisible and unimportant, the Greeks considered it essential. They believed when we find something beautiful we recognize how each element relates to a coherent whole. Proportion produces harmony, or "good flow"—eurythmy.

This idea of beauty reflects the legacy of thinkers like Pythagoras, famous for his theorem on right triangles. He also discovered that the lengths of strings which sound pleasant when plucked simultaneously form ratios of small integers: 1:2 is an octave, 2:3 a major fifth, 3:4 a major fourth. Pythagoreans believed this proved that the universe is structured according to consistent mathematical principles at every scale, from molecules to planetary orbits (long believed to be circular). Visual beauty, like musical harmony, results from the same proportions and geometric forms that undergird natural forms.

Our eyes may not distinguish 1:3.723 from 1:4, but Vitruvius would say we "feel" the difference. Harmonic proportions and pure forms resonate within our minds and bodies because we share them. The Greeks believed certain irrational numbers had mystical significance, including π, the ratio between a circle's circumference and its diameter. Another is φ, the "golden section," a ratio easily generated from a square with a ruler and compass, which, if repeated, generates a spiral form found throughout nature. That people have located harmonic ratios and the golden section in the Parthenon and many other much-admired artworks lends support to this theory. It suggests their beauty is a matter of fact, not opinion, because they reflect the structure of the cosmos.

Making beauty—a powerful commodity—objective and quantifiable is profoundly appealing. If beauty can be defined in measurable terms, a formula can guarantee it as an outcome. This hope still motivates many, including researchers who often find that subjects rate human faces with the greatest bilateral symmetry and specific proportions the most "beautiful." Some studies even correlate these "objective" measures of beauty to famously attractive people (U.S. actors Michelle Pfeiffer and Brad Pitt have both been cited).

Can beauty be explained scientifically? Are people judging faces revealing "objective" truths, or expressing views shaped by immersion in specific cultural ideals? Vitruvius' theory is vulnerable to many critiques, but the idea—the hope—that beauty is measurable and absolute, and that one design language is eternally valid across time and geography, would endure.

ALBERTI: THE POWER OF BEAUTY

A Gothic cathedral looks nothing like an Ionic temple, but medieval intellectuals and builders shared Vitruvius' view of proportion, harmonic ratios, and geometry. Christianity is filled with significant numbers: twelve apostles, a triune God, ten commandments, seven virtues and vices. Numerical relationships in design contributed to a church's Christian identity as much as Biblical imagery in stained glass or sculpture. These ideas were preserved in medieval mathematics and construction practice, and later inherited by Renaissance thinkers like Alberti. His mission to ensure enduring quality for modern buildings only changed their design expression. He agreed with Vitruvius that great architecture required both perfect numbers and the ancient architectural vocabulary.

Albert considered both Vitruvius and surviving ancient buildings to be authoritative sources on this design language. Unfortunately, they often disagreed. Rome's ancient temples seldom matched Vitruvius' temple descriptions; most had Etruscan-style layouts or were round, a type he mentions only briefly. The Colosseum must have been especially confusing. It combines four different orders in one building, one a later Roman order called the Composite (Ionic volutes on a Corinthian capital). The orders are also used as surface decoration to frame arches: the three lower stories have engaged half-columns and the attic uses flattened strips called **pilasters**. Such practices appear nowhere in Vitruvius.

Unlike Vitruvius, however, Alberti discusses beauty directly. He builds on ancient ideas and adds a distinctly moralistic tone, suitable for a cleric. For him, a building without beauty is not only unattractive, but offensive. It lacks dignity and wastes resources, showing poor judgment. Vitruvius' teachings imply that venustas is not a matter of taste or opinion, but Alberti declares this outright: beauty is an objective quality.

His book includes many definitions of beauty, including: "Beauty is a form of sympathy and consonance of the parts within a body, according to definite number, outline, and position, as dictated by harmony, the absolute and fundamental rule in nature."[2] The word translated "harmony" is **concinnitas**, a term from rhetoric meaning skillfully crafted and pleasing. This concept brings together good proportion, simple geometry, and bilateral symmetry, which Alberti considered essential to architectural composition.

BEAUTY, LINEAMENTS, AND ORNAMENT

Alberti also distinguishes beauty from "ornament": "Beauty is some inherent property, to be found suffused all through the body of that which may be called beautiful, whereas ornament, rather than being inherent, has the character of something attached or additional."[3] For Alberti, architectural beauty is based on a building's **lineaments**, his term for its geometric form, design features that could be captured by a three-dimensional outline drawing. Qualities like material, decorative details, or color fall under "ornament," "a form of auxiliary light and complement to beauty."[4] Significantly, Alberti classifies the ancient orders with ornament. Good geometry and proportions produce beauty, but Ionic columns do not.

Elsewhere, Alberti explains beauty as completeness: "Beauty is that reasoned harmony of all the parts within a body, so that nothing may be added, taken away, or altered but for the worse."[5] He also argued that beauty ensures buildings will make future generations respect, not mock, the leaders who commissioned them. Alberti even claims (rather optimistically) that a beautiful building can "restrain the anger" of an enemy and protect it from destruction.[6]

Alberti offers his readers convincing reasons to invest in architectural beauty, expressed through ancient examples (admired in both antiquity and his own time), mathematical rules (validated by authors from antiquity to the Renaissance), and the orders (promoted by Vitruvius)—a formula for buildings that would be beautiful forever. His message helped revolutionize architecture and turn

FIGURE 5.7   Donato Bramate, Tempietto, S. Pietro in Montorio, Rome (1502–1510).

elite taste toward Vitruvian ideals. Yet this formula was difficult to implement in practice: information about ancient buildings was fragmentary, and did not offer clear solutions to modern building needs. Renaissance architects applied what information they had creatively, producing architecture embodying an idea of beauty that was simultaneously old and new.

A little shrine marking the (supposed) spot where the apostle Peter was martyred in Rome is such a hybrid. Its design began with a rare find: a matching set of sixteen ancient granite columns that survived a millennium together. Their diameter regulated the design by architect Donato Bramante, who knew Leonardo da Vinci in Milan. The columns, which encircle a cylinder set on a stepped base, support a Doric entablature, following the example of many ancient round temples in and around Rome. The few surviving roofs are flattened and cone-shaped. But Bramante instead stretches the cylinder high above the entablature, where it becomes the drum of a dome. He embellishes its exterior with niches and pilasters, and crowns the surrounding entablature with a stone **balustrade** (ornamental handrail).

Despite its ancient columns and Doric details, the Tempietto would have probably looked very strange to Vitruvius. But he would have likely still found it beautiful, because of its geometry and proportions. Renaissance architects certainly did; they considered Bramante's "little temple" perfect, declaring it "as good as the ancients." Serlio and Palladio even published it alongside ancient temples as a model for future architects, the highest possible honor.

CLASSICISM: AN ENDURING STANDARD

The Renaissance's new, old-style architecture helped establish an enduring standard for "good design." Today, architecture that uses the ancient orders is called **classical**. To *classify* is to place things in an organized system, whether biological taxonomy or instructional units in a school (*classes*). The term *classic* also means something that sets a high standard. Classic films, classical music, or classic cars are all products whose quality has stood the test of time and remain worthy models to follow.

"Classical" architecture adopts a long-respected tradition rooted in ancient Greece and Rome, such as a new bank in Philadelphia from the 1820s that was modeled directly on a Doric temple. The architecture's dignity and stability inspired people to put faith in the institution, reassuring customers that their money was safe there (wrongly, it turned out). This pattern continues in many new banks today that still use columns and ancient details. These add cost without improving practical function; their purpose is to inspire confidence. Whether used in a shaky, brand-new nation or in front of a suburban strip mall, classicism helps make an institution appear timeless and secure.

FIGURE 5.8   William Strickland, Second Bank of the United States, Philadelphia, Pennsylvania, 1819–1824.

The prevalence of classical style architecture is in part due to the persistent appeal of Alberti's argument. If ancient-style, mathematically harmonic buildings are "objectively" beautiful, they belong everywhere, at all times. A universally, eternally valid design language also implies that everyone should admire it. Classicism would be widely adopted, in part, because people wanted to demonstrate they could appreciate and apply this "eternal" form of beauty.

ABSOLUTISM, CERTAINTY, AND RULES FOR ARCHITECTURE

France was the first culture outside Italy to embrace its Renaissance-era revival of classical architecture. French aristocrats interested in the "new" art and architecture hired Serlio and other artists from Italy to build and decorate their homes. In fact, Serlio's book on ancient buildings was first published in France, and dedicated to its king François I. A century later, Louis XIV's Royal Academy of Architecture officially adopted and promoted the classical tradition.

Louis XIV was an absolute monarch with unchecked authority over his kingdom. Like ancient Egypt, France had a strict political and social hierarchy, with one person at the pinnacle. Louis and his supporters believed God made him king, and whatever was good for him was good for France—among his famous quotes is "I am the state." But seventeenth-century French culture was not monolithic. Another influential figure was the philosopher René Descartes (famous for his Cartesian grid). Descartes did not believe knowledge derived from authority, but reason. In a famous thought experiment, he questioned the basis of knowledge by imagining that everything he "knew" might be an illusion produced by the mind: he disregarded anything seen, touched, or read as potentially deceptive. All that remains, that *must* be true, was his thinking mind, leading to his famous quote "*cogito ergo sum*" ("I think, therefore I am"). He declared that only knowledge built logically from this foundation was solid and sure.

The Royal Academies, established to ensure France produced the world's best art, poetry, and science, combined absolutist and Cartesian agendas. Rationality would define architectural perfection, and this would guarantee great buildings that would glorify the king. The first head of the Academy of Architecture entrusted with this task was François Blondel, a military engineer, mathematician, and scholar of ancient literature.

After his 1671 appointment, Blondel and his committee studied the problem and formulated a French architectural doctrine, published in 1675. It established an official position with three basic rules:

1. *All great architecture belongs to the classical tradition.* This creates a hierarchy, with one European design tradition firmly placed at the top. To ensure buildings will remain beautiful, dignified, and admirable forever, use the style still admired after thousands of years: classicism.

2. *Medieval architecture is bad.* Blondel condemns medieval design as "individual fantasy." Good architecture, he argues, is attained by following reliable methods and models. French architects must know their buildings will glorify the king and the nation for centuries. Current taste found the Gothic unattractive, which proved that departing from classicism was dangerous.

3. *Use the classical style correctly.* Designing an Ionic building is not enough; architects must be sure to use the best possible Ionic. Blondel took Alberti's belief in absolute, measurable beauty further. He believed there was one set of correct, harmonic proportions for each order—an equation for perfect, beautiful buildings. The king demanded no less.

PERFECTION, REALITY, AND DEBATE

Blondel's faith in one set of perfect, correct proportions for each order raised problems. Treatises by Serlio, Vignola, and Palladio had established five canonical orders—the three Greek ones, the Tuscan, and the later Roman Composite. But their drawings of the same ancient buildings often showed inconsistent details or measurements. In addition, proportions were seldom identical for each order. One building's Ionic column might be 8.5 diameters tall, another's 9 1/3.

Blondel wanted a system uniting Alberti's three sources of knowledge (Vitruvius, ruins, and proportions) into one absolute architectural truth. Certain that these must be reconcilable, Blondel decided that Italian architects were unreliable. The king paid for his own surveyors to go take new measurements. They returned years later with the most thorough and accurate results to date. But, to Blondel's dismay, they did *not* show the ancient orders each had one set of absolute, reliable proportions, but simply confirmed the inconsistency of their use. Reality conflicted with abstract ideals.

Although Blondel's hope that classicism would provide an objectively, eternally valid path to architectural beauty was dashed, French faith in classical architecture would last into the twentieth century. Debates about how to use the orders, and whether the certainty Blondel hoped for was possible, would continue even longer.

That debate began immediately with Blondel's contemporary Claude Perrault, a physician and scientist in the Cartesian rational tradition. Perrault reasoned that if ancient evidence and mathematical perfection were irreconcilable, one must choose which to privilege. He proposed simply calculating the average measurements of all surviving examples of each order and using the resulting (imperfect) ratios. To Blondel and the Academy, this was heresy. Perrault published his ideas on architecture anyway, establishing an important tradition: questioning official doctrines on architecture.

COMPETING CLASSICISMS

A century after Blondel and Perrault's disagreement, information about ancient design expanded exponentially. The eighteenth-century discovery of Pompeii and Herculaneum, buried by Mount Vesuvius' eruption in 79 CE, offered vastly expanded information about Greco-Roman cities and buildings. Improved relations with the Ottoman empire also allowed Western Europeans to visit ancient Greek homelands for the first time since before the Renaissance.

The resulting knowledge revealed that "classical antiquity" was not one uniform template, but many variable traditions that spanned ten centuries and two different civilizations. Greek and Roman architecture were interrelated, but represented two distinct forms of classicism with many chronological phases and geographic variations. Moreover, several temples in Italy were Greek, while some in Athens were actually Roman. Understanding "classicism" became more difficult, not less.

Another new eighteenth-century field, art history, emerged to make sense of ancient artworks. One of its earliest figures, Johann Winckelmann, was a German librarian fascinated by ancient writings about statues who worked for collectors of ancient art like the Pope, who owned Rome's largest collection of antiquities. Winckelmann compared ancient statues with descriptions by classical authors. He thus attributed many to specific artists, making it possible to know what famous ancient works looked like, and understand how ancient art changed over time.

Winckelmann's research led him to believe that Greek art was superior to all others. This was because it did not depict imperfect reality, like the Romans, but expressed idealized perfection. He considered one phase of Greek art the best of all: from the fifth to the early fourth centuries BCE (now called the "classical" period). The Parthenon was built during this period, making it "perfect," too. Winckelmann considered the later Hellenistic era second-rate, and dismissed the Romans as imitators.

Such assertions led to a debate among European architects: Greece or Rome? Their model was no longer a generalized "antiquity," but a specific place, period, and culture. Greece was the original and (in Winckelmann's view, at least) eternally perfect. But Rome had more and usefully varied ancient monuments, and many modern classical-style buildings. If classical design requires choosing the best model, that leads to an unresolvable debate over history and style.

LE CORBUSIER AND THE ESSENCE OF CLASSICISM

Or not; Alberti said beauty was not about orders and details, but harmonically and proportionally arranged geometric shapes. If so, buildings without classical elements might still be "classically beautiful." Le Corbusier saw the Parthenon as a model of architectural perfection, but never copied its details. He famously pronounced that "architecture is the masterly, correct, and magnificent play of volumes brought together in light."[7] Beauty comes from pure solids and voids, arranged well and perceived by an "eye that can see."

In 1947, architectural historian Colin Rowe demonstrated that Palladio's Renaissance classicism and Le Corbusier's stark modern designs of the 1920s were more similar than they first appeared. Rowe compared the proportions of Palladio's sixteenth-century villas with Le Corbusier's houses, and revealed convincing similarities. His argument suggests that both embody the same mathematically based idea of beauty through different surface styles. It suggests that the essence of classicism is a set of abstract qualities that reliably resonate with the human eye and the soul.

Swiss engineer Robert Maillart's bridge over a deep gorge lends support to Le Corbusier's belief that engineers produce beauty automatically through rational design methods. Maillart declared that the bridge's elegantly simple arch resulted from a strictly efficient use of concrete. If mathematics makes Le Corbusier's villas classically beautiful, we might believe this bridge also qualifies. So does the Hall of Supreme Harmony in Beijing's Forbidden City, which exhibits entirely

FIGURE 5.9   Le Corbusier, Villa Savoye, Poissy-sur-Seine, France, 1929–1931.

"classical" design values: balance, axial alignment, a systematically embellished structural vocabulary, clear hierarchy of elements, and proportional harmony that symbolizes the natural order of the universe. Classical beauty may be less about specific ancient Mediterranean styles than a widespread way of thinking about form, which supports beauty as an objective and universal quality.

FIGURE 5.10   Robert Maillart, Salginatobel Bridge, Switzerland, 1928–1930.

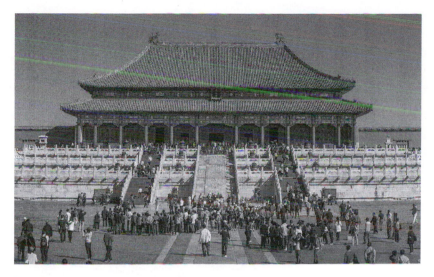

FIGURE 5.11   Hall of Supreme Harmony, Beijing, 1406–1420.

"ARBITRARY BEAUTY," AESTHETICS, AND THE IRRATIONAL

This view contradicts much of everyday experience, however. We disagree about fashion, films, and food so common sense suggests there can be no one standard of beauty. Different tastes produce different judgments. Perrault's critique of Blondel addressed this issue. Perrault believed in "positive" beauty, produced by universally admirable qualities (like fine materials, excellent craftsmanship, and magnificent size). But he also described another form of beauty that was "arbitrary," relating to qualities about which people can disagree, such as variations in column proportions and spacing. This makes some standards subjective, varying according to who judges. Perrault mentions differences in taste between cultural groups, but this logically extends to individuals. If opinions on beauty can be personal, is venustas different for everyone?

Aesthetics, today a synonym for beauty, comes from the Greek word for the physical senses (an "anesthetic" stops pain by shutting senses down). Aesthetics tie beauty to subjectivity: everyone has a unique sensory and experiential response which affects our judgment. This counters the classical idea of beauty that works everywhere, for everyone, forever. Instead, beauty is not (only) understood visually and mentally, but felt physically, and emotionally.

ROMANTICISM, BURKE, AND THE SUBLIME

An eighteenth-century European cultural movement celebrated emotion. **Romanticism** began in poetry, then influenced music, painting, and architecture. Participating artists tried to evoke intense feelings through their works. A non-artist, Irishman Edmund Burke, described Romantic aesthetic theory in his 1757 essay *A Philosophical Enquiry into the Origin of Our Ideas of the Sublime and the Beautiful*. Burke argues that aesthetics are irrational, located not in the mind but in the body, as sensations of pleasure. He defines beauty as an odd set of qualities: smallness, wholeness, delicacy and smoothness, unity and stability.

Burkean aesthetics primarily celebrate beauty's "opposite," the **sublime**. Burke's sublime is achieved through infinity, vastness, magnitude, magnificence, and difficulty. It describes an experience that overwhelms the senses and cannot be processed rationally. An example might be standing at the edge of the Grand Canyon: its enormity makes us feel small, and its revelation of the earth's geologic layers can make us feel very temporary.

For Burke, "beauty" provides a sense of physical and intellectual control. The sublime induces more intense feelings: terror at the brink of an abyss, insignificance amidst the vastness of time and space, and the exhilaration of experiencing something huge, eternal, and greater than ourselves. This provides a dramatically different vision of architecture's aesthetic goals. Are buildings supposed to be safe and comprehensible, or exciting and overwhelming? Is that possible?

One way is the ancient urge to build high: the Great Pyramids, or skyscrapers like SOM's 2,700-foot Burj Khalifa (over twice the Empire State building's height) both achieve sublime height. Building so tall satisfies an irrational, emotional impulse, a desire to challenge the laws of nature. The Pyramids and Stonehenge can also induce a sense of infinite time: we know logically that architecture cannot last forever, yet such buildings seem as if they could.

BOULLÉE, BARBIER, AND SUBLIME CLASSICISM

One eighteenth-century French architect, Étienne-Louis Boullée, left a successful career at age fifty-four to produce **paper architecture**, now better remembered than his buildings. Boullée was in the French Academy, and committed to the principles of classical design. His imaginary cathedral features pediments, colonnades, cornices, and domes, all abstracted to emphasize their pure geometric forms. Boullée believed different shapes each provoked a distinct "emotional impression" in viewers, so a compositional sequence of hemispheres, cubes, and cylinders choreographed a specific series of emotions. This linking of form and feeling is an architectural manifestation of Romantic sensibility.

So is Boullée's sense of scale. The blur in the lower left of Figure 5.12 is a vast crowd of people; he envisioned a colossal scale for his cathedral that would utterly overwhelm the viewer. His interior view shows light pouring in from the

FIGURE 5.12   Étienne-Louis Boullée, Project for a Metropolitan Cathedral, 1781.

drum of the dome and blazing fire on the altar, which exploit another of Burke's sources of the sublime: dramatic lighting. Even on paper, Boullée's imaginary world of superhuman-sized and dramatically lit space creates a sense of awe.

Another classically inspired design that captures the sublime was produced by one of Boullée's former students, François Barbier, for one of Boullée's former clients, an eccentric aristocrat, Racine de Monville. The drawings show a stump of an Ionic column, just the base and a ragged portion of fluted shaft. Yet this fragment is large enough to contain an entire house, suggesting the original stood hundreds of feet tall—an impossibly gargantuan monument. Barbier's design invites nostalgia for its lost grandeur, and also conveys great age through the column's ragged, weed-covered upper edge. He wants to inspire intense feelings about some long-lost civilization, whose ruins we inhabit like rodents.

The sublime was far easier to achieve in fantasy drawings than built reality, yet Barbier's pseudo-broken giant column house was in fact built. It was one of several fantasy structures known as "follies" that filled Monville's estate, manifesting the Romantic impulse to stage experiences through design. This movement cultivated a direct relationship with the garden, which produced another new Romantic aesthetic category.

LANDSCAPE, THE PICTURESQUE, AND LESSONS FROM CHINA

The Renaissance revival of villas increased interest in garden design. Most Italian gardens were laid out in symmetrical geometric patterns and enclosed by walls. The French continued this tradition of orderly walkways and plantings, but made them even more elaborate. The kingdom's power made protective walls unnecessary, so its wealthiest aristocrats could create enormous formal gardens at their country chateaux.

Like classical architecture, European formal gardens pursue beauty through control, symmetry, and rational compositional patterns. But in the eighteenth century, some British critics rejected this approach, exemplified by Versailles' acres of geometrically pruned shrubs, lacework flower beds, and straight gravel walks, as simplistic. The beauty of unspoiled natural landscapes, they observed, is composed of irregular and uncontrolled elements, and more powerful. Creating an environment that lives up to nature's complex aesthetic relationships is more difficult, and more worthwhile. Such qualities were called **picturesque** after those seen in landscape painting.

Picturesque aesthetics are expressed in a different, "English" approach to design, seen at such gardens as Stourhead Park. They feature no straight paths or intricately patterned planting beds. A bridge and two small structures in the distance are the only visible signs of human intervention within an otherwise natural environment. That sense of nature, however, is a carefully constructed illusion. This landscape is just as artificial as the gardens of Versailles. The topography was reshaped, the lake constructed, and clumps of trees and shrubs planted according to a plan. Its aim was to produce an environment that appeared undesigned, but fulfilled ideas of "natural" beauty by following aesthetic rules.

Both pursued pleasure, but in different ways. A classical French or Italian garden can be understood from one point, which reveals its geometric order at a glance. Its pleasure derives from rationality and predictability. The picturesque,

FIGURE 5.13   Flitcroft and Hoare, Gardens at Stourhead Park, Wiltshire, England, 1744–1765.

instead, pursues the pleasure of an experience that unfolds unpredictably through movement and time. To understand Stourhead, we must walk all over it in countless ways and see every possible sequence of views that change with the weather, the seasons, and the years.

These views are composed to create a pleasing, faux-natural irregularity through balanced asymmetry. The bridge in the middle distance balances the temple across the lake; the clump of evergreens on the left balances the lower shrubs and small trees across the bridge. The goal is an interesting, pleasant, and occasionally surprising environment. This response to Continental tradition might suggest the English were somehow more sensitive to the beauties of unspoiled nature. However, Britain learned this alternative form of landscape design from a distant culture's sophisticated, centuries-old tradition.

England established trade with Chinese coastal cities in the late 1600s, where British travelers learned to appreciate tea and fine porcelain, and were also exposed to an established tradition of garden design. One reported a Chinese saying that any child can plant trees in straight lines; what was more challenging and praiseworthy was to re-create the subtle, difficult beauty of an old, gnarled tree. China's gardens used artfully constructed juxtapositions of landforms, water, rocks, plants, and structures like bridges to create spaces of balance and visual variety.

Chinese garden design was just one facet of the world's oldest continuous cultural tradition, with ancient aesthetic canons for art and architecture. Compositions achieved balance by contrasting regular objects with irregular forms across media. The philosophical basis for this approach can be identified in ancient texts like the *I Ching* (fourth century BCE or older). Such writings on cosmology and philosophy present the universe as a dynamic balance of opposites, where events evolve as a process, and change is inevitable—all concepts adopted by the English picturesque garden.

PICTURESQUE ARCHITECTURE

Many British intellectuals absorbed and reprocessed Chinese aesthetic ideas. Among them was aristocrat Uvedale Price, who redesigned his estate's landscape and wrote essays about the picturesque. Price presented it as a Romantic aesthetic category occupying a midpoint between the beautiful and the sublime. A walled, geometric Italian garden is "beautiful" because it inspires a sense of order and control; a rugged, perilous Alpine landscape is "sublime" because it embodies nature's untamed power. A picturesque garden like Stourhead, neither boring nor terrifying, strikes a moderating balance between these aesthetic extremes.

Price also believed architecture should embrace picturesque values. To him, this meant buildings should be designed to enhance their surroundings' scenic quality, not as a separate element dominating the landscape. He found irregularity—whether designed or the result of decay—preferable to symmetry because it adds visual variety. The picturesque and sublime also provided new reasons to appreciate medieval architecture. The dramatic height and lighting of the Gothic appealed strongly to a Romantic sensibility, as did the many medieval structures that were built in separate phases, resulting in irregular "variety." Many in Britain were in ruins that evoked a sublime sense of time and death.

Only twenty years after Lord Burlington's Palladian villa at Chiswick, another British aristocrat, Horace Walpole, Earl of Orford, remodeled another

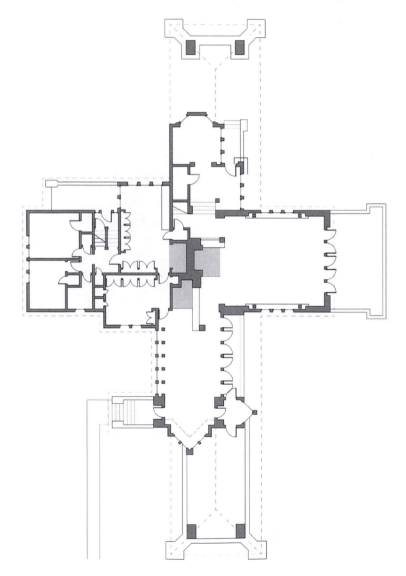

FIGURE 5.14   Frank Lloyd Wright, Willits House, Highland Park, Illinois, 1902, plan and view.

house near London into a pseudo-medieval estate called Strawberry Hill. He added castle-inspired crenellations and round towers, plus Gothic ecclesiastical windows. Mixed sources and asymmetrical composition were designed to suggest evolution over several centuries and create a picturesque composition.

Picturesque irregularity is also seen in later architecture that looked very different from Strawberry Hill, such as the Prairie Style houses designed by Frank Lloyd Wright at the turn of the twentieth century. The long, horizontal lines of their terrace walls, window banks, and low-pitched hipped roofs were meant to harmonize with the flat Midwestern landscape, echoing Price's emphasis on a building's relationship with the landscape. The Willits House plan has four distinct, carefully balanced wings that radiate from a common center. Wright's balanced asymmetry also recalls Strawberry Hill's play of distinct parts, albeit expressed in a very different design language.

Wright's designs inspired a generation of modern architects in Europe, including Ludwig Mies van der Rohe, whose unbuilt design for a Brick Villa (1923) abstracts Wright's "pinwheel" plan into its barest essence. Mies, famous for his dictum "Less is more," spent his career pursuing architecture of minimal purity. But his aesthetic ideal often conflicted with practical realities. His Farnsworth House, a country retreat for a Chicago doctor, expresses Mies' architectural ideas with elegant clarity. But it also caused a notorious lawsuit when his client found his transcendent jewel of a house impossible to live in. She loved it on paper, but the reality of an unventilated glass house on a mosquito-infested river was entirely different. Aesthetic success does not preclude real-world disaster.

FIGURE 5.15   L. Mies van der Rohe, Farnsworth House, Plano, Illinois, 1945–1951.

THE LIMITS OF BEAUTY: FUNCTIONALISM

Beauty is the most troublesome leg in Vitruvius' triad. Efforts to make it an absolute quantity have never eliminated differences in taste and judgment. Romantic
aesthetics accommodates its personal, irrational dimension, but no design can
guarantee a viewer will feel what was intended. In person, Barbier's broken-column
house might not seem "sublime" at all—just bizarre.

Vitruvius was hardly infallible, as we saw with the issue of the Doric's
gender. So why not give up venustas? With no way to guarantee success, perhaps
it should not be part of the equation. Some have argued that architects should consider structure and utility alone when they design. This idea, called **functionalism**,
gained a strong following in the early to mid twentieth century. One of its chief
proponents was Walter Gropius, founder of the Bauhaus. Gropius opposed the
Beaux-Arts method, which enforced predetermined (classical) standards of beauty:
all building designs must be symmetrical and have a clear hierarchy of axially
distributed shapes and forms.

Functionalists argued this "outside-in" approach was backward, and that
buildings should be designed from the inside out. Architecture should not squeeze
everything into an envelope that follows compositional rules, but generate forms
and arrangements from functions. To do this, they begin with a *program*: a list of
spatially specific jobs a building needs to accommodate. Big spaces receive big
volumes, small spaces can be clustered together, and all are arranged for the most
convenient, efficient access. The exterior form simply reflects and expresses what
happens inside.

Many buildings designed this way perform their appointed tasks efficiently. Some have their admirers; but such buildings are often condemned as "ugly." Would this concern Gropius? Not at all: he argued that trying to achieve beauty distracts from fulfilling architecture's primary job of meeting people's immediate, practical needs; beauty is irrelevant. Le Corbusier instead argued that deriving designs from function and reason Is the most reliable way to achieve beauty. So not thinking about beauty is the best way to achieve beauty—quite a contradiction.

BEAUTIFUL? SUBLIME? PICTURESQUE? FUNCTIONALIST?

We can now return to the ICA, and reconsider what we might mean if we declare it "beautiful" (Figure 5.1). Its design features no ornament, much less the classical vocabulary; but if its proportions are harmonic, its simple forms might fulfill an abstracted form of classical beauty. Yet Romantic aesthetics might be more relevant here: the drama of its huge cantilever is arguably sublime. Its volumes' asymmetrical arrangement provides a picturesque addition to the Boston waterfront. The forms also appear to be generated from interior uses: the upper block houses large galleries, and offices, cafe, lobby, and outdoor seating are all visibly expressed, so it could be considered functionalist.

The label "beautiful" seems inadequate to describe the ICA's many visual goals, which also encompass an anti-aesthetic attitude. Yet clarifying what sorts of aesthetic aims architects have pursued helps explain what this design was meant to achieve, why the museum chose it, and why Boston's architects gave it special recognition.

To insist, as Vitruvius does, that architecture should be "aesthetically successful" requires some system that explains what success looks like—a set of clear rules, like classical proportion; or looser but still definable goals, like the picturesque, the sublime, or functionalism. This suggests that architectural design should follow an established model, or obey a set of standards. Is this true?

The lack of consistent proportions in ancient buildings that troubled Blondel does not necessarily indicate classicism's "failure." It suggests that every time builders began a Doric temple or Ionic portico, they worked to produce something slightly better than last time. They were creative and innovative; not just following the rules, they challenged or transcended them.

Blondel found this side of design dangerous. But historically, architects who create something never seen or imagined before have gained the greatest glory (even divinity, for Imhotep). Architectural aesthetics also includes creativity, finding new solutions to old problems, and tackling brand-new ones. Vitruvius' belief in venustas goes beyond faith in a fixed, authoritative classical vocabulary; it includes a belief in the architect's capacity for creative innovation.

VOCABULARY

abacus, acanthus, aesthetics, anthropomorphic analogy, balustrade, cantilever, capital, classical, concinnitas, Corinthian, Doric, engaged column, entablature, entasis, foliate, functionalism, Ionic, lineaments, peripteral, picturesque, pilaster, podium, Romanticism, sublime, volute.

STUDY AND REVIEW QUESTIONS

1. How easy is it to demonstrate that a building is "beautiful"? Can this same adjective apply to both the Taj Mahal and the ICA in Boston? Why or why not?
2. Why did Vitruvius look to Greek standards and styles when describing how to achieve architectural beauty?
3. What do the Doric, Ionic, and Corinthian orders all have in common? What are their most important differences?
4. How does Vitruvius connect the Greek orders to the human body? Why are its proportional and geometric qualities significant for architectural design?
5. Where do Alberti's ideas of beauty overlap with Vitruvius, and where are they different? What is his distinction between beauty and "decoration"?
6. What is "classical" architecture? What is its appeal?
7. Why did Blondel define rules for architecture? What was Perrault's response? Whose position do you prefer?
8. Do you agree that Le Corbusier's abstract designs should be considered "classical"? Why or why not?
9. Define the term *sublime*, and describe how it can apply to architecture.
10. What is the "picturesque"? Where did this aesthetic idea originate, and what was its impact on architecture?
11. What is the benefit of eliminating beauty as an architectural requirement? Do you believe a functionalist approach to design produces good buildings?

APPLICATION AND DISCUSSION EXERCISES

1. Find two buildings in your environment that your believe achieve architectural beauty in two different ways. Describe their visual qualities, and why you think each is aesthetically successful.
2. Locate a nearby building that embodies "classical" ideas in some way (directly, abstractly, or through other compositional values). Do you believe these qualities make it a better building?

3. Find a building that inspires a strong aesthetic reaction from you—whether beautiful, sublime, picturesque, or anti-aesthetic. How does it achieve this, and do you consider it a successful work of architecture?

NOTES

1 Vitruvius. *The Ten Books on Architecture*, trans. I. Rowland (Cambridge: Cambridge University Press, 1999), p. 47.
2 Leon Battista Alberti, *On the Art of Building in Ten Books*, trans. J. Rykwert and J. Tavernor (Cambridge, MA: MIT Press, 1988), p. 303.
3 Ibid., p. 156.
4 Ibid., p. 156.
5 Ibid., p. 156.
6 Ibid., p. 156.
7 Le Corbusier, *Towards an Architecture*, trans. J. Goodman (Los Angeles: Getty Research Institute, 2007), p. 102.

FURTHER READING

Alberti, Leon Battista. *On the Art of Building in Ten Books.* Trans. J. Rykwert and J. Tavernor. Cambridge, MA: MIT Press, 1988.

Burke, Edmund. *A Philosophical Inquiry into the Origin of our Ideas of the Sublime and the Beautiful.* New York: Garland, 1971.

Le Corbusier. *Toward an Architecture.* Trans. J. Goodman. Los Angeles: Getty Research Institute, 2007.

Levine, Neil. *The Architecture of Frank Lloyd Wright.* Princeton: Princeton University Press, 1996.

Mitrović, Branko. *Philosophy for Architects.* New York: Princeton Architectural Press, 2011.

Perrault, Claude. *Ordonnance for the Five Kinds of Columns after the Method of the Ancients.* Santa Monica: Getty Center for the Study of Art and the Humanities, 1993.

Roth, Leland. *Understanding Architecture: Its Elements, History and Meaning.* Third edition. Boulder: Westview Press, 2014.

Rowe, Colin. *The Mathematics of the Ideal Villa and Other Essays.* Cambridge, MA: MIT Press. 1976.

Rykwert, Joseph. *The Dancing Column: On Order of Architecture.* Cambridge, MA: MIT Press, 1996.

Tavernor, Robert. *On Alberti and the Art of Building.* New Haven and London: Yale University Press, 1998.

Vitruvius. *The Ten Books on Architecture.* Trans. I. Rowland. Cambridge: Cambridge University Press, 1999.

Watkins, C. and Ben Cowell. *Uvedale Price: Decoding the Picturesque.* Woodbridge: Boydell, 2012.

Wittkower, Rudolf. *Architectural Principles in the Age of Humanism.* London: Academy Editions, 1949.

CHAPTER 6
ORIGINALITY

IF WE ACCEPT VITRUVIUS' DEMAND for venustas, then we must formulate some set of aesthetic rules for architecture; otherwise there is no way to determine success. Yet would we want all buildings to be variations on a single creative model, however "perfect"? The sublime also suggests that architecture should be exciting.

FIGURE 6.1   Jean Nouvel, Musée Quai Branly, Paris, 2006.

One way to achieve this is by introducing unexpected elements to a building, such as a straight, vertical façade punctured by a grid of conventional windows at a Paris museum that also happens to be a lush vertical garden. Whether or not we enter the museum, the surprise this portion of its design provokes makes us more likely to pause, ponder, and remember. This would likely please its architect, Jean Nouvel, who no doubt hoped this element would inspire viewers to think differently about walls and gardens, nature and architecture. He wanted his building to be original.

ANOTHER RENAISSANCE IDEAL

Serlio writes that his design system, which offers five orders and arrays of possible plans and elevations, allows even "mediocre architects" to make good buildings. Simply follow the rules, choose from the menu, and build. Easy—too easy. Who aspires to mediocrity? Or wants to design a building that follows a recipe? Both architects and their clients usually want something "different."

Alberti and Serlio emphasized how classicism guaranteed quality, but Florentine painter and architect Giorgio Vasari described the Renaissance differently in the mid sixteenth century. His book, *The Lives of the Most Excellent Painters, Sculptors, and Architects,* often shortened to *Lives of the Artists* (1550/1568), is a series of biographies that emphasizes the people who created Renaissance art. Vasari explains that when the Roman Empire ended, ancient artists' ability to capture the beauty of nature was lost. Art "declined" (in Vasari's opinion) to become flat, primitive, and pattern-like until a miracle happened in late medieval Tuscany. A few Florentines like Giotto began to paint more like the artists of antiquity, creating figures that appeared solid and spaces that seemed real.

Over several generations, as he tells it, Florentine art "advanced" until it eventually rivaled the ancients. Taken together, Vasari's dozens of lives show the collective, transformative effect of these figures' work. But he also presents artists as individuals whose achievements and limits reflect their innate talents and personalities. Vasari praises Leonardo da Vinci for his universal intellect and ability to master human anatomy, envision helicopters and tanks, and paint such works as the *Mona Lisa*, whose smoky shadows make her seem to "live and breathe." But Leonardo's wide-ranging curiosity and huge number of projects also meant he seldom finished anything. For Vasari, his career thus fell short of "perfection." Raphael, Leonardo's contemporary, also produced groundbreaking, stunningly lifelike portraits. Raphael might have attained "perfection" according to Vasari, except he died young, at thirty-seven.

But one extraordinary artist achieved Vasari's ideal: Michelangelo Buonarroti who "transcends and surpasses" every other artist to reign supreme in all three disciplines: sculpture (like his *David*), painting (the Sistine Ceiling), and

FIGURE 6.2   Michelangelo, *David*, 1502, and detail of Libyan Sibyl from the Sistine Chapel, 1508–1512.

architecture.[1] Moreover, Vasari claims that Michelangelo's art does not merely imitate Nature, but surpasses it. When his figures break nature's "rules"—seen in David's oversized head and hands, and the female Libyan Sibyl's astonishingly burly shoulders—these departures are not defects. Exaggerated proportions and expressive musculature serve higher ends, and prove the artist's greatness.

Vasari even claimed Michelangelo was the best artist who ever lived, anywhere on earth, at any time in history. Despite his conviction, we recognize that such an assertion is faith, not fact. But Vasari's reasons for believing Michelangelo was the best artist ever became very influential.

DISEGNO, INVENTION, AND "DIVINE GENIUS"

Vasari conjoined painting, sculpture, and architecture because all rely on **disegno**, an Italian word encompassing both "drawing" and "design." Drawing allows artists to communicate a work's formal essence (those qualities defining Alberti's lineaments), imitate nature graphically, and envision new solutions, an increasingly valued skill during the Renaissance. Imaginative creativity or "invention" also allowed artists to design new buildings that recapture the lost grandeur of ancient monuments, known only from fragments, words, and abstract ideas of beauty.

FIGURE 6.3   Raphael, Philosophy (*School of Athens*), Stanze della Segnatura, Vatican Palace, 1509–1511.

Raphael's famous fresco in the Vatican Palace, *The School of Athens*, does just that. He depicts the greatest ancient philosophers gathered inside a vast building with coffered barrel vaults and a "dome" of sky. It borrows elements from ancient sites in Rome, but Raphael's synthesis existed only in the imagination. The artist invented an architecture that no one had ever built—yet.

Vasari praises Michelangelo for "the power of his most divine genius."[2] Today we use the word **genius** to describe someone whose thinking is so new and radical it completely reframes how people see reality. *Genius* is Latin for a person's distinctive skills and talents (see Chapter 4). To ancient Romans, it could also describe an individual or family's guardian spirit. When Vasari calls Michelangelo's achievements "divine," it equates his work and his spirit with God himself, the ultimate Creator.

This account of Michelangelo's miraculous, unique, and individual talent also associated the pinnacle of artistic achievement with bold, creative rule-breaking. Although Vasari discusses Michelangelo's architecture very briefly, these passages emphasize the link between genius and originality. We can see Michelangelo's architectural originality in his research library for the monastery at San Lorenzo in Florence. It includes an entry hall that initially appears quite "classical." Its smooth Doric columns have standard proportions, and the pediments above the openings (some triangular, some rounded) were all conventional elements by Michelangelo's day.

But if we look more closely, some things look strange: like the odd, squarish shapes above window-like niches, and the columns' placement within the wall,

FIGURE 6.4   Michelangelo, Laurentian Library Vestibule, S. Lorenzo, Florence, Italy, 1530s.

seemingly supported by curved **consoles** or shelf brackets, instead of a solid foundation. Also, these elements are un-classically crowded with very little background space, barely enough to separate the niche pediments from the columns. The library door's pediment (obstructed in Figure 6.4) physically overlaps the flanking columns, and a door is squeezed into the corner so tightly it looks like a mistake. Photographs seldom capture how the grand staircase to the reading room fills the space—there is barely room to walk around it.

Michelangelo knew the rules of "proper" classicism. But he preferred to combine standard and his own invented elements to create tension and drama, much like the exaggerated anatomy of his human figures. Any "mediocre" architect can follow the rules; Michelangelo's only rule was his own creative vision. Vasari wrote that Michelangelo's architecture "broke the bonds and chains that made them all [architects of his generation] follow a common path."[3] His rule-breaking showed how his contemporaries were limiting themselves by striving to be "correct."

Anyone can make something that purposefully violates rules. The ability to produce something unorthodox that is also superior to conventional work—as Vasari believed Michelangelo did—is what demonstrates "divine" creative powers. This made him more than an artist who has genius; it proved he was "a genius," and defined a new standard of achievement.

GENIUS, PRECEDENT, AND INSPIRATION

Michelangelo was Vasari's model of a naturally gifted individual who rose above all around him. But he also had deep respect for certain earlier figures, such as Brunelleschi. Unlike the truism that copying is the sincerest form of flattery, Michelangelo's paid his highest compliment to a few respected forerunners by taking their work as a starting point for his own. He acknowledged the inspirational source while producing something entirely his own that surpasses the model.

This happened with Michelangelo's most prestigious architectural project: St. Peter's basilica in Rome, the mother church of Western Christianity (Figure 1.10). The task of replacing the original, unstable, thousand-year-old church began in earnest in 1506, forty years before the seventy-two-year-old Michelangelo was appointed in 1546. After eight years of progress under its first architect, construction ground to a halt. For thirty-two years, a series of chief architects had been busy—not with construction, for the most part, but dealing with ongoing disagreement over the new church design.

The chief architect preceding Michelangelo, Antonio da Sangallo, spent most of his twenty-six years in charge producing his own design. Seven years were occupied in building an enormous wooden model, 15 × 24 × 10 feet (2.6 × 7.3 × 3 meters). More expensive than some built churches, this model would ensure that Sangallo's design remained authoritative for any future architects.

Except Michelangelo. He had little respect for Sangallo (or most of his contemporaries), and no intention of building a design he disliked strongly. But instead of starting over, he returned to the first design by the first architect—Bramante, architect of the Tempietto, the tiny shrine deemed as good as ancient temples (Figure 5.7). Michelangelo greatly respected Bramante, thirty years his senior. The imaginary architectural space in Raphael's *School of Athens* was likely inspired by Bramante's design for the church next door, then in its earliest phases of construction.

Surviving evidence, including a medal showing an exterior view of Bramante's project (Figure 0.5), suggests he designed a symmetrical plan with a cross in a square. It would be crowned by a dome approaching the size of the ancient Pantheon in Rome (Figure 7.5) and Brunelleschi's dome in Florence (Figure 4.5). Most of the completed construction had followed Bramante's design, and all later redesigns incorporated the foundations and piers already in place. Part of the delay was because centralized plans remained controversial, and because the piers intended to support a vast dome 300 feet overhead had already developed cracks.

Michelangelo took Bramante's original plan and gave it muscle: to Sangallo's more robust piers for the dome, he added more solid perimeter walls, and a simplified cross-in-square layout. He retained the first scheme's essential strengths, ended decades of debate (for a while), and got it built. When

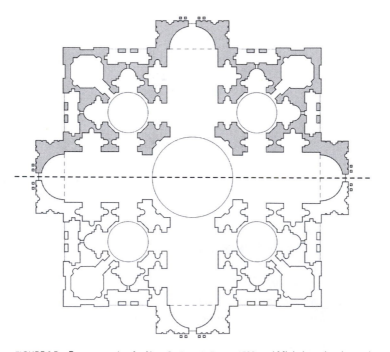

FIGURE 6.5   Bramante, plan for New St. Peter's Rome, 1506, and Michelangelo, plan and exterior view, New St. Peter's, Rome, 1546.

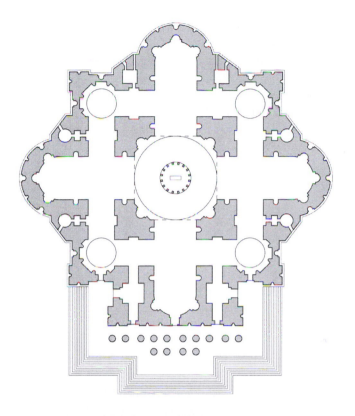

FIGURE 6.5 *(continued)*

Michelangelo died in 1564 after eighteen years on the project, at almost eighty-nine years old, the basilica was finished up to the dome's drum. His dome was built in slightly modified form, its hemispherical profile stretched into an egg-shape—an unintentional but appropriate homage to Brunelleschi, whom he also respected.

At St. Peter's, Michelangelo also had an opportunity Brunelleschi did not: to design a dome's exterior. There and elsewhere on the basilica's exterior, Michelangelo used his own innovative version of the classical vocabulary in architecture. It gave this massive structure a dignified and distinctive urban presence, one that has been identified with the Eternal City ever since.

AFTER THE GENIUS

We may not agree that Michelangelo's achievements actually live up to Vasari's estimation; he was certainly not an objective critic. Vasari considered himself one of Michelangelo's disciples, and his paintings and architecture quite obviously follow his style. He had a direct interest in depicting Michelangelo as a godlike genius, because enhancing his master's reputation increased his own reflected glory. Or not; how impressive is it to copy an artist whose greatness is defined through his originality? If we follow "the best artist ever," what can we possibly hope to achieve?

Perhaps we accept Michelangelo's supremacy and, like Vasari, work in his shadow; we could reject his greatness as exaggerated; or, given enough self-confidence, we might even challenge this supposed "god" of art and try to beat him. Gianlorenzo Bernini, a young virtuoso sculptor born over a century after Michelangelo, took the latter route. When he unveiled his own *David*, Bernini declared himself an heir, another genius whose original creations can build on the work of Michelangelo the way Michelangelo built on Bramante's designs.

Bernini's confidence paid off. His talent and charm made him the favorite architect of several popes, an architectural celebrity who lived like a courtier. The crowning achievement of his brilliant career was his own monumental contribution to St. Peter's in Rome. Bernini's great colonnades for the enormous keyhole-shaped piazza extend the basilica's imposing presence into the city, an urban-scaled signature that rivals Michelangelo's landmark dome (Figure 3.5).

Unfortunately, the convention-shattering originality associated with "genius" does not automatically earn recognition and success. Francesco Borromini, a contemporary of Bernini's in Rome, was just as brilliant an architect as Bernini, if not more so. He designed dynamic, exciting spaces from unexpectedly rational geometric foundations, and sculpted undulating, clay-like surfaces that stretched the classical vocabulary. At San Carlo alle Quattro Fontane, Borromini's sinuous floor plan resolves into an intricately coffered oval dome—a truly "ingenious" design for a minuscule church. He also had larger projects in

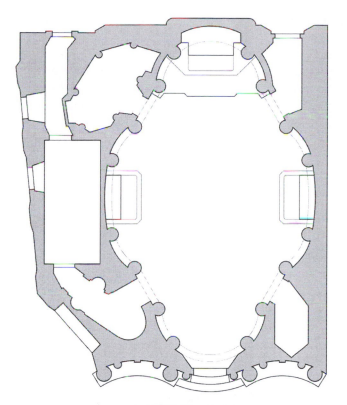

FIGURE 6.6 Borromini, St. Carlo alle Quattro Fontane, Rome, 1638–1667 (plan and dome view).

Rome, but nothing that could rival the enormous mark on the city Bernini left at St. Peter's square.

Like Michelangelo, Borromini had a difficult personality; he eventually committed suicide. Borromini's character and career can fit the modern model of the genius as an unstable outsider: someone whose ideas are too advanced to be fully appreciated in his own day, but are vindicated over time. We often assume that a genius will not be hailed as a prophet, but shunned as a threat.

TEACHING GENIUS?

If great architecture results from originality, invention, and the divinely, rebelliously inventive genius, this conflicts with the systematic knowledge necessary for a "discipline"—a word describing a subject that can be taught. Renaissance books and the French Academy both relied on rules that made architecture teachable, and expected creativity to happen within boundaries they established. Not everyone agreed with this approach. One nineteenth-century critic, Eugène-Emmanuel Viollet-le-Duc, called the École des Beaux-Arts a "mill," a factory producing uniform architects who all design the same way. He believed design schools should foster creativity, not obedience.

A young American named Louis Sullivan, part of a generation who studied architecture in Paris at the Beaux-Arts during the late nineteenth century, had a similar reaction. In his autobiography, Sullivan describes becoming dissatisfied with the world's most famous architecture school. When he traveled to Italy to see the buildings everybody studied in Paris, this was a revelation. Sullivan was overwhelmed by one space in Rome: the Sistine Chapel. For two whole days he "communed in silence with a Super-Man" and "felt and saw a great Free Spirit."[4] Sullivan, by his account, did not need rules and methods, but a direct , inspiring encounter with a genius—another genius, perhaps?—like Michelangelo to unlock his own latent creativity.

Sullivan soon returned to the U.S., and eventually moved to Chicago. There his architecture prominently showcased an original ornamental style of vibrant, geometrically structured botanical forms (Figure 7.8). Sullivan's work shares many of classicism's sources and formal principles but, like Michelangelo's, it is recognizably his own. Whether Sullivan qualifies as a "genius" (many of his struggles echoed Borromini's) is debatable. His pursuit of originality, however, is undisputed.

MILLENNIAL MEN

In *Towards an Architecture*, Le Corbusier scorns all his fellow architects—except two. One is Phidias, an Athenian sculptor who created the Parthenon's colossal cult statue and its exterior sculpture (see Chapter 1). Some believed Phidias was also artistic coordinator for the Acropolis reconstruction after the Persians destroyed Athens' mountaintop sanctuary. In this version of history, Iktinos and Kallikrates, the Parthenon's architects, were subject to Phidias' unifying vision for the entire site; Le Corbusier celebrates the creative "mastermind" with the greatest design authority.

The other architect Le Corbusier admires is Michelangelo. He sees St. Peter's as an inspirational manifestation of his architectural genius. Unlike Vasari, Le Corbusier does not claim Michelangelo was the best artist ever. But he does call him "the man of the last thousand years," a towering figure whose creative vision dominates a millennium. Similarly, for Le Corbusier Phidias was clearly "the man" of the previous thousand years; "his" Acropolis set a design standard unsurpassed until Michelangelo.

Le Corbusier never actually names the architect whose genius will define the next millennium—the reader is left to make that implied connection (he was not known for his modesty). Only one other modern architect, Frank Lloyd Wright, had an ego that could rival Le Corbusier's. Another commonality was that both had many apprentices, but few of them achieved a level of success that approached their masters'. Like Vasari, most became disciples who perpetuated the master's vision.

The idea of genius is both individual and unpredictable, a random, even once-in-a-millennium strike from above. If architecture is supposed to demonstrate originality—not just whenever an epoch's lone genius appears, but consistently—how can this be perpetuated? Can innovation be organized and harnessed for the wider good? And is it strictly personal, or can it apply to groups?

ORIGINALITY, CHANGE, AND PROGRESS

We might also wonder whether "genius" actually exists, or is a convenient but artificial way to understand original thinking. Physicist Thomas Kuhn's 1962 book *The Structure of Scientific Revolutions* provides a different perspective drawn from the history of science. He found that an existing explanatory model, or paradigm, will generate experiments, hypotheses, and discoveries that expand knowledge— for a while. But eventually, scientists will encounter evidence and pose questions that the model cannot satisfactorily address.

Kuhn finds that major breakthroughs often originate from people who view an existing paradigm as outsiders on the field's periphery. From this more detached position, they can formulate a new model, one retaining the original's strengths while adding the capacity to explain more evidence and answer new questions. Kuhn called such a fundamental change in thinking a **paradigm shift**.

Kuhn's theory does not refute the existence of extraordinarily gifted, visionary individuals. It does, however, suggest that revolutionary creativity is not only about who we are, but *where* we are. Our position within the world of ideas

FIGURE 6.7   Portrait of Menkaure and his wife, ca. 2500 BCE.

affects our ability to generate new ones. If architecture is supposed to demonstrate change, then greater participation by non-architects, or greater exposure to non-architectural fields among architects, should help this occur.

Today, as we enjoy ever-changing products like smaller, lighter, more powerful computers and telephones, we expect and generally welcome change as "progress." But this is not a universal value. For instance, a statue of Menkaure, builder of the last Great Pyramid at Giza around 2500 BCE, and his wife, follow a model of portraiture used for Egyptian royalty as late as the seventh century BCE. If artists are carefully following conventions established 1,800 years earlier, this shows that originality was not a priority. Ancient Egyptian culture did experience many changes over time—Imhotep's pyramid is one obvious architectural example—but it greatly privileged continuity, eternity, and the idea of stasis.

The modern embrace of change as a positive force has been shaped by major thinkers, including the philosopher Gottlob Hegel. Hegel believed that change is essential, even inevitable, particularly in the world of ideas. He developed a model that explains how change happens in human thought: one idea, a **thesis**, provokes an alternative or opposing explanation, or **antithesis**. Eventually the two ideas are reconciled into a **synthesis**, which becomes a new thesis and starts a new cycle. Hegel saw this process as increasing knowledge over time. Its momentum drives understanding forward, ever closer to the ideal of Truth.

Or rather, "upward:" Hegel originally studied theology, and he believed history not only changed, but advanced in a spiral, driven by what he called *Geist* or Spirit. Hegel would never accept that Michelangelo or the ancient Greeks were "the best ever," because later achievements are generally higher on the spiral. In his model, progress does not rely on the appearance of geniuses, or an outsider's perspective, but is itself an inexorable force. A few decades after Hegel's death, British naturalist Charles Darwin proposed that organisms, like ideas, also change through natural processes. His theory of evolution was an original extension of Hegel's ideas, and also a fundamental paradigm shift in the sciences.

REBELLION, SUCCESS, AND THE AVANT-GARDE

Change is often the rule in architectural thought as well. Even institutions that were created to provide stability and certainty, like the French Academy, would evolve. So did the École des Beaux Arts, which—despite Viollet-le-Duc's accusations—did occasionally produce rebels. One set of Rome Prize architects from the 1820s studied unapproved works in Italy, including archaic Greek temples in Paestum which the Academy found objectionably crude (see Figure 5.3). Yet most of these architects eventually found success within the system they flouted; one, Félix Duban, later designed the Beaux-Arts' main building in Paris.

Is independent creativity in architecture so natural that revolt against authority is inevitable? Are audacity and rebelliousness the best strategy for success? Such ideas define the **avant-garde**, the dominant paradigm in the arts for over a century. This military term (a synonym for *vanguard*) originally described a group of soldiers who led dangerous attacks. They would seize an enemy location, hold it until the main force arrives, then repeat the pattern. Aggressively claiming new territory requires a critical perspective on the status quo, so we can identify strategic opportunities to advance.

One famous example of an avant-garde challenge to cultural boundaries dates to 1917. That year, French artist Marcel Duchamp purchased a standard urinal, signed it with a pseudonym, named it *Fountain*, and placed it in an art exhibit. Duchamp's gambit succeeded; the scandal it provoked publicized the notion that the artist's originality is what defines art. This idea had been active in the art world for decades, but Duchamp audaciously took the strategy further than ever before. He found an unclaimed piece of territory and invaded, redirecting ideas about art for a century.

MODERNISM: DESIGNING THE NOW

The artistic avant-gardes that inspired Duchamp's *Fountain* were part of a wider cultural movement called **modernism**. The Industrial Revolution had made unprecedented, rapid upheaval from technological and social transformation an unavoidable reality during the nineteenth century. Within a changing and often alienating world, modernist art rejected fantasies of eternal truth, ideal beauty, or a nostalgically conceived past for an honest reflection of the artists' own reality and medium. Modernism advanced critical analysis of the now: a meaningful novel or painting should present the contradictions and tensions within a place and moment, and find new ways to express these.

The modernist avant-garde in France was sustained by an expanding urban middle class, for whom books and paintings were affordable luxuries. Unlike poetry or pastels, architecture must contend with vastly higher production costs and official oversight. Despite these challenges, various avant-garde ideas about "modernist" architecture began to emerge during the nineteenth century, and crystallized in the early twentieth.

One theme was industrial materials, which nineteenth-century architects had embraced far less comfortably than engineers (see Chapter 4). Most architects hid any use of modern materials like iron in traditional building types. Yet the first major project by one of the Beaux-Arts' 1820s rebels, Henri Labrouste, did otherwise. His Ste.-Geneviève library in Paris used iron arches and columns for a lofty, visually open main reading room, its main public space. Instead of hiding iron under historic skin, or limiting it to a separate "engineered" zone, his design made

FIGURE 6.8   Henri Labrouste, Bibliothèque Sainte-Geneviève, Paris, 1843–1851.

industrially produced elements architecturally central in a way that has long been considered modernist, even avant-garde.

ARCHITECTURAL EXTREMISM: LOOS AND FUTURISM

Another avenue to modernist architecture was radical simplicity in design, which can be traced back to Alberti's idea that beauty derives from pure, abstract forms. Boullée's elemental, unbuildable volumes were arguably avant-garde for the eighteenth century, and later historians like Emil Kaufmann would link them to modernism (see Figure 5.12). A century after Boullée, revolutionary simplicity was further advocated by Czech architect Adolf Loos, who spent most of his career in Vienna. Loos was a cultural critic in popular newspapers, writing harsh but witty columns mocking Viennese habits in everything from personal hygiene and table manners to clothing.

In 1908, Loos published a sensational statement on architecture, culture, and the cultural stakes of decoration. "Ornament and Crime" is full of extreme, prejudiced ideas of human culture. He accused people who like decoration—on their buildings, furniture, food—of "cultural immaturity." Loos compares patterns on a building façade with children or vandals scrawling on walls, and memorably associates tattooing with two groups: cultures that Europeans considered "primitive," and criminals. If we instead prefer unfrosted gingerbread, or an unengraved cigarette case (two of his many examples), we are appreciating a higher form of beauty. Loos writes: "Freedom from ornament is a sign of spiritual strength."[5]

Loos also asserted that any (European) person with a tattoo was either in prison, or would be soon. This claim is outrageous by design. His extreme rhetoric targeted a powerful school of Viennese architects with an ornately decorative style. Using a bold strategy as avant-garde as Duchamp's stunt a decade later, Loos associated his competitors' work with "lower" forms of humanity to discredit their authority, gain attention, and leverage it into professional opportunity.

Architecture's most revolutionary call for constant change was published one year after Loos' essay. Italy, with its centuries of venerated art and revered monuments, spawned an avant-garde movement called Futurism. Its writers, artists, and architects published their first **manifesto** in 1909. It declared racing automobiles more beautiful than Greek statues, and factories and power plants better than cathedrals or temples. They did not merely prefer the new, but said: "We will destroy the museums, libraries, academies of every kind."[6] To ignore or surpass is not enough; the old must be obliterated.

The Futurists believed Italy's cultural apparatus and centuries-old cities made it impossible for their culture to be "modern." In 1914, Futurist architect Antonio Sant'Elia declared that "each generation will have to build its own city."[7] They wanted the ancient ideal of architectural permanence to give way to transience.

Like this year's hit songs or fashion trends, today's buildings will soon be obsolete, and should be replaced. The avant-garde model demands it.

SOCIAL RELEVANCE, HOUSING, AND MODERNIST SYNTHESIS

Another approach to architectural modernism involved associating building design with radical social change. An important rationale for using industrial materials and simple forms was that they made architecture affordable and accessible to more people. This was evident after World War I, when avant-garde architects in Europe promoted using modern architecture to remedy a massive housing short-age. Instead of producing houses through traditional, labor-intensive construction methods, why not harness industry? Combining mass production with simplicity could provide comfortable, affordable, and beautiful (in Loos' sense) homes for everyone.

Le Corbusier's *Towards an Architecture* presents simple, industrially pro-duced modernist housing as a solution to a pressing social issue. He had worked on this problem since 1915, when Le Corbusier and Swiss engineer Max Du Bois developed a prefabricated system intended for large-scale housing construction. Their proposed system of horizontal reinforced concrete slabs supported by six columns per floor could be enclosed with an envelope made of any available

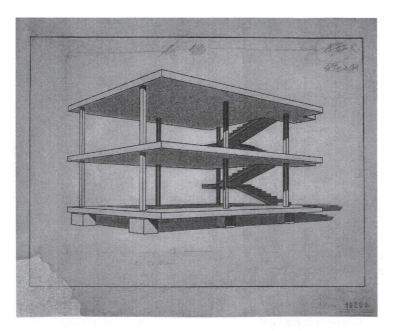

FIGURE 6.9   Le Corbusier and Max Du Bois, Maison Dom-ino, 1914–1915.

materials, and subdivided with interior partitions arranged as needed. It promised to serve immediate social needs through modern methods and simple forms.

In 1915, however, "Le Corbusier" was still called by his birth name, Charles-Edouard Jeanneret. Jeanneret came to Paris during World War I, fortunate that Swiss citizenship spared him from combat. Wartime Paris offered little architectural work (another job paid his rent), but provided an active artistic and literary avant-garde that included Pablo Picasso, Igor Stravinsky, and Ernest Hemingway. The young Jeanneret, his cousin, and painter Amédée Ozenfant participated through a journal, *L'Esprit Nouveau* ("The New Spirit"), presenting radical new ideas on art, culture, and architecture.

Jeanneret originally used the pseudonym Le Corbusier (which combines a family name and a nickname) to help make the startup, avant-garde journal appear to have a wider circle of authors. His book *Towards an Architecture* (whose title was first translated into English as *Towards a New Architecture*) is mostly a compilation of the articles he wrote for *L'Esprit Nouveau*. It was another manifesto, meant to be as provocative as Loos and as revolutionary as the Futurists. In it, Le Corbusier effectively integrated the three main ideas about architectural modernism—industrial-age, engineering-inspired design; a radically simple aesthetic; and an intent to serve the masses through architecture—into a call for radical change. *Towards an Architecture* also argued that architects belong in the vanguard of culture. This book's unequaled influence helped move the avant-garde from architecture's fringe to its center. An anti-establishment document of the 1920s became the discipline's gospel.

ACADEMIES FOR REBELS?

The Bauhaus in Germany, established to teach modern design, had a similar impact. It too was committed to industrial methods, abstract aesthetics, and a revolutionary cultural mission. The Bauhaus was an avant-garde, countercultural institution that encouraged students and faculty to reject the mainstream. Yet if authoritative teachers teach students to rebel, are they truly rebelling? Is an avant-garde academy an oxymoron? Contradictory or not, the experiment lasted only fourteen years. In 1933, Germany's new Nazi regime closed the Bauhaus for supporting modernist art and Jewish artists. Ironically, this only enlarged its artistic influence, as graduates and faculty scattered internationally. Some went east, to Russia and Japan. Many others went west, to Great Britain and North America.

Two former Bauhaus directors had a lasting impact on U.S. architecture and design education. Walter Gropius, the Bauhaus' founder, became chair of architecture at Harvard's Graduate School of Design. In another seeming contradiction, an exclusive Ivy League university taught the architecture of avant-garde revolution. The program's influence helped turn modernist aesthetics into the norm of American postwar architecture. Harvard's graduates and Bauhaus-influenced methods eventually reshaped how architecture was taught at most North American universities.

Mies van der Rohe, who directed the Bauhaus during its final three years, was another influential figure. He came to Chicago in 1937 to lead the architecture department at the Armour Institute, later the Illinois Institute of Technology, and enjoyed a prolific practice after World War II. In Berlin during the early 1920s, Mies imagined transparent, free-form glass, steel, and concrete towers that were impossible for that place and time. By the 1950s, this exiled prophet turned his avant-garde dreams into reality in Chicago and New York. Architectural modernism, born of avant-garde ideas, became the professional establishment, the authority to be overthrown by the next wave of new ideas.

FIGURE 6.10   Mies van der Rohe, Project for a Glass Skyscraper, 1922, and Seagram Building, New York City, 1956–1958.

FIGURE 6.10   *(continued)*

Histories of the modern movement resisted this seemingly inevitable fate by appropriating the idea of change. Swiss historian Sigfried Giedion's book *Space, Time, and Architecture: The Growth of a New Tradition*, first published in 1941, became the modern architect's gospel. Giedion embraces Hegel's idea of the **Zeitgeist**, meaning "spirit of the age." For him, a valid work of art expresses its moment's essence—modernism's central idea. Giedion defines great architects as interpreters of their own culture through design. Culture is always changing, so authentic modernism will too. Following the ever-changing Zeitgeist will keep architecture "modern" forever.

THE LIMITS OF RADICALISM

The avant-garde model accommodates our desire for originality in architecture, but it also carries risks. Is there an infinite amount of creative territory to be claimed for architecture? At what point does pushing a discipline's boundaries as far as they can go produce irrelevance? We might also wonder whether a deliberately radical approach is necessarily a good thing for buildings. Do we want the architect's primary job to be generating cutting-edge design ideas, or producing useful real-world structures?

Daringly innovative architecture can be a desirable commodity. This has been particularly true since the late twentieth century. In the 1990s, Frank Gehry's original and distinctive forms took him from relative obscurity to international stardom (Figure 0.1). Success comes with a price, however. After Gehry's projects demonstrated an increasingly recognizable, "signature" style, whatever their designs' creative origins, he was often criticized for a lack of originality. Avant-garde status demands perpetual novelty, it seems, as well as unpopularity.

Many famously original buildings also fail practically. Some of Gehry's projects have produced hazardous icicle showers and inflicted blinding glare on neighbors; stories abound of buildings by famous architects that have leaking roofs, useless spaces, and even car-melting façades. At what point does architects' daring creativity violate their basic professional obligations? While venustas may be the Vitruvian triad's most glamorous element, he promotes this in balance with utilitas and firmitas. How does that work in practice?

VOCABULARY

avant-garde, console, disegno, genius, manifesto, modernism, paradigm shift, thesis–antithesis–synthesis, Zeitgeist.

STUDY AND REVIEW QUESTIONS

1. What makes originality a more appealing architectural quality than Serlio's system?
2. Why does Vasari think Michelangelo is the best artist who has ever lived? What made Michelangelo's work and his architecture distinctive?
3. What problems does Vasari's exaltation of Michelangelo create for himself and future artists?
4. Compare how Bernini and Borromini personify different models of the "genius." Which is more inspiring?

5. Where did Louis Sullivan find his "true" creative education in Europe? What does this imply about architectural training?
6. How does Le Corbusier's book reinforce the architect as "genius"? Who qualifies?
7. Compare how Kuhn and Hegel explain how ideas change. What do their models imply about cultural innovation, and which do you prefer?
8. How does the avant-garde reward artistic rebellion? How have architects participated, and were any successful?
9. Describe various approaches to a "modernist" approach to architecture. Where and how did they come together into a unified vision?
10. How can the avant-garde model contradict architecture's realities as a profession?

APPLICATION AND DISCUSSION EXERCISES

1. Identify a building you know whose design seems "original" in some way. Do its innovative qualities make it a better building, and how? Do they have any drawbacks?
2. Investigate how a written discussion about an innovative architect explains his or her creative originality. Does it emphasize "genius," an outsider-driven paradigm shift, a cultural avant-garde, or another explanation? Is it convincing?
3. List at least three areas of culture where constant innovation is considered "normal." How is this good, and what problems can it present? Which of these apply to architecture?

NOTES

1   Giorgio Vasari, *The Lives of the Most Excellent Painters, Sculptors, and Architects*, trans. J. C. and P. Bondanella (New York: Oxford University Press, 1991), p. 282.
2   Ibid., p. 282.
3   Ibid., p. 454.
4   Louis Sullivan, *Autobiography of an Idea* (New York: Dover, 1956), p. 234.
5   Adolf Loos, "Ornament and Crime," in U. Conrads, ed., *Programs and Manifestos on 20th-Century Architecture*, Trans. M. Bullock (Cambridge, MA: MIT Press, 1970), p. 24.
6   Filippo Tommaso Marinetti, "The Foundation and Manifesto of Futurism," in C. Harrison and P. Wood, eds., *Art in Theory 1900–2000: An Anthology of Changing Ideas*, 2nd ed. (Malden, MA: Blackwell Publishing, 2003), p. 148.
7   Antonio Sant'Elia, "Futurist Architecture," in U. Conrads, ed., *Programs and Manifestos on 20th-Century Architecture*, trans. M. Bullock (Cambridge, MA: MIT Press, 1970), p. 38.

FURTHER READING

Ackerman, James. *The Architecture of Michelangelo*. New York: Viking, 1961.

Conrads, Ulrich. *Programs and Manifestoes on 20th Century Architecture*. Trans. M. Bullock. Cambridge, MA: MIT Press, 1970.

Droste, Magdalena. *Bauhaus 1919–1933*, Trans. K. Williams. Berlin: Taschen, 2002.

Giedion, Sigfried. *Space, Time and Architecture: The Growth of a New Tradition*. Cambridge, MA: Harvard University Press, 1941.

Kuhn, Thomas. *The Structure of Scientific Revolutions*. Chicago: University of Chicago Press, 1962.

Le Corbusier. *Toward an Architecture*. Trans. J. Goodman. Los Angeles: Getty Research Institute, 2007.

Marinetti, Filippo Tommaso. "The Foundation and Manifesto of Futurism," in C. Harrison and P. Wood, eds. *Art in Theory 1900–2000: An Anthology of Changing Ideas*. Malden, MA: Blackwell Publishing, 2003.

Sullivan, Louis. *Autobiography of an Idea*. New York: Dover, 1956 (1924).

Vasari, Giorgio. *The Lives of the Most Excellent Painters, Sculptors, and Architects*. Trans. J. C. and P. Bondanella. New York: Oxford University Press, 1991.

Vidler, Anthony. *Histories of the Immediate Present: Inventing Architectural Modernism*. Cambridge, MA: MIT Press, 2008.

PART III
WHAT IS ARCHITECTURE ABOUT?
PHYSICS, PLACES, PEOPLE

CHAPTER 7
STRUCTURE AND FORM

IN 2011, THE AMERICAN INSTITUTE OF Architects bestowed its Twenty-Five Year Award on the John Hancock Tower in Boston, the city's tallest skyscraper. Completed in 1976 by Ieoh Ming Pei and Henry Cobb, who both studied under Walter Gropius at Harvard, the tower's design innovations included newly developed reflective glass panel sheathing. Huge, almost seamless panes made it a pure, abstract prism that mirrored city and sky—until a 1973 windstorm.

Several 500-pound (227 kilogram) glass panels cracked, fell out, and damaged others on their way to the sidewalk, fortunately with no injuries reported. But the tower was soon nicknamed the "Plywood Palace" after temporary panels were installed. Its completion was delayed three years until the deadly peril—a tiny detail in the double-paned panel design—was identified. The entire building was expensively resheathed in low-tech single-pane sheet glass. In this case, new and original was not better.

Ludwig Mies van der Rohe, whose avant-garde visions helped inspire such all-glass towers, reportedly said: "It is much better to be good than original."[1] Mies was committed to expressing new ideas about form and space made possible by modern materials. But he was also committed to the craft of perfect making. Architecture—built architecture, anyway—is shaped by practical limits. These include the first item in Vitruvius's triad: firmitas, or structural stability. What is built always begins with an understanding of what available materials can, and cannot, do.

ADOBE: DESERT WALLS

One of the most ancient and abundant construction materials is the earth itself, mixed with water, sand, a matrix like straw or dung. If poured into small forms

FIGURE 7.1   I. M. Pei, John Hancock Tower, Boston, 1976 (photo from 1973).

and left to dry, the result is uniform blocks of sun-dried mud brick or **adobe**. This **modular** system, in which larger forms are built of small units, permits highly varied building shapes. When covered with an outer layer of mud, it is a **plastic** material that can be shaped into smooth, rounded forms, like clay.

These qualities are evident in two distant examples, one in North America's Southwest and another in the African Sahara. Adobe construction lends itself to solid, heavy walls. Their high **thermal mass** slows heat transfer, so it is ideal for both regions' arid climate: the interior stays cool in blistering hot weather, and warm on cold desert nights. Adobe is most practical in dry conditions, because water erodes exterior surfaces. Structures can survive over many years, even centuries, but only with constant, labor-intensive maintenance.

Adobe walls are often combined with beams—wood in New Mexico, palm sticks in Mali—to span interior spaces. Dried mud lacks elasticity, and flexible beams reinforce the structure by absorbing tensile forces. The result is a

FIGURE 7.2   San Francisco de Assis in Taos, New Mexico, 1772–1816, and Great Mosque of Djenné, Mali, first
built in the thirteenth century; current structure 1907.

composite system that brings together different materials to perform separate
structural jobs. At Djenné, the abundance of projecting palm sticks are also a
permanent scaffolding for annual repair. The Great Mosque's rhythm of slender

conical finials and towers would never be mistaken for the smooth, squat forms at San Francisco de Taos. But similar resources and methods shaped what both desert cultures built. Building technology sets basic parameters for design.

WOOD: FRAMES AND CONNECTIONS

Wherever trees are an abundant and economical resource, as in much of North America, wood is used for its strength, flexibility, and workability. Like adobe, wood construction takes units of a basic shape (usually long and thin, like trees) and connects them into a system. Most U.S. home building relies on nailed connections to join studs into a frame. While individual nails are weak and easily pulled out, the system's strength comes from redundancy; thousands working together are strong.

Wood is vulnerable to insects and moisture, yet exposed wood can endure if carefully designed and maintained. A number of softwood churches in Russia and Scandinavia have stood for centuries, and early Buddhist wooden architecture in Japan and China has lasted for well over a thousand years (Figure 1.8). In all cases, their designs consider wood's natural expansion and contraction with changes in temperature and moisture, and how to shed water.

China's oldest known building code, the 900-year-old *Yingzao Fashi* (*Treatise on Architectural Methods*) of 1103, presents timber design methods. Its author Li Jie (d. 1110) was a Song Dynasty bureaucrat who administered palace,

FIGURE 7.3   Detail of puzuo, following construction details illustrated in Li Jie, *Yingzao Fashi*, 1103 (courtesy Qinghua Guo, University of Melbourne, Australia).

bridge, and ship construction (echoing the Greek understanding of "architect"). He was also a scientist, painter, and author of other books—a builder, intellectual, artist, and administrator. The *Yingzao Fashi* standardized imperial construction terminology and roof slope calculations, and proposed improved building methods.

Li Jie illustrates many intricate carpentry joints that accommodate expansion in humidity, but remain mechanically locked when members dry and shrink. Diagrams show complex bracketed roof framing systems to support heavy roof loads, and how to place joists at gradually flattening angles, producing China's traditional sloping roof profiles. These slow rainwater's flow and carry it away from the foundation, helping wooden structures survive in a rainy climate.

HARD EARTH: MASONRY

China's robust wooden frames supported roofs covered with tiles of **terra cotta** ("baked earth"). Terra cotta, pottery, and brick are all related technologies. If a region's mud contains clay, it can be fired in high-temperature kilns. This requires abundant fuel, but the resulting units are stronger, fireproof, and more durable than mud brick or wood.

Fired bricks are joined into structural units with adhesive mortar, typically lime, sand, and water. This composite system gives brick great flexibility for design. It is most efficient to mass-produce bricks in standardized shapes and sizes, but mortar is plastic. By shaping mortar beds, builders can turn orthogonal blocks into curved arches, or the all-brick dome of Hagia Sophia (Figure 1.11).

Despite brick's many advantages, another form of masonry has the highest architectural prestige: stone. Stone construction requires access to geologically determined supplies, plus extraction technology and the resources to quarry, transport, and shape a resilient material. It thus indicates a high level of cultural organization. In fact, when some European archaeologists encountered the ruins of a great stone city and royal palace in southern Africa, they refused to believe it had been built by the local people. They mistakenly believed that African cultures had never been "civilized" enough to build a structure of precisely cut stone.

All evidence shows that the Great Zimbabwe, begun almost a thousand years ago, was indeed built by ancestors of the local people. The modern nation of Zimbabwe took its name from this site, whose name is similar to "stone house" in one of the local languages. This direct reference to a heritage of stone architecture asserted the dignity of its people and their past.

The world's oldest standing, all-stone large structure is also in Africa: the stepped pyramid at Saqquara, older than Stonehenge (Figures 1.3 and 4.1). Its piled form makes natural use of stone's compressive strength. But forming interior spaces with limestone blocks, which cannot span across large openings, is a

FIGURE 7.4   Great Zimbabwe, near Masvingo, Zimbabwe, begun eleventh century.

challenge. Greek stone temples were both objects for the public eye and interior spaces for the gods. Instead of a pile, they turned stone into a frame with a post-and-lintel system (see Figures 1.4 and 5.3). On top of transporting stone blocks, this entailed hoisting blocks up to form columns and the horizontal entablature above.

The Parthenon's 34-foot (11-meter) columns have multiple cylindrical drums, pinned with bronze dowels at the center. The entablature is a series of blocks each spanning two columns and joined with metal cramps, or horizontal connectors. Behind the marble pediment, the gable roof was built of wooden trusses. Most Greek temple roofs had terra cotta roof tiles, but at the Parthenon they were carved from the same stone used throughout the building, from Mount Pentelikus, 10 miles (16 kilometers) away. The whole temple was enveloped in glistening white marble, a triumphant luxury visible from afar.

LIQUID STONE: CONCRETE

Brunelleschi's predominantly brick dome in Florence shows that even enormous interiors can, with great effort, be enclosed with unit masonry (see Figure 4.5). Brunelleschi's dome was certainly inspired by a Roman dome 1,300 years old at

FIGURE 7.5   Pantheon, Rome, 117–125, interior view.

the time: the Pantheon. At 142 feet (43 meters) in diameter, the Pantheon was similar in scale to the octagonal drum in Florence. But had Brunelleschi known exactly how it was built, he might have given up.

The Pantheon's dome was made of a material unavailable in the fifteenth century: concrete. The Romans discovered deposits of an ash called **pozzolana** around Mt. Vesuvius, the volcano that destroyed Pompeii. While Vitruvius was writing his *Ten Books on Architecture*, builders were experimenting with this natural cement, which could harden underwater. They soon learned how to cast artificial stone in any shape wooden formwork permitted. The dry materials needed—cement, lime, sand, aggregate—were easy to transport and could be combined with water on site, delivered by Roman aqueducts. By the early second century, Rome's builders were using concrete to create colossal vaulted interiors for public buildings. They faced concrete construction with brick or small pyramid-shaped stones to create a smooth surface. This was usually plastered and painted, often imitating public buildings like the Pantheon. Their interiors were covered with panels of richly colored cut stone **veneer** from throughout the empire.

The resulting spaces were awe-inspiring. They also separated Roman buildings' visible skin from their supporting structure, entirely unlike the Parthenon's solid marble columns and walls, where visible forms reveal how the building stands up. In fact, according to Vitruvius, the Doric temple's decorative vocabulary reflects structural history. The first Greek temples were wooden shrines with posts made from tree trunks. Column fluting recalls the wood's vertical grain, and details like **triglyphs** and **guttae** are memories of the joists supporting the shrine's roof.

If so, then classicism explains its own structure and history: archaic wooden prototypes became more dignified, permanent stone temples, which preserved the memory of their origin in details. Understanding architecture's technological starting point helps explain its meaning.

THE PRIMITIVE HUT AND STRUCTURAL TRUTH

Many European Enlightenment thinkers believed primitive beginnings revealed essential truths. For instance, eighteenth-century philosopher Jean-Jacques Rousseau looked to a precivilized "state of nature" as a model for a more humane society. Rousseau's provocative writings would influence architecture through one of his many readers, Marc-Antoine Laugier. A French Jesuit priest and historian, Laugier became a Benedictine abbot after his outspoken cultural criticism cost him his position in Paris. His argumentative and widely read *Essay on Architecture* of 1753 deliberately incited more controversy in French intellectual circles.

Laugier did not reject the classical tradition, by then firmly established in France. But he argued that classicism was fundamentally misunderstood, and interpreted its meaning in a new and influential way. Laugier integrated Vitruvius's account of the archaic wooden temple with another passage describing how humans became builders. Vitruvius presented early wood shelters as one stage in a longer process (from fire to stone construction), in which technology produced civilization. Laugier similarly describes how early humans sought comfort from the elements, eventually building a forest hut out of trees and branches. That shelter prefigures the classical temple: the tree trunks are like columns, horizontal logs the entablature, and angled branches to shed rain the gable roof.

But for Laugier, this "rustic hut" is not a first draft that will evolve into later developments. He believes this archaic form is an authoritative model representing

FIGURE 7.6 *Rustic Hut,* frontispiece to Marc-Antoine Laugier, *Essay on Architecture,* 1753.

architecture's ideal. He insists that the hut's free-standing columns, horizontal entablature, and a triangular pediment are the only authentic classical elements. They are valid because they perform structural work as vertical supports, spanning elements, and roof. Laugier believed that a building's design must explain how it stands up.

This position contradicted contemporary design practice and entrenched ideas about classicism. Alberti had stated that the classical orders were "decoration," divorced from any structural role. Ancient Roman examples showed concrete walls and vaults providing support, with columns, pilasters, and pediments as embellishment. But Laugier said that Alberti, Vitruvius, and even the Roman builders were wrong. Using elements that served no structural function or violated the logic of construction was incorrect, no matter how popular in antiquity or his own day.

Laugier refers to several architectural elements and practices as "faults." He calls pilasters and engaged columns "unnatural" because they are attached to a structural wall. Anything that can be removed without compromising a building's stability is decoration, not architecture. Columns should be free-standing straight cylinders that do not twist or have projecting blocks (**rustication**) columns. This wastes extra material, there to provide visual interest but no support. Entablatures must be straight, solid beams that span an opening and support a roof, and a pediment should occur only at the end of a gable roof.

During Laugier's day, celebrated buildings by France's most prestigious architects used classical elements freely and decoratively in all the ways he considers improper. Their goal was to produce visually rich compositions, not explanations of construction logic. One of the few buildings Laugier admires is the ancient Roman Maison Carrée in southern France (Figure 5.5). Its portico columns are straight, free-standing cylinders supporting a load. The entablature is a straight beam, and its pediment is the roof's gable end. The engaged columns around the back are a pity (he tactfully overlooks them), but the rest, in his view, is properly logical.

How can a preacher with no architectural experience criticize an entire profession? Laugier had absorbed Descartes' message that truth does not come from authorities like Vitruvius, ancient buildings, or famous architects, but from rational analysis. He also insists that architectural forms consistent with structural logic are "honest"; otherwise, they "lie." Laugier argues that buildings have a moral obligation to be truthful. Violations of that structural truth are not simply poor design, but ethically wrong. Laugier's essay is a sermon.

HONESTY, MATERIAL, AND STYLE

Another eighteenth-century clergyman and architecture critic was Venetian aristocrat and Franciscan priest Carlo Lodoli. A mathematician and educator, his students found his unusual ideas about architecture significant enough to publish after his death. Like Laugier, Lodoli believed architecture should be rational, and design should obey construction logic. He was also interested in Vitruvius' account of how wooden temples were translated into stone. But for him, this story proved that classicism is illegitimate.

Lodoli appreciated the natural relationship between material, structure, and design. The choice of building material should affect the form you create: solid piles for stone, frames for wood, arches for bricks. Otherwise, the building is in conflict with its own physical tendencies. By this logic, "translating" a wooden hut into a stone shrine that retains the original form is wrong. Whenever materials change, building design should too. Thus, if classicism originates in stone pretending to be wood, it is an unnatural way to design. Although Laugier found an honest core within the classical vocabulary, Lodoli considered the entire system dishonest.

Laugier and Lodoli disagreed on classicism's validity, but agreed that the logic of a building's tectonics determines its form, a position called **structural rationalism**. The idea that buildings should explain their physical structure to a viewer had enormous influence on the modern era, when new ways of building made the relationship between technology and design a central issue.

VIOLLET-LE-DUC: GOTHIC WISDOM

New ideas about structure and style, plus Romantic aesthetics (Chapter 5) led some nineteenth century Europeans to look at medieval architecture with more appreciative eyes. One, Eugène-Emmanuel Viollet-le-Duc (1814–1879), grew up in an unconventional Paris family whose circle of artists, intellectuals, and writers included novelist Victor Hugo. Hugo's famous book *The Hunchback of Notre Dame* (1831) praises medieval cathedrals as embodiments of French heritage and culture.

Hugo inspired the young Viollet-le-Duc to study architecture, but he refused to attend the École des Beaux-Arts—it was he who, at age seventeen, called it an "architect mill." Viollet-le-Duc instead trained in professional offices and visited medieval buildings. Many of these structures were in dire condition because of damage inflicted during the French Revolution. The French government established an office to preserve them in 1834, but very few architects had suitable experience to do the work needed. Viollet-le-Duc's unusual education and interests led to his appointment at age twenty-six to direct restoration of the 800-year-old basilica of La Madeleine at Vézélay. He would spend his career repairing dozens of structures, gaining an unmatched understanding of medieval stone construction.

Vezelay's Romanesque interior is defined by solid forms and surfaces. Its 60-foot-high nave is crossed by round stone arches. These separate **groin vaults**, formed when two **barrel** (half-cylindrical) **vaults** cross at a right angle. Each pair of arches flanking a vault forms a unit called a **bay**. Construction proceeded one bay at a time, from ground to ceiling. Once complete, the masons moved to the next.

The Gothic modified groin vaults with thicker stone arches ("ribs") at intersections that provided a supporting framework (Figure 1.12). **Ribbed vaults** produced a more skeletal structure which, along with pointed arches, permitted enormous window openings and taller interiors. The tallest Gothic vaults in Beauvais Cathedral's choir soared over 157 feet (47.9 meters). But greater height added stress from wind loads. Instead of compensating with thicker walls and ribs, builders used **flying buttresses** that transferred loads to massive piers at right angles to the outer wall. These added stability, but still allowed light into the interiors.

Analysis and restoration gave Viollet-le-Duc profound respect for Gothic structure. He also admired its aesthetic and spiritual power, but was especially impressed with the flexibility and efficiency of the Gothic system. Its builders enclosed enormous, soaring volumes out of stone, at a fraction of the mass that the Romans required. Viollet-le-Duc also admired the Gothic's structural rationalism, its coherence between visible features and building support. A typical interior's vault ribs follow lines of force descending from roof to floor. Ribs become clustered colonnettes that run down the surface of massive supporting piers. Gothic design explains its structural essence as a stone skeleton.

FIGURE 7.7   E. E. Viollet-le-Duc, Structural system of Amiens Cathedral, *Dictionnaire Raisonné de l'architecture française du XIe au XVIe siècle* (1854–1868).

Viollet-le-Duc became a passionate advocate for medieval design through dozens of articles and books. But he also considered what lessons Gothic builders might teach contemporary architects. He wondered: what would Gothic architects have built if they had mass-produced, abundant, and inexpensive iron? They would, Viollet-le-Duc was certain, exploit its incredible efficiency to create glorious interior spaces with minimal materials. He imagined composite systems of lightweight masonry vaults, cast-iron struts, and wrought-iron tie bars—modern applications of Gothic structural values.

BÖTTICHER: SKIN AND BONES

Laugier, Lodoli, and Viollet-le-Duc's interest in the relationship between technology and form was also seen at a Prussian school of architecture, the Bauakademie in Berlin. Modeled on the École Polytechnique, the French engineering academy, rather than the Beaux-Arts, it emphasized both structure and history. Professor Karl Bötticher studied both Greek and Gothic architecture, and argued that they evolved from distinct approaches to stone construction. The Greek temple's balance of verticals and horizontals developed from **trabeated** (post-and-beam) construction. The Gothic expresses **arcuation**, construction with arches and vaults. But neither simply reveals raw construction as a transparent revelation of pure tectonics. Both Greek and Gothic architecture have exemplary coherence between the visible and the structural.

Laugier and Lodoli both suggest that honest buildings nakedly reveal structure to the eye. But Bötticher observed that most buildings, like the human body, require different systems for structure and enclosure. The hand's skin protects bones, muscles, and blood, and has its own features (creases, nails, and hair). But it also communicates what lies beneath: we can detect separate finger bones, the palm's cushions of muscle, round knuckles, long veins and tendons. Skin has its own nature as an enveloping membrane, but also reveals deeper truths.

For Bötticher, this represents good design: the surface should express the underlying structure. Like Laugier, Bötticher sees this relationship in ethical terms; a "dishonest" building skin is a deceptive costume, like Thomas U. Walter's U.S. Capitol dome (see Figure 4.11). Its cast-iron structural core—fireproof, light, strong, and inexpensive—is hidden beneath an inner dome's coffered shell and a colonnaded exterior dome. These suggest solid masonry, not industrial-age construction.

By this logic, any new structural system requires a new expressive style, and new forms should only arise from new structural developments. In the 1840s, Bötticher believed iron offered an opportunity to develop a new, authentically modern design language. Modern construction and architectural style should evolve together. A few decades later, some of the most far-reaching developments in structure and form would occur across the Atlantic.

SKYSCRAPERS, HEIGHT, AND STYLE

During the late nineteenth century, Chicago and New York experienced exploding demand for commercial office space in compact downtown areas. Technological developments like the elevator permitted the earliest skyscrapers of seven or eight stories. Their success led to taller office buildings built with iron, then steel frames. Skyscraper architects were often trained in the Beaux-Arts system, and adapted various historic styles to envelop metal structures—a disconnection Lodoli, Viollet-le-Duc, and Bötticher would find objectionable.

When Beaux-Arts-trained Boston architect Henry Hobson Richardson designed an eight-story skyscraper for Chicago-based department store Marshall Fields (1885–1887), he applied his favorite, early medieval style. But this was a wholesale store where buyers made bulk orders for resale, not an elegant retail space for public shoppers. Richardson's exterior used heavy rusticated stone with no decorative detail—just plain blocks with arches above some windows. Louis Sullivan, the Chicago architect who found Michelangelo's Sistine Chapel more instructive than the Beaux-Arts (see Chapter 6), admired Richardson's building. Its stone skin provided a dignified public covering for the metal frame, but also expressed the stacked horizontal floors beneath. To Sullivan, it represented an "honest" way to wrap a metal frame.

Sullivan's 1896 essay "The Tall Office Building, Artistically Considered" urged architects to express the skyscraper's essence. He believed its aesthetic potential should derive from its most unique quality: height. A skyscraper "should be every inch a proud and soaring thing," and celebrate its verticality through design.[2] Its exterior should explain the structural frame, layered structure, and functional zones within. Sullivan's essay contains his most famous quote, that "form ever follows function."[3] Although this idea had been expressed earlier (see Chapter 8), when Sullivan connected it to this entirely modern building type, it became a turning point.

The façade of Richardson's skyscraper was load-bearing masonry that stood on the ground, structurally separate from the interior frame. But by Sullivan's day, most skyscrapers used lightweight cladding systems that were hung on the frame itself, such as his Guaranty Building's abundant terra cotta ornament. The separation of structure and enclosure provided new freedom in thinking about the relationship between a building's skin and bones.

TOWERS OF GLASS

Although skyscrapers were prohibited in most European cities until the 1950s, an essay on "Modern Architecture" by Viennese architect Otto Wagner published in

FIGURE 7.8   Louis H. Sullivan, Guaranty Building, Buffalo, New York, 1896.

1896, the same year as Sullivan's essay, also considers the issue of how construction should affect design. Wagner classified building methods into two types. He called load-bearing masonry "Renaissance construction." In "modern construction," a frame does the structural work, while thin panels attached to the outside provide enclosure, the typical skyscraper system.

Wagner wanted to clarify what makes architecture "modern". Like Sullivan, he had focused on developing an original ornamental style for a period; Wagner was among the architects attacked by Adolf Loos for "tattooing" buildings (see Chapter 6). But he ultimately decided architectural modernity was about expressing this frame-and-cladding construction system. Works like his Postal Savings Bank in Vienna demonstrate how exterior stone panels are bolted to a supporting frame: visible bolt-heads were meant to be gilded to catch the sun, and the entry canopy is supported by a slender column in the form of an oversize threaded bolt.

Inside, the banking hall's framed structure and sky-lit vault uses simple piers and supports with panels of glass as infill. No material better dramatized the non-structural role of cladding. Like iron, glass is an ancient material that was hand-made and only available in small sizes until industrial production provided large, inexpensive sheets. Frame construction with glass infill was used where both weather protection and abundant natural light were important, such as factories, greenhouses, shopping galleries, and train sheds. But the possibility of an entirely transparent building was radical and inspirational.

Another liberating modern technological development was concrete. After artificial cement was invented in Britain in 1842, engineers learned to **reinforce concrete** with metal bars and mesh. This meant concrete could be used in ways the Romans never imagined. The thin concrete slab depicted in Le Corbusier's Maison Dom-ino scheme (see Figure 6.9) could only "float" on point supports because of extensive metal reinforcing. Without it the columns would puncture the slabs, and they would fail.

While not the most efficient way to engineer such a system, the Mainson Dom-ino conveys the design freedom offered by modern building technology. By concentrating all loads in slabs and slender columns, they can be wrapped with any cladding—even glass. Stack them higher, and the result is Mies van der Rohe's vision of a completely transparent tower (see Figure 6.10). It took many other technological developments—air conditioning, fluorescent lighting, and coated glass—to make giant all-glass towers buildable and livable. And, as the John Hancock tower shows, even simple versions of this model could still present huge construction challenges.

RADICAL TECH

To one critic, the glass towers of the post–World War II era realized the possibilities of building technologies that were new and exciting in the 1920s, but conventional and complacent by the 1950s. British architectural historian Reyner Banham had studied aeronautical engineering during the war, then earned his doctorate under Nikolaus Pevsner ("Lincoln Cathedral vs. bicycle shed"; see Introduction). Banham looked at the history of modern architecture through a technological lens. His dissertation was published as *Theory and Design in the First Machine Age* (1960), a history of modernism with a new emphasis.

There was no question that changes in construction methods helped create modern architecture. But Banham argued that new building technology was not just a contributing factor, but the essence of architectural modernism. For the discipline to remain "modern" requires more than discerning the Zeitgeist (however that might be accomplished). He argued that modern architects needed to focus on continuing technological changes, and pursue the most radical, discipline-altering possibilities they offer.

One of Banham's heroes was engineer and design revolutionary Buck-minster Fuller, famous for popularizing the geodesic dome. Le Corbusier had described the house as "a machine for living in" in *Towards an Architecture*, but his 1920s villas did not embody this slogan nearly as well as Fuller's Dymaxion house, first proposed in 1929. Still radical-looking today, this proposal for a floating aluminum volume on one cylindrical footing (also a conduit for utilities) was science fiction when first introduced. Fuller believed houses should indeed be designed like airplanes or automobiles, in a factory with non-traditional construction materials for maximum efficiency and economy.

Many of Fuller's ideas were never realized, and he spent most of his long career outside architecture's mainstream. But Banham admired his commitment to questioning assumptions about design through technology, and offered his own extreme proposals for the American house. His 1965 essay "The Home Is Not a

FIGURE 7.9   Buckminster Fuller, Dymaxion House, 1929.

House" argues that the essence of an American house was mechanically generated comfort in the frontier. A conventional suburban home is really a machine:
beneath siding and sheetrock lies a mechanical infrastructure of wiring, pipes, and
ductwork. Large windows, porches, and the indispensable lawn exist to connect
the machine to "nature."

Banham saw the Conestoga wagon and Airstream trailer as more authentic
forms for American living, offering the freedom to range across a continent. In fact,
he argues, an ideal house would be an inflatable plastic dome or an engine blowing
a minimally protective bubble of forced air—high-tech camping. His imagined shelters would (barely) keep out the elements without blocking views of nature, and
include a portable mechanical core for heat, cooking, and entertainment. When
ready to move on, just toss it into the car and drive on.

Such a home is hardly ideal for all; Banham breezily brushed aside
issues like security and privacy. But his celebration of freedom, mobility, and
radically applied technology inspired a number of architects to liberate themselves from stifling convention. Among them was a group in London that produced a series of graphic journals called *Archigram*. Drawing on science fiction and comic books, they used drawings, montage, and subversive humor
to push architects to consider how new materials and technologies could
challenge how we build.

If a house can be a mobile high-tech machine, why not make a mechanized city that walks around like a huge robotic insect, making urban culture
available to all? Cities have always changed and evolved, but slowly because of
politics, expense, and traditional ways of building infrastructure. What if new cities
were designed for change? Archigram's Plug-In City proposed a fixed structural
framework that provides utilities, with replaceable pods for all habitable spaces.
Its design eagerly anticipated that a new generation of developments would be
incorporated once current technology is obsolete.

Such futuristic, large-scale, high-tech design ideas may seem impossible, but during the 1960s and 1970s the U.S. and Soviet space programs
gave science, engineering, and futuristic building visibility as both reality and
popular entertainment. Towering gantries for rocket launch pads and portable
life-sustaining structures for space travel were inspiring icons of structurally
"honest" modern design. They demonstrated that humans can live in tiny
metal containers and mobile modular cities (like the International Space Station).
Many architects remain committed to exploring how new technologies can
redefine building.

But is that necessarily what people want from architecture? Should
the architect's gaze be focused on structure and the future? Should forces
besides gravity anchor buildings to the ground instead of letting them float
freely in space?

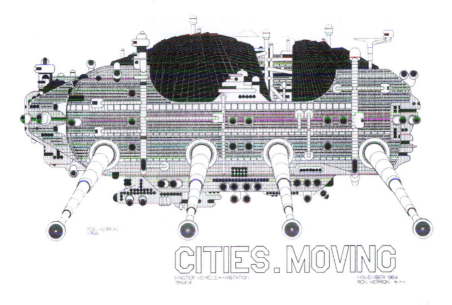

FIGURE 7.10   Ron Herron, "A Walking City," *Archigram* 5 (1964).

VOCABULARY

adobe, arcuation, barrel vault, bay, composite, flying buttress, groin vault, guttae, modular, plastic, pozzolana, reinforced concrete, ribbed vault, rustication, structural rationalism, terra cotta, thermal mass, trabeation, triglyph, veneer.

STUDY AND REVIEW QUESTIONS: STRUCTURE AND FORM

1. How does a culture's resources directly affect what sort of architecture they can create? Compare the design possibilities and limits of adobe and wood construction.
2. What resources are necessary to build with fired brick and stone? What advantages make masonry construction worth the additional costs?
3. How did concrete define ancient Roman architecture? What was the relationship between their buildings' visible surfaces and physical structure?
4. How did Laugier turn stories about the origin of architectural forms into a design ideal? Compare his understanding of the classical tradition with Lodoli's.

5. How did Viollet-le-Duc become an expert in medieval architecture? What did he admire about Gothic design, and how did he think it was relevant for modern architects?

6. Explain Bötticher's idea of how a building's visible exterior should relate to its internal structure.

7. What did Louis Sullivan believe a skyscraper design should achieve? How does this relate to ideas about structure, style, and "honesty"?

8. How does Le Corbusier's "Maison Dom-ino" scheme express the design possibilities provided by modern materials and construction? How does it anticipate Mies' Glass Tower of 1922?

9. Why did Reyner Banham believe glass and steel skyscrapers were no longer "modern" by 1960? How did his proposals for the American house reflect his view of modernism's essence?

10. What makes Archigram's radical urban proposals appropriate for the 1960s and 1970s?

APPLICATION AND DISCUSSION EXERCISES

1. Find Laugier's *Essay on Architecture*, and list all his design "faults." Then look at the East Wing of the Louvre, the Palais du Luxembourg, or the Panthéon (originally Ste.-Geneviève), all in Paris. How would Laugier probably view its design? Would you agree with his assessment?

2. Find a building in your area whose design expresses its structure and materials, and describe how it does so. Does this make it a better building?

3. Research two recently published designs that incorporate new technological developments. What (if anything) does this technology contribute to the architecture's significance?

NOTES

1 Reported by Philip Johnson; see "Obituary: Philip Johnson," *The Telegraph*, 28 January 2005, http://www.telegraph.co.uk/news/obituaries/1482161/Philip-Johnson.html (accessed 02 December 2014).

2 Louis Sullivan, "The Tall Office Building, Artistically Considered," *Lippincott's Magazine* 57 (March 1896): 406.

3 Ibid., p. 408.

FURTHER READING

Banham, P. Reyner. "A Home Is Not a House." *Art in America* (April 1965): 109–118.

_____. *Theory and Design in the First Machine Age*. New York: Praeger, 1960.

Conrads, Ulrich. *Programs and Manifestoes on 20th Century Architecture*. Trans. M. Bullock. Cambridge, MA: MIT Press, 1970.

Frampton, Kenneth. *Modern Architecture: A Critical History*. Fourth edition. London: Thames & Hudson, 2007.

Guo, Qinghua. "Yingzao Fashi: Twelfth-Century Chinese Building Manual." *Architectural History* 41 (1998): 1–13.

Hearn, Millard Fil. *Ideas That Shaped Buildings*. Cambridge, MA: MIT Press, 2003.

Lambert, Phyllis, ed. *Mies in America*. Montreal: Canadian Centre for Architecture, 2001.

Laugier, Marc-Antoine. *Essay on Architecture*. Trans. W. and A. Herrmann. Los Angeles: Hennessey & Ingalls, 1977 (1753).

Le Corbusier. *Toward an Architecture*. Trans. J. Goodman. Los Angeles: Getty Research Institute, 2007 (1923).

Levy, Matthys and Mario Salvadori. *Why Buildings Fall Down*. New York: W. W. Norton, 1987.

Riley, Terrence and Barry Bergdoll, eds. *Mies in Berlin*. New York: Museum of Modern Art.

Sullivan, Louis. "The Tall Office Building, Artistically Considered." *Lippincott's Magazine* 57 (March 1896): 403–409.

Viollet-le-Duc, Eugène-Emmanuel. *Discourses on Architecture*. Trans. B. Bucknall. New York: Dover, 1987 (1872).

Wagner, Otto. *Modern Architecture: A Guidebook for His Students to This Field of Art*. Trans. H. F. Mallgrave. Santa Monica, CA: Getty Center, 1988 (1896).

CHAPTER 8
MEMORY AND IDENTITY

IN 2013, 173,000 PEOPLE WERE allowed to enter an exclusive sacred space: the inner shrine of the Ise Jingu in Japan. Ise is a **Shinto** sanctuary, dedicated to the sun goddess Amaterasu; Shintoism is an indigenous Japanese religion honoring ancestors and natural forces. A walled inner precinct contains Ise's three most sacred shrines, built of cypress wood with reed-thatched roofs. Only priests can enter the walled shrine except during one two-month period every twenty years, when selected worshipers from across Japan each deposit a white stone from the sacred Isuzu river.

The 2013 ritual was the sixty-second **sengu**, a complete reconstruction of the shrine every twenty years, a tradition that dates to 690. The seventeen-year reconstruction process begins with the harvesting of cypress trees planted centuries earlier. The wood is seasoned and shaped with hand tools, with no nails used. Although wooden architecture can last for centuries, Ise embraces the material's natural tendency to decay. The shrine is perfect and worthy of the divine, not by using an enduring building material like stone, but by regularly offering the goddess a brand-new temple.

This process works because the inner shrine consists of two sites, side by side: the sengu ends when Amaterasu's sacred mirror is transferred from the old shrine to the new. Six months later, the old one is dismantled, its wood now a sacred relic. Ise is therefore both over 1,300 years old, and always less than twenty. Its design and construction techniques, passed on by generations of builders, are ancient, but its physical substance is ever young.

The way Ise's materials and traditions connect it to one unique location illustrates an idea called **genius loci**, Latin for "the spirit of a place." Its manifestation of one group's rituals and views of sacredness, time, and continuity also evokes Gottlob Hegel's concept of the **Volksgeist**, the spirit of a people or culture. The shrine cannot exist apart from Japan, its people, and their politics: Ise's high

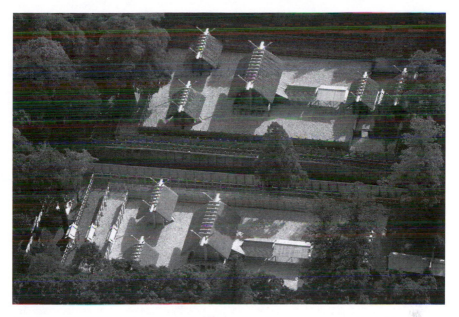

FIGURE 8.1   Grand Shrine at Ise Jingu, Japan, 690; sixty-second reconstruction completed 2013.

priest must be a member of the imperial family (the Japanese flag depicts the sun, today a red circle). Occupying U.S. forces after World War II understood its importance, and prohibited the 1947 sengu to suppress nationalist pride. It only resumed when they left in 1953.

ANYWHERE, OR ONLY HERE

Architecture can express who builds, and where, much like design can "explain" structure. But this seems to contradict how certain traditions, such as European classicism and modernism, have spread across countries and continents. Vitruvius argued that the ancient Greek style of building expressed universals about the body, the universe, and tectonics; this meant it belonged to anyone, anywhere. But Greek builders did not intend to invent a global style. They built to fulfill immediate needs, using their own traditions and local resources.

Despite Renaissance authors' emphasis on ideal proportions and perfect forms, their revival of ancient-style architecture was also about place and culture. When Alberti completed a façade for a church in Florence, his scheme used harmonious geometric forms and proportions along with classical elements like columns, round arches, and a triangular pediment. The outcome resembles two nearby eleventh-century buildings: the Baptistery in front of Florence's cathedral, and the monastery church of San Miniato al Monte just outside the city. All share similar surface patterns of local white, pink, and green marbles; solid, flat walls with regular rhythms of semicircular arches; and simple geometry and roof structures. The earlier structures appear as "classical" as Alberti's hybrid façade.

Centuries of French influence had brought the Gothic to Italy—the pointed arches at the base of the façade of S. Maria Novella, which had to be incorporated into Alberti's scheme, are one example. But in Italy, the Gothic seldom exhibited the transparency or verticality seen in the north. An enduring regional preference for solid walls, simple geometry, and harmonic proportions suggests classicism better fit Italy's genius loci. One reason the Renaissance style revolution succeeded was because it promoted a "native" way of building. The new architecture already belonged in Italy.

Even in antiquity, Vitruvius' decision to include the obsolete but indigenous Tuscan style along with the imported Doric, Ionic, and Corinthian suggests that he wanted to show that Italic and Greek traditions were related. When Renaissance authors like Serlio and Palladio codified five "orders," they included two native to Italy: the Tuscan, and the Roman-invented Composite. They believed in classicism's universality, but making two-fifths of its vocabulary "Italian" also asserted cultural ownership. The first French architect to write a treatise on the orders, Philibert de l'Orme, also invented a "French" order (odd-looking and never used). The idea that a style can simultaneously belong everywhere and belong to a particular place is appealing, but difficult to sustain.

BUILDINGS THAT BELONG

This problem was discussed in the early nineteenth century by philosopher and mathematician Heinrich Hübsch. Hübsch studied architecture by travelling for four years in Italy and Greece, and greatly admired their ancient buildings. But he concluded that classical architecture, though ideal for its place, people, and period, should not be reused. He argued that styles should not be transferred across places and cultures, but respond to local conditions and immediate needs. The answer to the title of his 1828 essay "In What Style Should We Build?" was: our own.

But how do we generate "our own" architectural style? Many authors argued that styles should evolve from construction materials and methods (see Chapter 7). While this seems distinct from geographic and cultural association, architect Gottfried Semper argued that culture, technology, and aesthetics were directly connected. As people develop different ways of making things, these methods in turn shape form and style.

FIGURE 8.2   Leon Battista Alberti, façade of S. Maria Novella, Florence, 1456–1470; San Miniato al Monte, Florence, begun 1013.

Semper argued that historically, humans could have four basic technologies: fire to make ceramics and bricks, themselves fireproof to become a hearth; earth and stone, to make mounds or foundations; wood, to create a frames and roof for shelter from the rain; and fibers to create flexible woven surfaces that provide protection from the wind. Semper believed that architecture integrates all four ways of making, to the extent they are available to a given people. Groups without clay can never make pottery, but might produce sophisticated baskets and textiles in rich patterns. The forms of any products they make expresses who and where they are.

Semper spent several years in London where he built displays for the 1851 Great Exhibition, the first World's Fair held in the Crystal Palace, a glass and iron building in Hyde Park. There he saw exhibited a traditional house from the Caribbean island of Trinidad. Wood poles supported a lightweight roof, enclosed by a woven walls, with a ceramic hearth at the center—a nearly perfect echo of what he had recently theorized about architecture resulting from separate technologies. Semper was particularly interested in how ways of making can change over time. He concluded that new resources or evolving techniques will alter how technologies are used, and the forms that result. Any building, therefore, is a multi-dimensional cultural snapshot that conveys who, where, and how it was made. Architecture provides a portrait of its makers' world.

That world, as Semper realized, is dynamic. But modernity's accelerated distribution of new developments introduced the problem of global homogenization, which challenges architecture's ability to embody distinct cultural identities. As twentieth-century Egyptian architect Hassan Fathy observed the growing popularity of glass, steel, and concrete modernism among his nation's elites after World War II, he denounced the absurdity of glass boxes in Egypt, which had to be heavily air conditioned to be livable. The burdensome costs of imported materials, mechanical systems, and wasteful energy use made such architecture a form of conspicuous consumption, accessible to only the wealthiest Egyptians.

Knowing that people had lived in the Nile valley for over 5,000 years without air conditioning through intelligent use of the local climate and resources, Fathy experimented with Egypt's oldest building tradition: mud brick. Traditional techniques and forms—heavy, solid walls; shaded and carefully oriented openings; and high ceilings—could provide comfortable, naturally ventilated spaces for minimal cost. Among Fathy's projects was a new village for an impoverished community outside Luxor whose residents could never afford houses made out of industrial materials. Fathy also argued that building with centuries-old forms and materials resulted in architecture that inhabitants could consider their own because it connected to their land, traditions, and cultural memory.

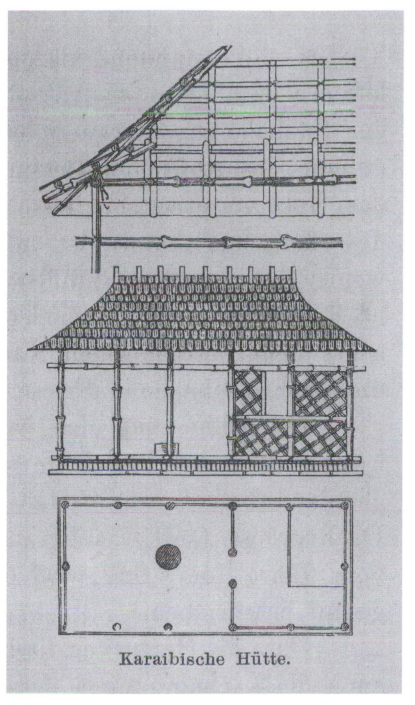

Karaibische Hütte.

FIGURE 8.3   Gottfried Semper, drawing of House from Trinidad, 1863 From *Der Stil in den technischen und tektonischen Künsten*, 1878.

FIGURE 8.4   Hassan Fathy, New Gourna, Egypt, 1947–1953.

PAST, POETRY, AND PHENOMENOLOGY

Fathy's projects in Egypt have had a complex legacy, but the argument that architecture should convey a sense of place and the past derives from an influential philosophical position. Although Descartes located the basis of knowledge entirely in the mind, others (most famously Aristotle) have argued that knowledge is gained through experience in the physical world, a position called **empiricism**. The empiricist conviction that objective truth is reached by observing physical phenomena gave rise to modern science. Enlightenment philosopher John Locke believed the human mind begins life as a "blank slate" (*tabula rasa* in Latin). Our brains record sensations, gradually "writing" what we see, touch, smell, taste, and hear into our understanding of the world.

Many ways of evaluating architecture are based on abstract, supposedly objective measures, like harmonic proportion. But Romantic concepts like the sublime (see Chapter 4) reveal architecture's less rational, more emotional side. **Phenomenology**, a branch of philosophy that investigates such forms of understanding, studies how knowledge is shaped by subjective forces like consciousness and experience. A descendant of the empiricist tradition, phenomenology also considers how we gain information about the physical world: through our bodies and minds.

To experience anything—a tree, say—the body registers multiple phenomena: light, forms, and color; the sound of rustling leaves in the wind, odors of wood, needles, or decaying leaves; rough or smooth bark, the coolness of shade beneath it. What we absorb is determined by our senses; a colorblind and a full-spectrum viewer will see the same tree differently. Our individual past and emotions also intervene to shape our perception of the tree as familiar or strange, for instance, or associated with positive or negative memories. All input from the physical world is filtered and modified by the senses, feeling, and experiences. The result: no one ever sees the same tree. Each mind constructs a picture of that tree, one that varies in small or large ways from everyone else's, and from images it produced during another time.

Phenomenology suggests that no account of architecture's meaning is complete without considering how this variable, subjective world of bodies, memories, emotions, and dreams can shape people's experience of buildings. Twentieth-century philosopher Martin Heidegger tied phenomenological concepts to the built environment directly in his writings. While investigating what it means to "be," Heidegger emphasized that being necessarily happens somewhere, in some moment. His 1951 essay "Being, Dwelling, Thinking" noted that the German words for "being" and "building" share a common origin in a word meaning "to dwell," or occupy a defined place. Existence is inextricable from spaces created for human life—architecture. And fully evaluating the built environment entails understanding its meaning for people.

OPENNESS OR ENCLOSURE

One concrete example of architecture's phenomenological dimension can be found in a simple design element, the fireplace. English phrases like "home and hearth" connect a fire's provision of physical warmth with something emotional—a place to experience a sense of security and connection to family and community. Even when their heat is unnecessary, fireplaces are often considered desirable features in homes or hotel lobbies because they convey a psychological message of welcome and comfort.

Many modernist architects, including Frank Lloyd Wright and Mies van der Rohe, made fireplaces prominent in otherwise radical house designs because they appreciated their emotional resonance for occupants (see Figures 5.14 and 5.15). The living room fireplace in Mies' Farnsworth House is a counterpoint to an otherwise completely transparent space open to the landscape on all sides. For Mies, the ideal of maximum visual openness within a structurally minimal frame dominated his late career, after his move to the U.S., seen in houses, office towers, and museums alike. His ideal exterior wall was a pane of glass, as nonexistent as possible.

Philip Johnson, designer of the similarly transparent Crystal Cathedral (see Figure 1.13), began his career as a disciple of Mies. His Glass House, a weekend home he built for himself in 1949, was directly inspired by the unfinished Farnsworth House; he saw Mies' drawings while curating a 1947 exhibition on his work at the Museum of Modern Art. Both houses reflect an ideal of a life fully connected to nature, like Reyner Banham's later mechanized bubble-house (see Chapter 7).

They also demonstrate the phenomenological limitations of the glass box. In both cases, apart from a solid interior form containing bathrooms and a fireplace, the occupant's life is entirely exposed. Some might find this liberating. For others, such houses fail to fulfill the two most basic functions of domestic architecture: privacy and a sense of safety. Constant, total exposure can make occupants feel vulnerable and anxious. Edith Farnsworth, the client for Mies' glass house, said she felt like a caged animal on display. Even Johnson soon found that he could not sleep in his own dream house.

While Farnsworth sold her house to find relief, Johnson had a solution just across the lawn. His Glass House was built with a solid brick twin, the "Guest House," with laundry and mechanical equipment. Johnson transformed its guest bedroom into his own. He slept in a cave-like enclosed space, then crossed the lawn to enjoy its opposite. Over time, Johnson also built a solid library and study with controlled views (squirrels distracted him at his desk), and an underground bunker for his growing collection of paintings. He discovered that the openness of his transparent pavilion was most enjoyable in contrast to enclosed, protective spaces.

FIGURE 8.5   Philip Johnson, Glass House, New Canaan, Connecticut, 1947–1949 and later.

Over fifty years, Johnson's country retreat grew from two to ten pavilions, each one designed in whatever new style he was using at the time. The Glass House complex vividly demonstrates both the potential and the limitations of the transparent box for human habitation. Its multiplicity also provides a built portrait of Johnson and his long career as an architectural changeling.

PORTRAYING A PEOPLE

The Ise shrine might also be considered an architectural portrait, depicting Japanese identity. It conveys many values associated with the archipelago's ancient culture: a veneration for handicraft and tradition, respect for social hierarchy, pursuit of perfection, and embrace of ephemerality. But, apt or not, Ise provides only one possible portrait. The late seventh century, the period of the first sengu, also produced the very different sanctuary at Hōryū-ji (Figure 1.8).

Ise's raised, open-framed, thatch-roofed architecture relates to that of other Pacific islands to the south, a reminder of Japan's links to coastal Asia. Ho¯ryu¯-ji demonstrates the influence of continental Asia; Buddhism and the pagoda form both arrived by way of China. These structures, conceived around the same period, express two different sides of Japan: an island nation shaped by the sea and typhoons, and an Asian power in dialogue with China's continental empire.

At different times one portrait may be preferred over another. During the early twentieth century, Ise was somewhat neglected, its cultural evocations considered uncomfortably "primitive." But after World War II ended with bitter defeat, nuclear devastation, and foreign occupation, Ise provided newly appealing associations: a nation of survivors who can rebuild again and again, who honor beauty, tradition, nature, and their own land most of all. The impulse for architecture to express identity by following tradition is both natural, and complicated. It raises a difficult question: which tradition?

Architecture can tie a group of people to a specific place, as Neolithic barrows did. But nomadic people might occupy an expansive region instead of one specific spot, while many other people leave their home region to settle elsewhere. Culture can be portable, and many migrants want to transplant their own in new locations. The Doric temples scattered across southern Italy are traces of its colonization by Greek settlers (Figure 5.3). They built such temples in their newly founded cities to proclaim to others, and themselves, that they remained "Greek."

Yet emigrants must compromise between a desire to retain their original identity and the realities of their new environment. Successful building necessarily adapts to available resources and local climate. The English colonists who landed in what is now Plymouth, Massachusetts, in the early seventeenth century settled near cultures with established architectural traditions. One, the Wampanoag, built wood and bark oval-shaped houses with rounded roofs that stayed warm in a cold, snowy climate. For the hot, humid summers, they built smaller, better-ventilated houses covered in dried reeds that stayed cooler.

The English might have borrowed their neighbors' designs, which clearly worked well. Instead they made houses resembling those they knew in Europe: prismatic boxes with square corners and gable roofs. These required more work and material, had more volume to heat in the winter, and were hotter during the summer. But providing shelter was only one of the houses' functions. They were also meant to assert identity—not that of the "primitive," "heathen" Wampanoag, but to remind settlers they were still English, even on the other side of the world.

BUILDING A NEW NATION

After thirteen British colonies in North America revolted 150 years later to form a new and independent nation, asserting identity became more complicated. The new United States was fractured by many internal divisions. Only a minimal federal government held the separate states together. A majority of the new country's population was ethnically English, but it also included substantial Scotch-Irish, German, Dutch, and enslaved West African populations. Religious differences also divided New England Puritans from Pennsylvania Quakers, Maryland Catholics, and Virginia Anglicans. An enormous difference existed between the North, with an economy centered increasingly on trade and manufacturing, and the South's reliance on plantation-based agriculture. How could any building represent a young nation divided in so many ways?

Independence Hall in Philadelphia, built to house Pennsylvania's colonial legislature, shows a typical approach to public architecture in the early U.S. It used locally manufactured brick with painted wood details. Stone was available, but far more costly, and brick was deemed both practical and dignified. Its simple volumes were ornamented with hints of the classical: a white cornice with Ionic **dentils** ("teeth") under the main roofline; brick pilasters; an arched window flanked by two rectangular ones above the entry, a motif introduced by Serlio; and a pediment halfway up the tower.

Like English settlers' houses at Plymouth, such architecture translated European models—in this case, the popularized Palladian classicism known as "Georgian"—into local materials. The strategy is similar to, if less scholarly, than Thomas Jefferson's plantation at Monticello (Figure 2.7). But Jefferson also formulated ideas about what the new nation's architecture should be, and was convinced that adapting British styles conveyed ongoing subservience. An audacious political experiment deserved buildings worthy of its idealistic ambitions.

FIGURE 8.6   Old State House (Independence Hall), Philadelphia, 1732–1753.

FIGURE 8.7   Thomas Jefferson, Virginia State Capitol, Richmond, 1785–1796.

As the first U.S. ambassador to France from 1784 to 1789, Jefferson interacted with leading architects in Paris. They convinced him that the architectural inspiration for his brand-new nation should be antiquity itself, not modern adaptations. Jefferson never traveled to Italy or Greece; the only ancient temple he visited was the Maison Carrée in southern France, then believed to date to the Roman Republic (Figure 5.5). Since the founding fathers' primary political model was this period's representative democracy through a Senate, it seemed appropriate for U.S. architecture to echo this inspiration. Jefferson's design for the Virginia State Capitol transformed the Maison Carrée into a practical home for governmental functions, and an emblem of a new Republic.

CLASSICISM AND CRITICISM

America's official architecture would be shaped by Jefferson's conviction that classicism best expressed its political ideals through the 1940s, when his own memorial was built as a white Pantheon on the Potomac. But applying Jefferson's ideas posed a range of problems. The President's House (now the "White House," because its porous stone requires protective whitewash) by Irish architect James Hoban was modeled on a Renaissance palazzo rather than an ancient temple. This was more practical than a temple form; Jefferson had effectively turned the Maison Carrée's cella into a palazzo so it could house government offices. But Hoban's design also mimicked recent estates for British aristocrats. America's chief executive deserved a dignified home, but should he live like an English lord? Would housing him in a temple like a cult statue be any better?

The U.S. Capitol building for the federal legislature (originally designed by a physician, William Thornton) also used the ever-practical palazzo form to house congressional offices. Its two symmetrical wings for the House of Representatives and the Senate were joined in the center by a low, Pantheon-like dome (never built). Constructed under a series of later architects, the incomplete building was mostly destroyed during the War of 1812. Two surviving columns have capitals by Benjamin Latrobe that substitute corn, native to North America, for Mediterranean acanthus leaves—an effort, like Philibert de l'Orme's "French" order, to make classicism explicitly "American."

Thornton's structure remains visible as the core of the current Capitol, but it and its first, helmet-shaped dome (built by Charles Bulfinch as part of its restoration) were dwarfed by the expansion begun in 1851 under Thomas U. Walter. As America's western "wilderness" gradually became states with legislative representation, Congress outgrew its home. Walter's new wings at either end more than doubled the building's length. His colossal new dome restored compositional balance and made the Capitol a more dominant landmark. However "dishonest" its combination of cast-iron engineering and classical skin (Chapter 7),

FIGURE 8.8   U.S. Capitol; first design by William Thornton, 1792; remodeling and dome by Charles Bulfinch, 1818–1826 expansion by Thomas U. Walter, 1851–1868.

the dome's scale and style conveyed the nation's high aspirations. Its schizo-phrenic split between interior and exterior may even be a most appropriate expression of a practical, forward-looking, divided nation that readily wraps itself in idealism.

Congress had originally commissioned a portrait of George Washington by American sculptor Horatio Greenough to be placed beneath Bulfinch's Capitol dome. Greenough's 1840 marble statue portrays Washington as a bare-chested Zeus seated on a throne, pointing to the heavens like an orator and offering a sword's hilt like a peacemaker. While depicting Washington as a god echoed Amer-ica's architectural approach, it was inconsistent with his personal modesty, and the political character of the presidency. The statue, today in the Museum of American History, was never installed in its intended location. Its artist, ironically, insisted that America should not express itself through classical architecture.

Greenough's 1843 essay "American Architecture" boldly contradicted Jefferson himself. He argued that U.S. architects should not only reject British models, but all Old World architecture—modern or ancient. America has its own landscape, culture, freedoms, and priorities, he observed. A new society with new institutions deserves a style of architecture that expresses its unique character. Greenough invoked a successful U.S. design industry: shipbuilding. No one sug-gests a clipper ship should resemble ancient Greek sailing vessels. A ship's design is based on its function, and its success is easy to evaluate: does it arrive safely, or end at the bottom of the ocean?

Fifty years before Sullivan extended the idea to skyscrapers, Greenough argued that form should follow function. As a sculptor, he saw bodies as model of good design: their forms reflect the structure beneath and achieve beauty without added adornment. His argument's similarities to Hübsch's ideas, Bötticher's "skin and bones," and Lodoli's views about material and form were not accidental (see Chapter 7). While living in Italy for nine years sculpting his Washington, Greenough was exposed to European debates regarding how style should relate to place, technology, and culture. He felt their relevance to his home country, but these questions arose because European nations faced similar problems.

OLD COUNTRIES, NEW NATIONS

Although European countries occupy long-settled territories with centuries-old building traditions, their architectural identities were far from settled in Gree-nough's day. As Japan demonstrates, geographic stability and an ancient culture do not end debate. Many European nations are also politically recent, including Italy, a peninsula governed by multiple powers before 1861, and Germany, until 1867 a cluster of politically and religiously divided states. Devastating invasions in the early nineteenth century spurred a German unification movement that enlisted architecture as an instrument. Bötticher, Hübsch, and Semper's ideas all emerged from intense debates about "German" architecture, as architects considered how style might promote political unity.

Art historian Johann Winckelmann's belief in the supremacy of Greek art convinced some that Germans should adopt Greek classicism. They included Bavarian architect Leo von Klenze, who built Walhalla, a temple to heroes of German culture overlooking the Danube, as a copy of the Parthenon, and a gateway to Munich as a latter-day Propylaea. But decades earlier, essayist Johann Herder had asked why Germans should imitate "foreigners" like Romans or Greeks. After all, German states had their own centuries-old medieval traditions.

An essay by poet Johann von Goethe called "On German Architecture" lyrically praised the Gothic cathedral of Strasbourg and one of its master builders, Erwin von Steinbach. Strasbourg is inconveniently located in France, however—today, anyway. A contested border city provides a problematic source for any "national" style. Other writers praised the Gothic cathedral of Köln, a more reliably Germanic city. Although its cathedral was unfinished, this problem presented an opportunity. A completion campaign helped mobilize support for national unity, which occurred before the cathedral was finished in 1880.

The debate over German architecture initially focused on two historic traditions: Greek or Gothic, the eternal or the local. Karl Friedrich Schinkel, this period's most influential architect, was initially an early Gothic advocate, then

FIGURE 8.9   Leo von Klenze, Walhalla, near Regensburg, Germany, 1830–1842.

he promoted a less archaeological, more practical classicism than von Klenze's. Hübsch studied both Greek and Gothic to break the deadlock, and his call for a new style would influence Bötticher, Semper, and many others. But well into the twentieth century there would be no fixed consensus about what German architecture should look like.

REVOLUTION, STABILITY, AND STYLE

Even France, despite over a millennium of national unity, has had to reassess its architectural identity many times in recent centuries. For much of its history, French architecture simply echoed the monarch's authority. Monuments like the Palace of Versailles for Louis XVI used overwhelming scale and splendor to intimidate subjects and foreign powers. But after the French Revolution of 1789, the same people living in the same place became a completely different country. A nation subject to king, aristocracy, and church became one espousing liberty, equality, and fraternity.

The new France radically redefined nearly every aspect of its society. The revolutionary regime abolished the church and established rationalized systems including the metric system and a new calendar, with ten-day weeks and 1792 designated year "I". Amidst these drastic changes, architectural classicism would persist, but be used to send a different message. Instead of Versailles' ornate ostentatiousness, the new Republic adopted a purified, idealistic classicism. J.-N.-L. Durand, former pupil of Boullée and supporter of the revolution, proposed a peripteral "Temple of Equality" with square piers supporting a pedimented roof. Their capitals were heads of figures symbolizing the new France's virtues: wisdom, economy, work, peace, courage, and prudence. The entablature inscription proclaims that "the virtues of the people provide the firmest foundation of equality." Durand's temple was never built, but he became influential through his teaching at France's new school of engineering, the École Polytechnique (Chapter 4).

France's idealistic and brutal First Republic was short-lived. A young military officer named Napoleon Bonaparte rose from the Reign of Terror's bloody chaos to seize power in 1799. He proclaimed himself "emperor," revolutionized modern warfare, and conquered most of continental Europe by 1810—it was his invasions that spurred German unification. Napoleon's reign ended at Waterloo in 1815, and instability followed. From 1789 to 1870, France had a revolution every ten to eighteen years, with radical republics succeeded by empire, monarchy, and another republic. Architecture was slower than politics; projects initiated to symbolize one France were often completed during another. A church honoring the patron saint of Paris was completed during a secular Republic, becoming the

FIGURE 8.10   A. B. Vignon, La Madeleine, Paris, 1806–1842.

Panthéon, a temple to French cultural heroes—patron saints of another sort. A secular temple to honor Napoleon's great army, still unfinished at his defeat, became the church of La Madeleine.

Amidst such turmoil, the classical vocabulary and Beaux-Arts system of architectural training provided a crucial combination of stability and flexibility. They provided a volatile nation with dignified buildings whose style could be conveniently reinterpreted as needed to mean different things for different governments.

NATIONAL BRANDING

Although Great Britain avoided the upheaval seen in France, it had to contemplate its national style during the nineteenth century after a politically significant building burned down in 1834: the medieval Palace of Westminster, home to the British Parliament since the thirteenth century. Architect Sir Charles Barry won the competition to design its replacement with a rationally planned classical scheme.

Although classicism dominated British architectural practice at that time, medieval architecture had vocal and influential advocates. They included author and architect A. W. N. Pugin, who argued that Gothic was Britain's only truly national style. Despite its French origins, the English Gothic had its own distinct flavor, seen in the square towers and screen-like façade at Lincoln Cathedral (Figure 0.2). Unlike "pagan" classicism, it was also an entirely Christian style. Religion was a divisive issue in the U.S., France, and Germany (which had a mix of Protestant and Catholic states). The British monarch, instead, is also head of the Church of England, which officially links national identity with a particular faith.

This structure, along with the medieval origins of the original structure and the thirteenth-century Magna Charta establishing British democracy, determined the new building's style. Barry was convinced to have Pugin "medievalize" his classical design by adding finials along the roof and tracery on the windows. He also broke its symmetry with the clock tower for Big Ben, and the square Victoria Tower. Inside, carved wood paneling and ecclesiastically inspired details provided Gothic flavor to Britain's halls of government.

Pugin made himself ill by working obsessively on the project, dying prematurely at age forty. But his efforts gave Britain's most recognizable building its neo-Gothic style and associated it with the nation's architectural identity, as he wished. Both the new Palace of Westminster and the nearly contemporary U.S. Capitol building were built to house national legislatures, but also used carefully chosen historic styles to project a national political identity through architecture.

As the Eiffel Tower demonstrates, a nongovernmental structure in no familiar style can achieve the same status over time. It can also happen with great speed. In 1957, Danish architect Jørn Utzon won the competition for a new opera

FIGURE 8.11 Sir Charles Barry and A. W. N. Pugin, Palace of Westminster, London, 1836–1860.

house in Sydney, Australia, with an abstract proposal. Its ambiguous white shells could be interpreted in many ways—birds' wings, ships' sails, or ocean waves—dynamic, appealing associations for another young, forward-looking nation. The project became legendary for construction difficulties, cost overruns, and functional limitations. Yet Utzon's problematic, impractical form was never abandoned, because Australia had already embraced it as an emblem.

READING BUILDINGS: SEMIOTICS

To see a building and think "Australia," "Britain," or "America" suggests that architecture can work like a visual language, in which form communicates ideas. Certain eighteenth-century French architects promoted an *architecture parlante*, a "**speaking architecture**" that explains a building's essence or "character" through design. For this to work, however, architects and viewers must share a common language. Early townhouses by Claude-Nicolas Ledoux that portrayed their wealthy owners through references to mythological characters assumed that an erudite audience would understand the connection.

If the goal is for buildings to be legible to a wider public, however, architecture must use a more accessible language. Ledoux's design for a new town for the French royal salt mines at Arc-et-Senans includes a Doric gateway with a wall whose masonry rustication becomes a rough stone pattern, clearly resembling the entrance to a cave. Everyone, from illiterate miners to educated administrators, could understand the association to the nearby mines.

After the Revolution interrupted Arc-et-Senans' construction, Ledoux continued to develop it on paper into a utopian community he called Chaux. The symbolic forms and aspirations of his designs became more extreme: a House for the River Inspector was a hollow cylinder cradled on a flat base, a section of pipe to express the occupant's role of ensuring the water supply for the mines and town. The Oikema, an educational facility to initiate young men into sexuality (the name means "brothel" in Greek), had a memorably phallic floor plan.

Such forms were absurd and inefficient for either function or communication. A few decades later, Henri Labrouste took a simpler, clearer approach at his Bibliothèque Ste-Genevieve in Paris (Figure 6.8). The building's exterior, a sedate palazzo, could accommodate many sorts of institutions. But on the outside of solid panels beneath the arched second-floor windows are inscribed the names of every author in the library's collection. Words often declare a building's identity as signage, but these correspond to the bookshelves behind the panels; they are more expressive and more permanent than a name above the door. Like the sacred descriptions of Paradise at the Taj Mahal, here the text is integrated with the architecture and amplifies its expressiveness.

FIGURE 8.12   C. N. Ledoux, House for the River Inspector and Oikema plan, Chaux, 1804.

Ideally, however, the idea of a "legible" building requires a comprehensible form. Before we decipher a building's inscriptions, we have often already absorbed its forms, volumes, layout, and materials. Architecture does most of its communication without words—visually, physically, and spatially. Understanding the mechanics of this process is the realm of **semiotics**, the study of how images acquire and convey meaning. American philosopher Charles Sanders Peirce (1839–1914) explained that **signs** work by pointing to something external—a **referent**, the "content" of the visual message. He discerned three distinct ways signs communicate their referents: as *icon*, *index*, or *symbol*.

An **icon** is familiar as our computers' graphic interfaces. Clicking on the image of a printer lets us print; a folder holds documents; the (obsolete) disk allows us to save. These are also icons in the Peircean sense, because each resembles its referent. Icons are often instantly comprehensible because of this direct, intuitive association. Another type of sign is an **index**, an image created physically by the referent. When pressure from our feet or fingers leave prints, or we leave skid marks after hitting car brakes, the resulting signs communicate information about our actions. Indexical signs can require greater interpretation than icons, since we must read them in reverse, from effect to cause.

Peirce's third type of sign is the **symbol**. He defines this familiar term in a specific way, as a sign that communicates information by convention. A symbol has meaning simply because a group of people have decided that it should. If while driving we see a red octagon, even if the letters "s-t-o-p" are invisible, we hit the brakes. But red octagons do not "resemble" stopping, nor are they physically

FIGURE 8.13   Monopoly house.

produced by stopping cars, like skid marks. Stop signs could have easily been made some other shape or color—yellow squares, or white circles. One group's decision when traffic signs were standardized, and its later proliferation, made red octagons a symbol for "stop." They only make sense if we know the code.

Peirce's categories can be used to interpret how architectural forms communicate, beginning with a simple, familiar example: the green plastic house from the classic board game Monopoly. The tiny plastic object has few details, but its cubic form, gable roof, and tiny chimney efficiently convey the idea of "house." It resembles its referent closely enough for us to call it an iconic sign—which is how it works in the game. It is not physically produced by a real house, however, so it cannot be an indexical sign of the same concept. We can, however, call it a symbol if we think its association with "house" is an arbitrary, socially determined convention. Around the world, this idea could be expressed with many very different forms. It would therefore be a symbol anywhere people do not automatically associate domestic architecture with gable-roofed boxes.

LEGIBILITY AND HISTORY

Understanding how architectural form can convey meaning helps explain the different public reactions to competing designs. Buckminster Fuller's Dymaxion House and Levittown offered different models for economical U.S. housing (Figures 2.9 and 7.9). While both were modern houses that benefitted from industrial mass-production, only one became popular. While Fuller's design boldly defied the familiar image of "house," the Levittown design, like the Monopoly house, borrowed just enough features from tradition, like an unnecessary fireplace, to make it a legible icon. Its success was due to a semiotic strategy.

This was not a priority for most modern architects. Le Corbusier cared little whether the public understood the Villa Savoye's form (Figure 5.9). It was meant to change people's ideas about what a house could be. The modern architect's job was not to recycle familiar forms, but to provide new icons for a new way of life. One young Philadelphia architect, Robert Venturi, questioned this philosophy. Venturi combined modern architectural training with extensive travel in Europe. His observations became an influential book, *Complexity and Contradiction in Architecture* (1966), a "gentle manifesto" comparing the glass and steel boxes winning design awards during the 1950s with the buildings he most enjoyed visiting.

Venturi felt that "pure" expressions of technology and abstract form neglected the qualities that made buildings meaningful to people. To Mies' dictum that "less is more," Venturi impudently replied: "Less is a bore."[1] His book presents over 200 examples demonstrating principles like ambiguity and "double-functioning elements" that the author believes produce more visually rewarding buildings. Its mosaics of illustrations juxtapose modernist works with centuries-old monuments to show how design can delight the eye and the mind—a return to venustas. Venturi saw buildings as visual texts that should be read and enjoyed, and inspire thought and creativity.

Venturi argues that for architects to produce buildings that say something new, they must first master a language of form grounded in history and culture. Absolute originality is impossible; to design a house, we necessarily start from our past experience of "house." History, whether ancient or modern, teaches fluency in a creative language, just as writers learn their craft by reading widely. Venturi presents buildings—famous and unknown, high style and vernacular—as his discipline's literature, to be read critically. They teach architecture's vocabulary of design.

Venturi's house for his mother in the Philadelphia suburbs used a gable, fireplace and symmetry—the familiar vocabulary used in the Monopoly and Levittown houses. But the design is hardly a mass-produced copy of the iconic house. A few legible elements are folded into a composition whose complexities and ambiguities are hinted on its flat, street-facing façade, but only revealed through the house's complex volume and intricate interior. This house attempts to demonstrate something all writers know: used thoughtfully, standard vocabulary and conventional forms can become poetry.

FIGURE 8.14   Robert Venturi, Vanna Venturi House, Chestnut Hill, Pennsylvania, 1960–1964.

In architecture, we often understand those conventional forms by asso-ciating specific buildings with a general category or **type**—cottage, skyscraper, pagoda, and palazzo are all examples. The word *type* originally meant "stamp" or "imprint," like letter blocks in printing presses or typewriters. It takes repetition and consistency to make a form recognizable. Among all the fonts in our word processors, each capital "T" must follow a basic structure: a horizontal cross-piece over a (more or less) vertical, centered line. Similarly, for us to understand a particular building as an instance of a general type, its form must retain some essential, defining characteristics: height for a skyscraper, or vertical layers of multiple roofs for a pagoda. These are only learned through regular exposure to an existing corpus of buildings; comprehensible architecture requires that we under-stand the past.

OLD BUILDINGS AND PUBLIC MEMORY

Venturi's position that historic architecture is an essential creative resource con-tradicted prevailing modernist doctrines during the 1960s. Many older buildings like McKim, Mead and White's Pennsylvania Station in New York City, with a classical skin and soaring interior modeled on ancient Roman baths, were consi-dered an impediment to cultural progress. Walter Gropius considered the station an embodiment of a "pseudo-tradition . . . only a throwback to the empty man-nerism inspired by the dependence of the American businessman on European prototypes of the so-called 'ageless masterpieces.'"[2] To him, Such architecture offered a fictitious memory that detached people from their own cultural reality in an unhealthy way.

The station's underground track system still functioned well, but its grandiose architecture was deteriorating and expensive to maintain. It also occu-pied lucrative Manhattan real estate at a time when railroads were losing public subsidies. When the Pennsylvania Railroad announced its intentions to demolish the fifty-year-old station and build an income-generating replacement, this spurred public debate about the value of old, outdated buildings. While many shared Gropius' negative view, others protested that losing a dignified gateway into New York would be tragic.

Despite many who considered the station a public amenity that sup-ported the city's quality of life, as private property its redevelopment could not be stopped. The station was demolished in 1964 and a new Madison Square Garden was built in its place. By 1968, Pennsylvania Station was a forgettable underground space that as of 2015, less than, a half-century later, will be replaced yet again.

Grand Central Terminal, another classical-revival station with a magni-ficent 80-foot-high interior concourse, was also slated for redevelopment for the

FIGURE 8.15   McKim, Mead and White, Pennsylvania Station, New York City, 1910.

same reasons as Penn Station. In 1954, the young I. M. Pei proposed moving the station underground and replacing the Beaux-Arts station with the world's largest office building, an hourglass-shaped tower taller than the Empire State Building. A decade later, Gropius' colleague Marcel Breuer designed an office tower that would hover above the existing station and generate rental income.

Breuer's project was only halted by a lawsuit from the New York City Landmarks Commission, created in 1962 because of outrage over Penn Station. The commission was given oversight over structures, including private ones, whose significance was considered important enough to justify public interest in their preservation. In a nation that normally privileged private property rights and new development, at a time when modernism dominated the architectural profession, this marked a new emphasis on historic architecture's value for collective memory and civic identity.

CITIES, PERSISTENT FORMS, AND DOUBLE-CODING

This issue was even more pressing where cities were far older than New York, such as Italy. Architect Aldo Rossi's 1966 book *The Architecture of the City*

MB-11

FIGURE 8.16   Marcel Breuer, redevelopment proposal for Grand Central Terminal, New York, 1965.

drew from his analysis of the peninsula's many ancient cities. Rossi was less interested in individual historic buildings than in the way castrum grids, ancient walls, or major monuments can structure urban environments for centuries. He showed how despite changes in use—a defensive wall becomes an encircling road, or a medieval city hall a museum—certain elements enduringly shape urban form.

Both change and continuity are necessary for any city to survive. But Rossi believed that what defines a city are structures that persist through its constant transformations. He called elements that provide continuing points of reference **urban artifacts** (*fatti urbani*). Street patterns, districts, or prominent structures like towers can all function this way. One example is Rome's Piazza Navona, whose long, narrow form with one rounded end to the north reveals its origin as an ancient

stadium, an oblong track for chariot races. Over the centuries, the walls supporting its tiered seating became foundations for buildings. The open space of the track remained as the city adapted around it.

Italy presents many similar cases, like ancient amphitheaters whose form survives as oval-shaped rings of houses in Florence and Lucca. The fabric of Rome's great amphitheater, the Colosseum, survived because of its size, and also because multiple plans to transform it into a wool factory ringed by workers' housing, or a piazza containing a church, were never carried out. Even so, the Colosseum has been many different things: a venue for bloody sports, a source of building stone, a sacred shrine, and a tourist attraction.

Rossi wrote: "The form of the city is always the form of a particular *time* in the city."[3] Time, like community, was not part of CIAM's modernist formula for the city (Chapter 3). This was consistent with Italy's Futurists, who wanted each generation to build a new city with new forms to serve altered needs (Chapter 5). Yet buildings everywhere often serve different functions than those they were designed for: churches become mosques, townhouses become commercial space, office towers are adapted into residences. Rossi's approach counters the modernist truism that form follows function by asking: what usually lasts longer? Our experience shows how often form does outlive function.

Considering this longer time horizon has implications for designing new structures. Rossi's own architecture drew from a menu of simple geometric solids—cubes, cylinders, pyramids—that recur in Italy's historic cities. He used them in compositions that intentionally recall traditional structures. The San Cataldo Cemetery project for Modena uses a huge brick-covered cube with square openings within an enclosing solid wall, pointing toward a truncated cone tower. This linked them to their location and its cultural traditions, while formal abstraction made the design references "universal" instead of archaeological. But the effect of Rossi's stark volumes could be alienating, communicating both heritage and emptiness.

Architects attempting to produce original buildings that also belong to a specific place, whose people will understand its message, must walk a creative tightrope between legibility and poetry. They might reconcile these different imperatives by using historic forms in new ways, or anchoring a formally innovative work with traditional materials. Such solutions often use the complexity of design to address different audiences simultaneously. Certain references are widely recognizable by the public, while others are accessible only to a circle of architectural professionals and critics. Charles Jencks called this "double-coding" in *The Language of Post-Modern Architecture* (1977); Venturi's house for his mother, with its mix of iconic referents, compositional subtleties, and obscure historic quotations, is a famous example.

One peril of this approach is that distilling complexities of place, history, and culture can easily end in oversimplification and superficial clichés. Sincere and necessary attempts to understand a building's public audience can involve

FIGURE 8.17   Aldo Rossi, San Cataldo Cemetery, Modena, Italy, 1971–1978.

defining and categorizing people. The outcome of any such exercise will vary greatly according to the participants' knowledge and values. The stakes are high. Architecture mediates between the powerful forces that produce buildings and the public; as Rossi demonstrates, built forms can also shape places and communities for generations. This makes it important to know whose interests architecture serves. Who should the architect work for?

VOCABULARY

dentil, empiricism, genius loci, icon, index, phenomenology, referent, semiotics, sengu, Shinto, sign, speaking architecture, stadium, symbol, type, urban artifact, Volksgeist.

STUDY AND REVIEW QUESTIONS

1. Describe the various ways in which the Ise shrine belongs to one specific geographic location and one cultural tradition. Could another one be built in, say, Seattle? Why or why not?
2. How might classical-style architecture "belong" to one specific location or people more than others? Why would this idea support both its revival in Renaissance Italy and its rejection by Hübsch?

3. How does Semper's theory of "four elements" make architecture a product of both technology and culture? Explain his model of how style changes.

4. What was Fathy's critique of universal versus local architectural styles? Describe his architecture for post-World War II Egypt, and why he used that approach. Do you accept his solution?

5. According to phenomenology, what sort of criteria or qualities make buildings successful? How did Johnson's Glass House succeed and fail from this perspective?

6. Compare the challenges of expressing a "national identity" through architecture in Japan and the early U.S. What was Jefferson's solution to this challenge, and how influential was it?

7. How might the U.S. Capitol building be considered a fitting symbol for the nation, and how would it be criticized by Greenough? What makes his criticism ironic?

8. What different issues shaped debates about a national style of architecture for Germany, France, and Britain? How were the results similar and different in each case?

9. How can architecture be considered a visual "language" that uses iconic, indexical, or symbolic signs? How can this affect a design's meaning, or its success?

10. Explain Venturi's criticisms of modern architecture, and his views about what good design is like, and how architects can learn it.

11. Why did demolishing Pennsylvania Station make sense in the early 1960s? How would this decision affect other historic buildings in New York, like Grand Central Terminal?

12. Explain Rossi's concept of the *urban artifact*, and find two features of your own environment that might fit his definition. How does this suggest form does not follow function?

13. How does "double-coded" design help architecture communicate to a complex public? What difficulties and potential problems does it pose?

APPLICATION AND DISCUSSION EXERCISES

1. Find a building you know whose design makes it "belong" to its location or community. Describe elements that anchor the building to its context: does it achieve this through form, materials, or accommodations to climate? Or to the local culture or rhythms of life?

2. Consider the environment where you are reading. Describe its size relative to your body, its shape, lighting, materials, and where you are positioned in the room. How do these variables affect your experience? Describe in detail what you like and what you would change if you could.

3.   How might you express your own national or cultural identity through architecture? Which traditions or references would you look to? What significant periods or moments would you choose from? Identify an environment that provides a meaningful model and explain why.

NOTES

1 Robert Venturi, *Complexity and Contradiction in Architecture* (New York: Museum of Modern Art, 1966), p. 25.
2 Walter Gropius, "Tradition and Continuity in Architecture," *Architectural Record* 136 (July 1964): 152.
3 Aldo Rossi, *The Architecture of the City*, trans. D. Ghirardo and J. Ockman (Cambridge, MA: MIT Press, 1982), p. 61.

FURTHER READING

Adams, Cassandra. "Japan's Ise Shrine and Its Thirteen-Hundred-Year-Old Reconstruction Tradition." *Journal of Architectural Education* 52, no. 1 (Sept. 1998): 49–60.

Fathy, Hassan. *Architecture for the Poor: An Experiment in Rural Egypt.* Chicago: University of Chicago Press, 1973.

Frampton, Kenneth. *Modern Architecture: A Critical History.* Fourth edition. London: Thames & Hudson, 2007.

Goethe, Johann von. "On German Architecture," in H. F. Mallgrave, ed., *Architectural Theory, Volume I: An Anthology from Vitruvius to 1870.* Malden, MA: Blackwell Publishing, 2006.

Greenough, Horatio. "American Architecture" in *Form and Function: Remarks on Art, Design and Architecture.* Berkeley: University of California Press, 1947.

Heidegger, Martin. "Building, Dwelling, Thinking" in *Basic Writings from Being and Time (1927) to The Task of Thinking (1964).* New York: Harper & Row, 1977.

Hübsch, Heinrich. "In What Style Should We Build?" (1828), in H. F. Mallgrave, ed. *Architectural Theory, Volume I: An Anthology from Vitruvius to 1870.* Malden, MA: Blackwell Publishing, 2006.

Huyssen, Andreas. *Present Pasts: Urban Palimpsests and the Politics of Memory.* Stanford: Stanford University Press, 2003.

Jencks, Charles. *The Language of Post-Modern Architecture.* New York: Rizzoli, 1977.

Levine, Neil. *The Architecture of Frank Lloyd Wright.* Princeton: Princeton University Press, 1996.

Mallgrave, Harry F. *Gottfried Semper: Architect of the Nineteenth Century.* New Haven: Yale University Press, 1996.

Mitrović, Branko. *Philosophy for Architects.* New York: Princeton Architectural Press, 2011.

Rossi, Aldo. *The Architecture of the City.* Trans. D. Ghirardo and J. Ockman. Cambridge, MA: MIT Press, 1982.

Venturi, Robert. *Complexity and Contradiction in Architecture.* New York: Museum of Modern Art. 1966.

CHAPTER 9
POWER AND POLITICS

FEW BUILDINGS ARE MORE DIRECTLY ASSOCIATED with power than the Pentagon, begun in 1941 to centralize administration of the U.S. armed forces. Although its five-sided design resembles many Vauban-era star-shaped fortifications, it actually derives from the project's original, irregular site. After a late decision to relocate the building, the basic layout was retained to save time. President Franklin D. Roosevelt also liked its unusual form.

The Pentagon is twice as large as the Empire State Building, built instead as a sprawling low-rise structure of load-bearing concrete. When

FIGURE 9.1   George Bergstrom, The Pentagon, Arlington, Virginia, 1941–1943.

designed, U.S. involvement in World War II was already anticipated and metal was a strategic material, so concrete was preferable to a steel-framed skyscraper. Its layout was largely pragmatic, but symmetrical façades with projecting pavilions and square piers gave it an austere dignity, a style often called "stripped" classicism. During this period, similar designs were also used for government structures in other countries, including Hitler's Germany. Berlin's Templehof Airport, the intended transportation hub of the Third Reich's global empire, was another vast, strategic project. Like the Pentagon, its low, sprawling design features heavy, load-bearing walls with punched window openings and abstract colonnades of square piers.

That one style could serve both New Deal democracy and fascist totalitarianism illustrates how incomplete semiotic interpretations of architecture can be without information about a building's political context. Changing circumstances can also profoundly alter a building's political significance. In 1948, when occupied Germany was divided into western and Soviet-controlled zones, the Soviet Union blockaded West Berlin to seize the divided city. For over a year, Allied airplanes flew in and out of Tempelhof around the clock to provide supplies and thwart Soviet intentions. Hitler's airport, which finally closed in 2008, became associated with the Berlin Airlift and the Cold War. In order to understand any building's meaning, we must know who built it, and how it is used. These issues are part of a larger question: how does power operate in architecture?

FIGURE 9.2   Ernst Sagebiel, Tempelhof Airport, Berlin, Germany, 1935–1941.

MARX AND THE CATHEDRAL

In *Twilight of the Idols*, Friedrich Nietzsche wrote that "architecture is a kind of eloquence of power in forms."[1] Eloquent or not, architecture is always an act of power that requires a command of material, space, and people. Considering how resources, politics, and culture influence each other follows a tradition charted by nineteenth-century philosopher and social historian Karl Marx (1818–1883). Marx is most famous for co-creating (with Frederick Engels) the political and economic model called **socialism**. His *Communist Manifesto* (1848) presents a revolutionary solution to modernity's dysfunctional relationship between resources and society, and *On Capital* (1867) analyzes capitalism as a system.

Marx was influenced by Hegel's ideas of historic change (see Chapter 5), but believed human events were driven by competition for material resources, like food and property. He emphasized how groups with common interests—social and economic **classes**—struggle to retain what they have, and gain more if possible. Marx also argued that distribution of resources affects how people think. In a society with a hereditary aristocracy that controls all land, the idea that everyone is equal would seem strange because it contradicts observed reality. In the same way, a culture with widespread equality is less likely to believe that a minority deserves greater power. Such a system of underlying beliefs is an **ideology**. Ideologies help us make sense of the power structures in which we operate, and also justify them by correlating experience with beliefs (i.e., "aristocrats should own more because they are naturally superior people").

While the popularity of Marx's political model has diminished recently, his focus on how distribution of money and power affects history and culture continues to influence many fields, including architecture. This approach adds an important layer to interpretations of building phenomena, like the medieval cathedral. Constructing any large structure demands great political and economic resources, and generates wealth by creating jobs for builders, material suppliers, and a market for workers' lodging, food, and services. In medieval Europe, religious pilgrimages were a form of religiously sanctioned tourism, and architecturally impressive destinations drew crowds whose spending supported the local economy. A cathedral was, among other things, an expensive investment made by leaders because it increased prosperity—an engine of wealth.

PATRONAGE AND THE ARCHITECT

The land and resources needed for building are often controlled by powerful groups and individuals. An intimate relationship with power makes the architect's job easier, but not necessarily simple. Vitruvius recounts the story of Dinocrates, an architect during the reign of Alexander the Great, the fourth-century-BCE Macedeonian general who conquered an enormous amount of territory from Egypt to the Indus river. According to Vitruvius, Dinocrates requested an audience with Alexander, but after waiting for days without result, he took action. Probably noticing the general's appreciation of attractive young men like himself, he stripped nude, draped a lion skin over one shoulder, and sauntered where the general would see him. Alexander did notice and invited him to approach and speak. Dinocrates laid out a grand proposal to carve a mountain into the portrait of a man (Alexander, naturally) holding a city in his hand. The general complimented Dinocrates on his bold idea, then posed an astute question: is there enough farmland nearby to feed this magnificent city? The architect, a bit embarrassed, admitted he had not considered this important issue. Despite this, Alexander was sufficiently impressed to retain Dinocrates, who later designed his new Egyptian capital city: Alexandria.

Dinocrates's gambit ultimately succeeded, securing his career and fame. But it portrays a professional relationship with a very clear hierarchy. The architect—colorful, creative, inventive—is also subservient. He sells his talents to a patron, a powerful person able to provide work and security. When Alexander questions Dinocrates, this shows that his greater authority and responsibility as a leader were a necessary check on the architect's imagination. Vitruvius was writing for another newly established world leader, the emperor Augustus, who liked being called a "second Alexander." Vitruvius adds that, while neither young nor beautiful like Dinocrates, he hopes his book will demonstrate his abilities, and that Augustus, like Alexander, will welcome someone able to help him build gloriously. Elsewhere, the author complains about incompetent architects who advance through social connections or beauty. Whether we find such appeals for patronage degrading or strategic, Dinocrates and Vitruvius show that self-promotion has long been part of the architect's job.

Dinocrates appears more deferential than the cunning Daedalus who subverted King Minos (see Chapter 4). But Daedalus' apparent independence simply meant that he worked for a series of rulers. Like most people, architects work for those with the wealth and power to provide jobs, whether in ancient Greece or in modern capitalist economies. Philip Johnson bluntly summarized the architect's position by saying "We are whores."[2] Strutting nude to catch a client's eye like Dinocrates did certainly resembles prostitution, or seduction at least. Johnson claimed this is the architect's fundamental role: to offer clients a flattering, fantasy reflection of themselves. He had no problem with this asymmetrical relationship. Johnson cared little about what forms of power his works celebrated, only whether clients could afford magnificent architecture. He built dozens of skyscrapers for multinational corporations, but also said, "I'd build for Lenin, too. I don't care."[3] Capitalism, communism, no matter; any opportunity to build was welcome.

Ironically, Johnson had less need to sell his services than any other twentieth-century architect: while still an undergraduate at Harvard, he became a millionaire. Johnson studied classics, but became interested in the modern

FIGURE 9.3   "International Architecture: An Exhibition," Museum of Modern Art, New York, 1932.

architecture emerging overseas. He toured Europe with Henry-Russell Hitchcock, an architectural historian who shared his modernist enthusiasm. They visited architects like Le Corbusier and Mies van der Rohe, saw dozens of new build-ings, and collected photographs and drawings. They then staged an exhibition at a new museum started by the Rockefeller family in one of their townhouses, the Museum of Modern Art (MoMA).

Johnson's wealth underwrote the 1932 exhibition of the "International Style," and his position as curator of MoMA's Architecture department. But he wanted to become more than a self-made architectural critic, curator, and expert. Johnson wanted to build. At age thirty-four, he returned to school to study archi-tecture under Walter Gropius at Harvard's Graduate School of Design. Soon after, he finished building his Glass House in Connecticut, the project that launched his practice (see Figure 8.5). Like Lord Burlington and Thomas Jefferson before him, Johnson was able to be his own patron. He had many talents, including an uncanny ability to predict the discipline's next direction, but Johnson's wealth pro-pelled or—as some criticized—purchased his career.

WHITEWASHED WALLS

An intimate relationship between architecture and wealth is evident in several exceptionally affluent U.S. families' patronage of grand public projects during the early twentieth century. The Vanderbilts were behind New York's Grand Central Terminal—they owned the railroad—and the Metropolitan Museum of Art. Rockefeller wealth from Standard Oil, now ExxonMobil, sponsored the Museum of Modern Art, Rockefeller Center, the United Nations, the World Trade Center, and Lincoln Center (see Figure 3.10). Such families' extensive philanthropy played a major role in defining some of the most impressive and beloved public spaces in many U.S. cities. But their architectural generosity was not necessarily disinterested. Private sponsorship of gleaming temples to the arts and diplomacy also encourages public acceptance of concentrated private wealth, seducing citizens into accepting otherwise disadvantageous power systems.

While Rockefeller Plaza was under construction during the 1930s, architecture was actively deployed by two European governments to sustain **fascism**, a political ideology that binds capitalist power to strong, authoritarian central government. Its name derives from the *fascio*, a ceremonial bundle of rods carried by the guards protecting ancient Rome's leaders. The symbol conveys the idea of strength through tightly bound unity. Fascism opposed Marxist transfer of economic ownership to workers, as well as democratic individualism. Both Fascist Italy (1922–1943) and National Socialist (Nazi) Germany (1933–1945) rallied citizens to sacrifice personal rights in exchange for glorious empires and global dominance. Their regimes made extensive use of film, radio broadcasts, mass ceremonies, and architecture to convince the public to unite and join movements defined by obedience to strong leadership.

Italy's two decades of Fascist rule produced an unprecedented quantity of new buildings—housing, train stations, government offices, even brand-new cities. This campaign met practical needs in a country whose industrial development lagged behind that of northern Europe. It also conveyed a politically potent sense of order and progress. Benito Mussolini was a pragmatic leader who supported a variety of architectural styles, including modernism (called **rationalism** in Italy) in many contexts. Most practicing Italian architects were also party members. Many of its most stylistically progressive rationalists strongly supported a regime that promised to bring order, industry, prosperity, and modernity to their nation.

Over time, Mussolini increasingly wanted new projects to reference Italy's classical heritage, and thereby associate his own rule with Rome's ancient empire. By the mid-1930s, most of Italy's nationally symbolic projects used an abstracted, modernized classicism to appear both forward-looking and eternally glorious. The design of a new satellite city built outside Rome for the planned 1942 Universal Exposition (EUR), described as a "cultural Olympiad," was intended to demonstrate Italy's architectural superiority. EUR's axially arranged buildings featured load-bearing volumes with simplified columns, piers, arches, and the same local travertine cladding found on the Colosseum. The harsh precision of

FIGURE 9.4   View of Guerini, La Padula and Romano, Palace of Italian Civilization, Esposizione Universale di Roma (EUR), 1938–1943.

their crisp, sharp edges was appropriate to their original purpose: the exposition's proceeds were intended to fund an invasion of Europe.

The Nazis' preference for monumental, modernized classicism reflected the strong opinions of Adolf Hitler, a rejected applicant to the Vienna Academy of Arts. Hitler opposed modernism for official buildings, and closed the Bauhaus because of its avant-garde aesthetics and its inclusion of international, Jewish, and Communist artists. The Nazi architectural policy reflected Hitler's intention that the Third Reich would endure for a thousand years, as long as Roman civilization had lasted. Governmental structures such as the Imperial Chancellery in Berlin housing Hitler's office used design to intimidate. Visitors followed a labyrinthine, quarter-mile-long (400-meter-long) corridor that crossed the ornate Marble Gallery, twice as long as Louis XIV's colossal Hall of Mirrors at Versailles, and ended at the super-human-sized door to the Führer's 4,000-square-foot (372-square-meter) office, his desk looming at the cavernous void's far end.

This and other works by Adolf Speer, who was Hitler's chief architect, armaments minister, and close adviser, aspired to sublime scale, drama, and eternity. Speer advised building out of solid stone to ensure that the German empire's ruins, like those of Rome, would inspire awe for millennia. Much of the Chancellery's building stone was quarried by prisoners at Flossenbürg, part of the Nazi system of concentration camps. The camps were partnerships between private companies and the government, which provided highly profitable slave labor for German mines, factories, and quarries. Most of Flossenbürg's inmates were intellectuals and clergy condemned to death by hard labor and maltreatment for opposing the

FIGURE 9.5   Albert Speer, Reich Chancellery, Berlin, 1939.

regime, only some of the 11 million civilians (including 6 million Jews) exterminated under Hitler. The Nazis' architecture was inextricable from their atrocities.

When architects cooperate closely with power structures, they often gain great professional opportunities. Had the Germans won World War II, their histories of twentieth-century architecture, might have honored Speer as Hitler's Imhotep. Instead, he was tried at Nuremburg and sentenced to twenty years in prison for war crimes. Speer was spared execution because he expressed remorse, the only top Nazi official to do so. Today, his chosen career path stands in contrast to the many artists and intellectuals (including Nikolaus Pevsner; see introduction) who fled Nazi Germany either because they expected persecution, or they did not wish to support the regime. Many who remained have since been judged complicit in the events that followed. These include Martin Heidegger, the philosopher behind modern phenomenology, who was an open anti-Semite and Nazi supporter. Debate over whether Heidegger's beliefs make his ideas intellectually illegitimate still continues. So does the discussion about the architecture built under and for Italy's Fascist regime. During the 1930s, Philip Johnson also supported Nazi Germany, and a fascist movement in the U.S. Should architects' personal politics affect our judgments of their architecture?

FOLLOWING LEADERS

Le Corbusier's wartime activities also raise uncomfortable political issues, because he cooperated with the Nazis' puppet government in France. He hoped the Vichy administration would appoint him as director of the nation's postwar rebuilding, so he could realize his ideas for modern housing and rational cities. Le Corbusier's writings express a desire to improve conditions for common people, and make direct appeals to the elite leaders with the power to authorize his plans. *Towards an Architecture*'s final chapter "Architecture or Revolution?" claims that workers will revolt unless we build housing better suited to modern life. Social problems are not about inequity, he argues, but the result of inadequate architecture. Le Corbusier promises powerful patrons that his designs will preserve their wealth and privileged position. He means to serve the masses by convincing elites to provide for them, arguing that we need visionary leaders to give people what they need instead of what they want.

Yet how much should leaders be trusted? One person's enlightened leadership can be another's dictatorial insanity, a quality that has emerged among absolute monarchs, capitalist oligarchs, fascist despots, and communist leaders, supposedly executing workers' collective will. When Josef Stalin ruled the Soviet Union from 1924 to 1952, he wanted to eradicate lingering nostalgia for the private wealth, religion, and royalty that communism rejected. Stalin decided to eliminate a popular architectural symbol of all three: the Cathedral of Christ the Savior in Moscow, a marble and gold monument to the motherland's glory built to celebrate Russia's victory over Napoleon with donations from impoverished peasants. To Stalin, it was so ideologically inappropriate to the new society that it needed to go. He announced a design competition for its replacement, a Palace of the Soviets celebrating communism. Dozens of architects from around the world, including Le Corbusier, submitted designs to express a new egalitarian order.

The winner was a marble-clad classical wedding cake of a tower by Russian architect Boris Iofan, its scale and style more bombastic than the cathedral it would replace. The tower would rise higher than the Empire State Building and dwarf the adjacent Kremlin. Its crowning statue of Lenin with 20-foot (6-meter) fingers was larger than the Statue of Liberty. For an agrarian nation struggling to feed its starving people during an era of famine and global depression, the tower was a colossal folly. It represented the will and interests of one leader rather than the Soviet people. Regardless, Konstantin Kon's beloved cathedral was demolished in 1931. By 1938, its enormous foundations were dug and lined with concrete. The tower's steel frame was complete to the eleventh floor by 1941. Only the German invasion finally halted Stalin's skyscraper, whose steel was soon dismantled for the war effort. In 1959, its foundation, a huge, concrete-lined hole in the ground in central Moscow, was resourcefully transformed into a 425-foot-diameter outdoor swimming pool.

In 1991, the Soviet Union ended, and the Cathedral of Christ the Savior's return began. After seventy-four years of atheistic communism, enough affection for the lost building had survived to make its recreation a top priority for the new Russian Federation. The rebuilt cathedral, a replica of the original, became a

FIGURE 9.6   Boris Iofan, project for Palace of the Soviets, Moscow, 1931.

theater of conflict again when the feminist punk group Pussy Riot staged a 2012 protest performance, for which two members were imprisoned. The persistence of this complex, ideologically charged site, despite Stalin's best efforts, demonstrates that popular will can exercise its own power over architecture. Amidst many competing sources of authority, where does the architect belong?

ELITISM AND CULTURAL CAPITAL

In their 1962 essay "Absolute Architecture," Austrian architects Hans Hollein and Walter Pichler wrote: "Architecture is not the satisfaction of the needs of the mediocre, is not an environment for the petty happiness of the masses. Architecture is made by those who stand at the highest level of culture and civilization, at the peak of their epoch's development. Architecture is an affair of the élite."[4] Like Le Corbusier, Pichler and Hollein believe that Architecture (with a capital "A") is produced by a small group that sits above the common majority, and knows best.

Hollein's elite is an aristocracy of ideas and tastes, part of what is called "high" culture. Today this is often located within a network of institutions—universities, museums, performing arts centers, publishing venues—that establish hierarchies of knowledge. Cultural elites are not necessarily identical to those of politics or wealth, although they do depend on government and private donors for support. We can consider them indirect manifestations of a society's systems of power.

Furthermore, cultural knowledge exercises its own form of social power, one studied during the late twentieth century by French sociologist Pierre Bourdieu. Bourdieu examined how taste in art, music, films, even furniture, provide what he calls **cultural capital**. Cultural capital is a valuable resource because it connects people to social groups ("fields" in Bourdieu's lexicon) that control opportunities. Belonging to a group requires that we share experiences and common interpretation of symbols: Is a Rolex watch impressive, or tacky? Is opera annoying or splendid? Hundreds of seemingly personal decisions—what education and jobs we pursue, our religious or political beliefs, how we eat or spend our leisure—may not be "personal" at all. In essence, Bourdieu argues that our tastes reveal the preferences of the social groups to which we belong, or hope to belong.

When some of society's overlapping circles are given higher status, they form a cultural elite. For architects, alignment with such groups can confer valuable prestige and opportunities while, providing greater independence from economic and political power compared to direct patronage. Promoters of the culturally elite architect have included Peter Eisenman (b. 1932), among the late twentieth century's most controversial architectural thinkers. Eisenman's academic and intellectual career, which includes a doctorate from Great Britain's Cambridge University, faculty positions at top U.S. architecture schools, and establishing and directing a center for architectural theory research, preceded his professional practice. Like contemporaries Robert Venturi and Charles Jencks, Eisenman was influenced by semiotics. He did not accept the Peircean model, also known as structuralism, which aims at decoding signs' meanings (see Chapter 8). He was interested in the **post-structuralism** advanced by such thinkers as French philosopher Jacques Derrida, which declares this project to be futile because signs and referents have an inherently unstable relationship. Words and images change meaning over time, and signify different things to different people. Post-structuralism claims that any interpretation supported by the original text is correct, which means none is ever definitive.

Eisenman applied these challenging ideas to architecture. His 1976 essay "Post-Functionalism" critiques one of the discipline's articles of faith: that architectural modernism results from the use of industrial materials, **curtain walls**, and dynamic asymmetry. This definition relies on stable associations with outside referents: a building is "modern" because it resembles a factory, uses exposed I-beams, or is composed like a modernist painting. Eisenman argues that, just like classicism, this architecture's meaning comes from simply "pointing" to something else. Fifty years after the Bauhaus, he insisted that architects had not yet expressed modernism, which he defines as "a sensibility based on the fundamental displacement of man."[5] In his view, modernist architecture must express human alienation in an unstable, meaningless world. He even asserted that architecture should not meet our needs, but shake us out of them. All architects can do is accept and explore architecture's instability through endless debate, knowing that this process will not produce truth—just ever-greater fragmentation of meaning.

This vision asserts architecture's **autonomy**, the idea that the field's value does not depend on service to governments, clients, or the public, but on its own internal conversations. What makes a building Architecture (again, capitalized) is not its physical, useful presence, but its role as a "text" that provides subject matter for architects to contemplate and discuss across generations. Eisenman collapses theory and architecture into one endeavor, accountable only to participants in its own hermetic discourse. His writings' difficult language can seem designed to keep that conversational circle small and exclusive.

To define architecture as a strictly intellectual field is to reject the practical profession serving public needs described by Vitruvius for cultural status and insularity. This model's inward focus highlights an important fact: architecture is itself a social system with its own forms of cultural capital. If architecture's highest aims are detached from human needs, this elevates the field's intellectuals—for whom writing and teaching often come before practice—above those who make their living designing buildings for people. This elevation of certain architects above others can be traced to Vasari's ideal of quasi-divine creative individuals, a myth that conflicts with the complicated realities of producing buildings (Chapter 6). But myths are powerful. They affect what people expect from architects, what architects expect of themselves, and who has the opportunity to become one.

FEMINISM AND CREATIVE CREDIT

According to the American Institute of Architects, in 2009 only 14 percent of registered architects in the U.S. were women, despite the fact that for decades nearly half the nation's architecture students and graduates have been female.[6] The many efforts to study and overcome this disconnect typically employ **feminism**. This occasionally controversial label applies to a set of cultural philosophies which accept two basic points: that gender differences affect human reality, and that women should not be automatically assigned a lower position in society. A feminist perspective on architecture can transcend the issue of gender by asking whose voices and ideas dominate the discipline, and how valuable but suppressed perspectives can be recognized.

Gendered categories have been applied to architecture since antiquity. Classicism invokes explicitly male and female bodies, and many designs establish gendered spatial realms. The architect's assumed role as form-giver is another example, because for most of history creativity was understood through analogies with reproduction, whose mechanics remained mysterious until the modern era. Aristotle believed the female body contributes physical matter while the male seed gives it life and form, resulting in a child "designed" by its father. Aristotle's influential model defines creativity as an intrinsically male capacity, and women as biologically unsuited for creative or intellectual work. This assumption endured well into modernity: Victorian-era physicians, for instance, believed that education diminished female fertility. Twentieth-century American architect Bruce Goff was a bit more generous: "Women are just as imaginative as men. They just have the wrong kind of imagination for architecture."[7]

Historically, women have been involved in shaping architecture in many ways. In some cultures building is a traditionally female responsibility. Many women rulers like Russia's Catherine the Great were influential architectural patrons. In Britain, a few aristocratic women, educated in mathematics and drawing, helped design improved cottages or new manor homes on their own estates. Non-wealthy women, however, faced consistent obstacles to working as architects. They were not allowed to apprentice with construction trades, or enter the workshops and academies that trained artists. During the nineteenth century, as professional offices grew, some did hire women to trace plans, an uncreative and poorly paid task. Male apprentices began the same way, but received opportunities to advance that were only rarely extended to women.

In addition, early professional programs in higher education were reserved for men, although women began challenging their exclusion in the late nineteenth century. One, Julia Morgan (1872–1957), was the University of California at Berkeley's first female graduate in civil engineering in 1894. She worked for an architect who encouraged her to attend the École des Beaux-Arts in Paris. After her third attempt at its entrance exams (the first time she was not permitted to even take them), Morgan was officially admitted in 1898. In 1902 she became the first woman from any country to earn an architecture diploma from the Beaux-Arts. Morgan's world-class credentials helped her establish a successful California practice. She produced hundreds of works in a half-century career, one of America's most prolific architects.

The first women graduated from U.S. architecture programs at Illinois (1879), Cornell (1880), and MIT (1890), years earlier than their counterparts in other countries. These were all land grant institutions legally required to admit all qualified students, although they imposed quotas that limited the number of women allowed in order to preserve male dominance in the profession. But many of America's private universities, including most Ivy League schools, traditionally excluded all female applicants, often along with anyone non-white, Jewish, or Catholic. Harvard, Pennsylvania, and Columbia began admitting a few women to their graduate design programs during World War II, to fill seats left by men in military service. Access to the nation's most prestigious design programs helped expand those few women's professional horizons.

One 1944 Columbia graduate was Natalie de Blois. She established a successful career at the large corporate-structured firm of Skidmore, Owings and Merrill (SOM), where she worked on major commercial projects like the modernist Pepsi Headquarters in New York. De Blois was the first woman to design a sky-scraper, the fifty-two-story Union Carbide building at 270 Park Avenue in New York. Her position at SOM began, however, after she was terminated by another firm for refusing to date a colleague, who thereafter refused to work with her. SOM was in the same building, and hired her immediately.

For twentieth-century women architects, personal decisions affected professional opportunities in ways most male colleagues never experienced. Morgan, like most of the few professional women of her day, never married, which permitted her to prioritize practice. De Blois did marry and had four children, and continued working with almost no interruption. Her determination to succeed in a context defined by male expectations and ideas of professional decorum entailed

FIGURE 9.7   Nathalie De Blois for SOM, Pepsi-Cola Headquarters, New York, 1960.

sacrifices, such as being excluded from one of her own buildings' opening cer-emonies because she was visibly pregnant. SOM's size and structure provided the framework for her success, but it also made her more anonymous than many of the firms' male partners. De Blois's work merited a partnership but she was never offered one, and partner Gordon Bunshaft sometimes received credit for her work.

Other postwar women architects worked in partnership with their hus-bands, including Alison Smithson in Britain and Ray Eames in Los Angeles. A partnership kept their names visible, but also meant credit was always shared. For decades the Pritzker Prize, first awarded to Philip Johnson in 1979, was reserved for architects perceived to be successful individuals; architecture's "Nobel Prize" was first given to a team in 2001. Some late twentieth-century women achieved independent success—the Italian-born Brazilian modernist Lina Bo Bardi is a nota-ble example. But only in 2004 did the Baghdad-born, London-based Zaha Hadid win a Pritzker, the first woman admitted into architecture's most elite club. In 2011, when Chicago architect Jeanne Gang received a MacArthur "genius" grant, this officially installed a woman on Vasari's creative pinnacle, alongside Michelangelo.

AUTHORITY, ETHNICITY, AND OPPORTUNITY

Professional registration in architecture certifies competence in objective areas like fire codes, budget estimating, and mechanical systems. But much of an architect's expertise is completely unquantifiable, and relates to complex cultural issues. In an architect–patron relationship, such as Dinocrates and Alexander, the patron clearly holds higher authority. But like most modern professions, the archi-tect–client dynamic relies heavily on the architect's ability to inspire confidence. Clients must trust an architect to both meet their practical needs and convey their identity and aspirations through design.

Trust is easiest to establish when architect and client share similar social identities, or if clients perceive the architect's status to be higher than their own. Degrees from famous schools and award-winning projects can establish an archi-tect's cultural authority, but this can also be influenced, often unconsciously, by such factors as gender, class, ethnicity, and religious affiliation. The low percentage of U.S.-registered architects representing the nation's many minorities is probably a legacy of both overt exclusion and subtle bias. As of 2011, only 3 percent of American architects identified themselves as Hispanic (versus 16 percent of the 2010 U.S. population) and 1 percent as African-American (versus 12 percent of the U.S. population).[8]

This latter group is dramatically underrepresented in proportion to African-Americans' contributions to the U.S. built environment, most often as skilled builders, enslaved or free. After slavery's final abolition in 1865, a small number found professional opportunity through office apprenticeships and higher education. The first African-American to graduate from a U.S. architecture school was Robert Robinson Taylor, valedictorian of his class at MIT in 1890. Only small numbers of minority students were accepted by majority-white institutions before the Civil Rights era. Many more received training through programs at historically black colleges, the earliest begun at Virginia's Hampton Institute (now Hampton University) in 1871. Its mechanical industries curriculum combined craft and design education to provide competence in all aspects of construction and design.

Finding opportunities after graduation was another challenge. In 1892, Taylor was hired by the Tuskegee Institute (now Tuskegee University) in Alabama, another historically black college, to lead its building program. Taylor's Beaux-Arts-style MIT education augmented Tuskegee's emphasis on practical training and self-reliance (early students helped build their own campus). He also designed many of its new campus buildings. Non-white architects throughout the U.S. often found greatest support in minority institutions and communities. Julia Morgan's early practice similarly benefited from projects for women's organizations. But many non-traditional architects, including Morgan, transcended the assumption that they would limit their practice to "peripheral" clients.

Another was Paul Revere Williams (1894–1980), the first registered African-American architect west of the Mississippi River in 1921, the first to join the American Institute of Architects in 1923, and the first named an AIA Fellow in 1957. Williams built a successful career crossing racial boundaries decades before the Civil Rights movement. The Los Angeles native earned an engineering degree from the predominantly white University of Southern California in 1919, then studied architecture independently through a local Beaux-Arts club. The black community in Los Angeles commissioned some of Williams' first independent projects, but in the 1920s it was too small to sustain an entire practice.

Williams devised many strategies to succeed in a majority-white environment. He entered mail-order design competitions where his work would be judged without knowledge of his race. Williams even learned to draw upside-down so he could sit opposite, not next to, prospective white clients. Over time, his talent, professionalism, and remarkable sensitivity to clients' biases allowed him to succeed within a racist culture. Williams built a successful practice serving a range of clients, including famous entertainers like Lucille Ball and Desi Arnaz, Bill Robinson, and Frank Sinatra, designing many homes where he, as a non-white person, was forbidden to live. Williams' clients became famously loyal to him and his architecture, known for its refined elegance.

Compared to the violently segregated South or stratified Northeast, California's more open cultural climate helped Williams and Morgan find opportunities to exercise their talents. Admitting everyone of ability strengthens any discipline, but considering diversity also illuminates architecture's loyalties. Architects' individual values and experiences shape their priorities, and how well

FIGURE 9.8   Paul R. Williams, 28th Street YMCA, Los Angeles, 1928.

they understand the complex public affected by their work. Diversity, measured not only by categories of identity but by perspectives and agendas, can ensure architecture does not work only for the rich and powerful, or for itself. Architecture may be an affair of the elite, but it touches everyone.

PROFESSION AND PUBLIC

In 1991, architectural historian Diane Ghirardo wrote, "The most fundamental questions [about architecture] address *what is built for whom*: expenditures for museums, skyscrapers, concert halls, and other objects of bourgeois gratification come at the expense of important and necessary social services, not to mention adequate housing at modest prices."[9] She asserts that what is built, and whose interests it serves, demonstrate architecture's true priorities. In contrast to those who see architecture as a luxury good, Ghirardo suggests that the architect's highest calling is not to glorify power or showcase their creativity, but to use design to benefit all.

Vitruvius focused on elite building types, but he also made the architect responsible for public welfare through urban design. What this means in practice can vary greatly: the architect might be a leader's deputy, a public advocate, or a bridge between power and the people. It depends on the economic, political, and social matrix within which buildings are produced, and the relationships between all human actors, from laborers to leaders.

Nineteenth-century British critic John Ruskin believed that architecture's ethical status depends on the social conditions that produce it. He placed particular emphasis on the design and production of ornament. What distinguished architecture from mere buildings for Ruskin was embellishment—but only if made in a certain way. He believed classical architecture was "invented to make plagiarists of its architects, slaves of its workmen, and sybarites [luxury addicts] of its inhabitants."[10] The charge of plagiarism or copying makes some sense; any Ionic building must follow the order's template. But how can a style turn builders into slaves?

Ruskin was an ardent medievalist, and believed that "true" Gothic—his favorite style—was not the result of flying buttresses, pointed arches, and ribbed vaults. It emerged from the builders' hands, minds, and souls, reflecting their character ("mental tendencies"). A Gothic builder must be northern European, at home with long winters, forests, and gray skies, so their work reflects this landscape and its people—a "mountain brotherhood between the cathedral and the Alp."[11] Even more importantly, builders must also be free to express their character in what they make. This permits ornament to reflect their own natural environment and cultural imagination of myths and images. Ruskin's model makes style "belong" to one place and culture, as promoted by Heinrich Hübsch (see Chapter 8).

Although he romanticizes the Gothic mason's creative liberty, the most audacious argument in Ruskin's *The Stones of Venice* (1851–1853) is that any architecture produced by workers in a state of freedom who can invent independently should be considered "beautiful." People should prefer the inconsistent, rugged products of dignified labor to polished products of oppression; let taste follow justice. Ruskin says "the function of ornament is to make you happy"; this extends to both builders and architecture's public.[12] We should all rejoice, he insists, whenever we see liberated creativity in stone.

BUILDING UTOPIA

Ruskin rejected modern industry because it replaced the independent craftsman with soulless machines and unskilled, poorly treated labor. Yet many later architects who saw the factory differently, as a new liberation in design, also absorbed Ruskin's social consciousness. Leaders of the Modern Movement argued that machine age architecture, combining industrial production and design efficiency, could improve living conditions for everyone. Although architects' personal views varied, modernism was most often affiliated with progressive politics, such as in 1920s Germany when the Socialist Weimar Republic supported modernist public housing and the Bauhaus.

During this same decade, the Soviet Union witnessed particularly dramatic attempts to transform society through modern architecture. After the 1917 Revolution, a flood of radical designs by young Soviet architects proclaimed a new culture based on equality and a bright industrial future. *Constructivist* works celebrated the aesthetic potential of modern structure, and tried to construct a new communist society through bold design. Among the most famous are Vladimir Tatlin's Monument to the Third International, intended to house the new government in suspended, rotating volumes in a steel frame soaring 100 meters taller than the Eiffel Tower, a spiraling emblem of Hegelian progress.

FIGURE 9.9   Vladimir Tatlin, "Monument to the Third International" project for Petrograd (St. Petersburg), 1919–1920.

Moisei Ginzburg's Narkomfin Housing project in Moscow was a **social condenser**, designed to instill communist values through design. Its apartments, ingeniously interlocked in section, are tiny units that feature a living room, bedroom, and bathroom—but no kitchen. The complex included a communal kitchen serving meals in a public dining room, plus an on-site laundry, child care, library, and gymnasium. The apartments were really dormitories, their minimal size encouraging the **proletariat** (workers) to spend more time in common spaces. There they would become more attached to their comrades and the social collective, instead of the private sphere of family—or rather, that was the plan. This experiment in architecture's capacity to promote an egalitarian society soon met the post-revolutionary state's harsh realities. Moscow's housing shortage was so dire that the Narkomfin's miniscule apartments were immediately assigned to multiple families, and its social project was never fully implemented. The building, dilapidated in 2014, remains a testament to faith in architecture's power to transform society, and a reminder of its limits.

FIGURE 9.10   Moisei Ginsburg, Narkomfin Housing, Moscow, 1928–1932.

PROPAGANDA OR POPULISM

The Soviet avant-garde only lasted about a decade, until a short-lived convergence of communist ideals, government policy, and visionary artistic proposals fell apart. After Stalin consolidated personal power in the late 1920s, his totalitarian rule of the communist state cost millions of Soviet lives. He preferred Iofan's tower, as impossible and impractical as Tatlin's, because Stalin believed its classical style would buttress public respect for his authority. Like other dictators, he deployed architecture as propaganda, and gauged popular response to building types to make it effective. But considering the public's perspective is not necessarily about manipulation.

While Robert Venturi was designing his mother's house (see Chapter 8), he began working with Denise Scott Brown, a fellow faculty member at the University of Pennsylvania. They became another successful married architectural team, although despite decades of collaborative work, Venturi won the 1991 Pritzker Prize alone. Scott Brown studied architecture in South Africa and London before coming to Philadelphia for graduate study in urban design. She was fascinated by U.S. cities' low-density fabric, which critics decried as a manmade wasteland. Scott Brown was especially enthralled by Las Vegas, whose flamboyant neon-lit casino strip exaggerated the structure of the typical American city. She brought Venturi there in 1966, and they returned with students in 1968. The result of their study, *Learning from Las Vegas* (1972), promoted a different view of the built environment, and of who designers should serve.

In automotive-scaled urban environments, commercial structures are designed to communicate across great distances to attract customers. Venturi and Scott Brown identified two architectural strategies to achieve this. One, the **duck**—inspired by a duck-shaped roadside stand selling duck products—uses the building's entire physical form as a three-dimensional sign. Their other category is the **decorated shed**, in which a neutral building provides generic space, while separate signage communicates its contents. Although ducks invite more extensive design expression, Venturi and Scott Brown argue that the decorated shed is usually a better choice. It costs less to build, often serves practical functions better, and its explicit signage communicates more efficiently and legibly.

A revolutionary feature of Venturi and Scott Brown's approach was their "non-judgmental" attention to ordinary structures that most architects only noticed to condemn. The idea that banal environments offered worthwhile design lessons was considered preposterous. But this had been the driving idea behind the recent Pop Art movement, which used advertising, comics, and product labels as sources for "high" art. Scott Brown's 1971 essay "Learning from Pop" argued that commercial structures and images are just as relevant to architects. She observed that market-driven structures reflect reality and ordinary consumers' preferences, which architects' abstract schemes often ignore. While it usually reflects corporate interests more than popular will, commercial architecture offers insights into how to connect with a public audience, valuable for any architect who wants regular people to understand and enjoy their work.

Venturi and Scott Brown propose anti-elite architects who do not dictate from a pedestal, nor abdicate their expertise and critical perspective. They respect the general public while offering informed, improved solutions for the built environment that can work in the real world. In the decades since their book's publication, however, accepting the status quo of low-density, car-dependent development has become harder to justify. The architect's obligation to promote public welfare has been extended to encompass how buildings impact life on a far broader scale.

BEYOND POPULAR OPINION: SUSTAINABILITY

In 1962, biologist Rachel Carson's *Silent Spring* demonstrated that modern industry inflicts incalculable damage on the natural environment. Since then, a growing understanding of how human activity can damage ecological systems has expanded debates in many fields. When we adopt this perspective, it extends our ethical obligations beyond people and their immediate needs to include all life, into the foreseeable future. Architecture displaces and alters natural environments by creating artificial ones, and has an enormous impact on physical and biological systems. In the U.S., buildings and cities account for over half of energy use, and construction produces an estimated 40 percent of landfill waste, so discussions of environmental ethics necessarily include architecture.

Traditionally, most construction used local resources, and cities only worked long-term if their inhabitants maintained a sustainable equilibrium with their natural surroundings. This wisdom was part of the architect's basic competence; as Alexander reminded Dinocrates, no city without reliable food and water supplies can survive long. The problem of over-exploiting nature has always been one of civilization's dangers. But with modern industry's unprecedented capacity to change the environment quickly and broadly, the problem's scope and severity became critical. Modern architecture absorbed an industrial model of design focused on efficiency, defined as maximum production in minimal time and economic cost. The equation excluded other costs, however, like the effects of resource extraction and energy use on the natural world.

Despite early critics of decontextualized design and profligate energy use, including Hassan Fathy (Chapter 8), Ian McHarg, and Victory Olgyay, the issue of sustainability remained marginal in architecture through the 1970s. Advocates gradually returned this problem to a more central position in design practice and ethics by the 1990s. By the turn of the twenty first century, many architects considered minimizing energy use through design to be as important as aesthetics

FIGURE 9.11   Ken Yeang, Mesinaga (IBM) Tower, Kuala Lumpur, Malaysia, 1990–1992.

or budget. Malaysian architect Kenneth Yeang (b. 1948) spent decades developing an appropriate tropical response to modernism's iconic glass tower. Instead of a sealed, air-conditioning-dependent container, Yeang's "bio-climactic" skyscraper opens up to natural ventilation and uses orientation, sun screens, and berms to maintain comfort without profligate energy use.

Even more than design, sustainability challenges how architects manage professional politics and cultural values. If clients do not prioritize environmental responsibility, they are unlikely to support additional investments to achieve it. In the U.S., where this remains a widespread issue, one useful tool has been the Leadership in Energy and Environmental Design (LEED) system established in 1998, which offers the opportunity to certify buildings' sustainability. Many clients decide that the positive associations and long-term financial benefits that a LEED-rated building brings compensate for any additional costs involved.

Critics, including architect William McDonough and chemist Michael Braungart, have also pointed out the LEED system's shortcomings. Their book *Cradle to Cradle* (2002) argues that any measure of architecture's sustainability must include site design and biodiversity; the impact of extraction, production, transport, toxicity, and projected life cycle of each material used; and all the building's energy use into the foreseeable future. Quantifying any building's full environmental impact is a daunting task beyond any official checklist. Yet however difficult to achieve, McDonough and Braungart's central assertion—that buildings, like all human products, are part of a closed ecosystem, and should make the environment healthier instead of more stressed—has gained widespread acceptance as one of the architect's core ethical obligations.

The Brundtland Commission Report of 1987 influentially defined sustainable development as that "which meets the needs of current generations without compromising the ability of future generations to meet their own needs."[13] This expansive definition defines sustainability in ways that are physical, temporal, and social, promoting communities where all can live healthy lives. In recent decades, more architects have used their skills for humanitarian purposes, to serve people with few resources and great need who can least afford architects' expertise, but stand to benefit from it most. In the U.S., an important catalyst for these efforts has been the Rural Studio established by Samuel Mockbee at Auburn University in 1993. Mockbee brought architecture students into impoverished communities of rural Alabama to attempt to address residents' needs through economical and environmentally responsible design. In other cases, this focus derived from the architect's own background. In 1990, Diébédo Francis Kéré, a builder from Burkina Faso, one of Africa's poorest nations, received a scholarship to study architecture at Berlin's Technische Hochshule. While still a student, Kéré designed a much-needed elementary school for his home village that used local and economical materials, and provided comfort in a challenging climate without mechanical systems. His work and that of countless others demonstrate how architectural knowledge can empower anyone, anywhere, to build a better world.

FIGURE 9.12   Diébédo Francis Kéré, Primary School in Gando, Burkina Faso, 2001.

VOCABULARY

autonomy, class, cultural capital, curtain wall, duck and decorated shed, fascism, feminism, ideology, post-structuralism, proletariat, rationalism, social condenser, socialism.

STUDY AND REVIEW QUESTIONS

1. What design qualities are shared by the Pentagon and Berlin's Tempel-hof Airport? What other factors complicate these buildings' meaning?

2. Why are politics and economics an essential part of architecture? What does Vitruvius' story of Dinocrates suggest about the architect's relationship with authority?

3. What was Philip Johnson's position on patronage? What are the benefits and disadvantages of this model?

4. Compare how the fascist regimes in Italy and Germany used architecture for political ends.

5. How does the Cathedral of Christ the Savior in Moscow's history reflect the power of both political leaders and of the people?

6. Describe at least two ways that "cultural capital" can affect architecture. How does this relate to Peter Eisenman's ideas about the architect's ideal role?

7. How can feminist ideas be used to critique architecture? What barriers have limited women's participation in the profession?

8. What were the benefits and disadvantages of working independently, within a larger firm, or in a partnership for twentieth-century women architects?

9. Compare how Robert Taylor and Paul Williams constructed careers as minority architects in the U.S. How do they demonstrate the complexities of the architect's cultural role?

10. Explain John Ruskin's logic regarding ornament, labor, and morality in architecture. How does it focus attention on buildings' social and technological context?

11. What did Constructivist architects hope their work could achieve for the Soviet Union?

12. Why did Venturi and Scott Brown think architects should take Las Vegas seriously? How do the "duck" and "decorated shed" relate to the pub-lic's view of architecture?

13. Describe how ecological and social sustainability can apply to architecture, and alter ideas of who architecture should serve.

APPLICATION AND DISCUSSION EXERCISES

1. Find a building in your community that was built by a powerful entity, such as a governmental body, a corporation, or a religious organization. Describe design features that you believe serve that client's agenda. Can you detect others that suggest the architect is also meeting other priorities?

2. Choose some facet of identity—gender, ethnicity, religion, class, sexual orientation, disability, age or any other—and analyze your built environment through that lens. Where and how do spaces and structures welcome, exclude, or ignore that set of people through design?

3. Identify a building in your area that has made life better for your community, whether through the design and building process, its use, or its impact on the social or physical environment. How do architecture and people interact there, and what are its greatest successes?

NOTES

1 Friedrich Nietzsche, *Twilight of the Idols*, trans. T. Common (Dover Publications, 2012), <http://www.myilibrary.com.ezaccess.libraries.psu.edu?ID=567271> (accessed 3 December 2014), p. 35.

2 Alan-Paul Johnson, *The Theory of Architecture: Concepts, Themes & Practices* (New York: Van Nostrand Reinhold, 1994), p. 127

3 Ibid., p. 127.

4 Hans Hollein, "Absolute Architecture," in U. Conrads, ed., *Programs and Manifestoes in 20th-Century Architecture*, trans. M. Bullock (Cambridge, MA: MIT Press. 1970), p. 181.

5 Peter Eisenman, "Post-Functionalism," *Oppositions* 6 (Fall 1976): 3.

6 The National Architecture Accreditation Board reports that as of 2013, 43 percent of U.S. architecture students were female, and 42 percent of U.S. architecture degrees were awarded to women. See http://www.acsa-arch.org/resources/data-resources/women (accessed 9 December 2014).

7 Gwendolyn Wright, "On the Fringe of the Profession: Women in American Architecture," in S. Kostof, ed., *The Architect: Chapters in the History of the Profession* (Oxford: Oxford University Press, 1977), p. 280.

8 This represents data collected as of May 31, 2011. This excludes the 18 percent of respondents who responded "Unknown." See "Diversity within the AIA," http://www.aia.org/about/initiatives/AIAS076703, accessed 9 December 2014.

9 Diane Ghirardo, *Out of Site: A Social Criticism of Architecture* (Seattle: Bay Press, 1991), p. 15.

10 John Ruskin, "Conclusion," *The Stones of Venice*, vol. 3 (New York: John W. Lovell, 1851), pp. 193–194.

11 Ruskin, "Nature of the Gothic," *Stones of Venice*, vol. 2, p. 158.

12 The immediate context for this sentence is Ruskin's belief that ornament should depict nature, and viewers should find joy in the handiwork of God. However, it also encapsulates efficiently what he says at greater length elsewhere regarding appreciation of the liberated craftsman's work. Ruskin, "The Material of Ornament," *Stones of Venice*, vol. I, p. 219.

13 World Commission on Environment and Development, *Our Common Future* (Oxford: Oxford University Press, 1987), p. 43.

FURTHER READING

Adams, Annmarie. "Gender Issues: Designing Women," in J. Ockman, ed. *Architecture School: Three Centuries of Educating Architects in North America.* Cambridge, MA: MIT Press, 2012.

Bourdieu, Pierre. *Distinction: A Social Critique of the Judgement of Taste.* Trans. R. Nice. Cambridge, MA: Harvard University Press, 1984.

Colomina, Beatriz, ed. *Sexuality and Space.* New York: Princeton Architectural Press, 1992.

Frank, Susanne S. *Peter Eisenman's House VI: The Client's Response.* New York: Whitney Library of Design, 1994.

Friedman, Alice T. *Women and the Making of the Modern House: A Social and Architectural History.* New Haven and London: Yale University Press, 2006.

Hudson, Karen E. *Paul R. Williams: Classic Hollywood Style.* New York: Rizzoli, 2012.

Larson, Magali Sarfatti. *Behind the Postmodern Façade: Architectural Change in Late Twentieth-Century America.* Berkeley: University of California Press, 1993.

Lima, Zeuler Rocha Mello de Almeida. *Lina Bo Bardi.* New Haven: Yale University Press, 2013.

Lu, Duanfang. *Third World Modernism: Architecture, Development and Identity.* New York: Routledge, 2011.

McDonough, William and Michael Braungart. *Cradle to Cradle.* New York: North Point Press, 2002.

McHarg, Ian. *Design With Nature.* Garden City, NY: American Museum of Natural History, 1971.

Rendell, Jane, Barbara Penner and Iain Borden, eds. *Gender Space Architecture: An Interdisciplinary Introduction.* London and New York: Routledge, 2000.

Ruskin, John. *The Stones of Venice.* London: Smith, Elder & Co., 1851–1853.

Schulze, Franz. *Philip Johnson: Life and Work.* New York: Knopf, 1994.

Scott Brown, Denise. "Learning from Pop." *Casabella* 359/60 (December 1971): 15–23.

Speer, Albert. *Inside the Third Reich: Memoirs.* Trans. R. and C. Winston. New York: Macmillan, 1970.

Sudjic, Deyan. *The Edifice Complex: How the Rich and Powerful Shape the World.* London: Allen Lane, 2005.

Twombly, Robert. *Power and Style: A Critique of Twentieth-Century Architecture in the United States.* New York: Hill and Wang, 1995.

Venturi, Robert, Denise Scott Brown and Steven Izenour. *Learning From Las Vegas.* Revised edition. Cambridge, MA: MIT Press, 1977 (1972).

Wilkins, Craig L. "Race and Diversity: African Americans in Architecture Education," in J. Ockman, ed., *Architecture School: Three Centuries of Educating Architects in North America*. Cambridge, MA: MIT Press, 2012.

Wright, Gwendolyn. "On the Fringe of the Profession: Women in American Architecture," in S. Kostof, ed., *The Architect: Chapters in the History of the Profession*. Oxford: Oxford University Press, 1977.

CONCLUSION
TWO FILMS, TWO ARCHITECTS, YOUR IDEAS

THE MOST FAMOUS AMERICAN ARCHITECT, without doubt, is Frank Lloyd Wright. After Wright, the second most famous is fictional: Howard Roark. This character was born on the pages of Ayn Rand's 1943 novel *The Fountainhead*, then portrayed by Gary Cooper in a 1949 film directed by King Vidor, the screenplay written by Rand herself, directly involved in the film's production.[1] Neither version was a critical success, but their parallel portraits of a heroic architect's slow journey from obscurity to triumph, obtained through absolute commitment to his own creative vision, stoically resisting all seductive temptations (fame, wealth, love), inspired decades of devoted fans. It made Roark an indispensable point of reference for any discussion about the architect.

Rand did extensive research about modern architecture that included reading books by Le Corbusier and Frank Lloyd Wright, and worked in the office of a New York City architect. However, she was primarily interested in politics, not architecture. *The Fountainhead* was created as a vehicle to promote Objectivism, her neo-Nietzschen philosophy of radical individualism, in which born leaders must be left to pursue their dreams unimpeded by concerns about responsibility to others, and thereby benefit all—"rational egoism", in Rand's phrase. The film in particular was a purposefully anti-communist project at a time when the Cold War between the U.S. and the Soviet Union began to escalate. Its carefully vetted participants anticipated Senator Joseph McCarthy's Hollywood "blacklists" (accusations of Communist sympathies among actors, writers, and directors that damaged many careers) during the early 1950s.

Sixty years after Rand's book was published, Nathaniel Kahn released a 2003 documentary film titled *My Architect: A Son's Journey*, about his father, renowned Philadelphia architect Louis Kahn (1901–1974). Kahn's enigmatic persona contrasts with the heroic, commanding Howard Roark, but possesses a warmth and humanity lacking in both Rand's icy prose and Cooper's stiff performance. Despite stark differences in their characters, however, Roark and Kahn's stories have much in common: a difficult professional start; a slow road to success; a puzzlingly complex romantic life; a stubborn commitment to their own design ideas against many practical impediments; and late, hard-won architectural glory. Kahn's exalted reputation among his fellow architects can be considered a real-life vindication of Rand's fictional portrait. He embodies the idea that an artist who lives for his work, and works with absolute dedication and rare brilliance—genius, even—can produce sublime works that touch and inspire millions.

But the portrait of Kahn also has a far bleaker side, one the film presents with brutal honesty: his path to immortality is littered with overworked colleagues, mistreated women, a bankrupt practice, neglected families, a rootless life, and lonely death. In *The Fountainhead*, the many victims of Roark's unyielding idealism and commitment are presented as unworthy or confused. They suffer because they lack faith in his vision and integrity. In contrast, *My Architect* shows many people who suffer precisely because of their faith in Kahn, not its absence. The documentary's poignant conclusion suggests that his son has gained an appreciation of his father's legacy, sympathy for his chosen path, and perhaps forgiveness for his many failings. But it leaves open the question of whether faith in Kahn was justified or misplaced. If *The Fountainhead* proclaims stridently presented "truths" about how great people must be given complete freedom to create great things for the good of all, *My Architect* poses the same question many ask of the famously "priceless" Taj Mahal: how much is great architecture worth?

Viewed together—which I recommend—these two films revisit the themes we have considered in this book: architecture's power to produce meaningful and spiritually uplifting environments, to express the dream of comforting domesticity, and to allow strangers to dwell together in a harmonious communities. They insist that the architect should construct a more beautiful world, one that embodies a new vision of what can be. Both films accept the notion that buildings should be honest about their own substance; that they should belong to their location, culture, and moment, but also transcend these limits so that anyone can appreciate them. In each, great architecture is the product of larger, powerful forces and also the expression of an individual imagination. They also reinforce persistent assumptions about who the architect should be (evident in the treatment of women and lack of non-white characters in both films). *The Fountainhead* and *My Architect* also celebrate how buildings, those mundane products of material, space, place, and needs, can become phenomena that transcend the limits of their makers and situation, and meet needs that people never knew they had.

Sometimes architects' designs appear strange, even inappropriate to the rest of us. Occasionally that first impression, unfortunately and expensively, proves correct. But sometimes, although we may not see it right away, an architect's unfamiliar vision offers precisely what we need, and a building opens the door to an unimagined dream that we are grateful to experience. If it can be dangerous to idealize the architect's power and be seduced by visions of what might be, it is also unwise to ignore the power of the architect's insights into what our tangible, real, messy, magnificent built world can become. It is also important to remember the power of our own participation in the many processes that produce, alter, and preserve the environments that shape our lives. Despite the myths of Roark and Kahn, architecture is never a solo act.

How did you define "architecture" when you began reading? What do you think architecture means now? Perhaps your thoughts have changed substantially while reading, or maybe they remained more or less the same. You may have started with certainty and arrived at confusion, or moved from a vague set of ideas to something more concrete. This matters little if this book has achieved its primary goal: to provide questions, concepts, and examples that help you articulate and explore your own values, insights, and ideas about architecture. If you find yourself looking at buildings differently and asking questions, wanting to learn more about architecture and thinking about how it can help make a better world, it has succeeded. Best of all would be if you keep reading and thinking, and feel empowered to participate in conversations about architecture. As you encounter opportunities to help shape buildings, neighborhoods, and cities—opportunities available to everyone, no matter their walk in life—keep asking what architecture means, for you and for all of us.

STUDY AND REVIEW QUESTIONS: EPILOGUE

1. Describe what you consider to be each film's most meaningful or powerful moment. How similar or different are they?
2. In both films, decide which character you consider most admirable, and which one you find most pathetic. Challenge your own reactions by writing a short critique of your two "admirable" figures and a brief defense of the two "pathetic" ones.
3. Imagine how each story might be told from the perspective of a different character. In what way might this change the overall message of each film? How would this different narrative change your opinions about Roark or Kahn?

APPLICATION AND DISCUSSION EXERCISES

1. Which of the ideas discussed in this book do you consider the most closely aligned with your own opinions about what architecture should be about? Find three concepts that express your own values.

2. Look for a building in your immediate environment that you consider an architectural success. Imagine that this building has been targeted for demolition, and write the strongest possible defense you can for its survival.

NOTE

1 Merrill Schleier, "Ayn Rand and King Vidor's Film 'The Fountainhead': Architectural Modernism, the Gendered Body and Political Ideology," *Journal of the Society of Architectural Historians* 61, 3 (Sept. 2002): 310–333.

ILLUSTRATIONS

INTRODUCTION

CHAPTER 1: SACRED SPACES

CHAPTER 2: THE HOUSE

CHAPTER 3: THE CITY

CHAPTER 4: THE ARCHITECT

CHAPTER 5: AESTHETICS

CHAPTER 6: ORIGINALITY

CHAPTER 7: STRUCTURE AND FORM

CHAPTER 8: MEMORY AND IDENTITY

CHAPTER 9: POWER AND POLITICS

THE AUTHOR

Denise Costanzo is an assistant professor of architecture at The Pennsylvania State University, University Park, Pennsylvania, USA. During 2014–2015 she was the American Academy in Rome's Marian and Andrew Heiskell Post-Doctoral Rome Prize Fellow in Modern Italian Studies.

GLOSSARY

abacus: a thin, usually square-shaped block placed between a column capital and the entablature of ancient Greek and Roman orders

academy: under Louis XIV, a committee charged with defining a particular field's principles of excellence and overseeing their instruction

acanthus: indigenous Mediterranean plant; whose leaves are depicted in Corinthian capitals

adobe: building material of sun-dried blocks made from mud, sand, water, and a binding agent

aesthetics: principles and ideas that define beauty and other forms of sensory perception

agora: an open space in ancient Greek cities, usually framed by major civic structures and used for public gatherings

ambo: a raised platform for reading and preaching in a Christian church; also pulpit

andron: area of an ancient Greek house reserved for men

anthropomorphic analogy: the belief that the ancient Greek orders mirror the proportional relationships and beauty of the human body

apse: in a basilica, a semicircular niche with a half-dome

archetype: an authoritative model to which other works refer

arcuation: a structural system that spans openings with arches and vaults

atelier: French for an artist's or architect's studio

atrium: in ancient Rome, an interior courtyard open to the sky with an impluvium; in contemporary architecture, a glazed interior void

authenticity: a state of genuineness, as opposed to artificiality or falsehood

autonomy: a state of independence from outside forces

avant-garde: in art and culture, a movement that seeks to advance creative progress by making a decisive break with past beliefs and practices

axis: a straight, organizing line of alignment within a spatial composition

ballista: an ancient weapon related to the catapult and crossbow that used torsion to launch a projectile

balustrade: an ornamental handrail

barrel vault: a roof shaped like a half-cylinder, with its semicircular cross-section perpendicular to the ground plane

barrow: an earth-covered burial mound, usually with an internal chamber

basilica: in ancient Rome, a large building for legal and judicial functions; in early Christianity, a type of church adapted from the courthouse design

bastion: in fortification design, an angled projection from a defensive wall

bay: a vertically oriented architectural unit repeated laterally

bimah: a raised platform for reading scripture and preaching in a synagogue

bourgeois: French for "city-dweller"; later, a prosperous urban professional or business owner

cantilever: a solid form that suspends over open space and is structurally anchored at only one end

capital: in ancient Greek and Roman architecture, a mediating decorative and structural element between the vertical column shaft to the horizontal entablature

cardo and decumanus: two primary roads in an ancient Roman castrum, oriented north-south and east-west, respectively, that connect the four main gates centered on each wall and cross in the center

castrum: an ancient Roman military fort laid out in a grid pattern within a square-shaped perimeter; many became permanent cities that preserved this structure, with the cardo and decumanus as the two main streets

cathedral: Christian church that is also the seat of a bishop

centering: temporary wood framework used during the construction of masonry arches and vaults

centralized plan: a design in which elements are distributed evenly around a central point or axis

chatra: an honorific canopy; a three-tiered symbolic tree on top of a stupa

citadel: a fortress located on high ground, often overlooking a city

class: any grouping within a rational ordering system; in the social sciences, a group of people with similar resources, status, and interests

classical: something designated exemplary, of lasting value as a model; in architecture, the design vocabulary developed in ancient Greece and Rome

clerestory: a row of windows placed along the top of a high wall

column: a vertical support with a round cross-section and generally cylindrical form

composite: a classical architectural order developed in ancient Rome combining Ionic and Corinthian capitals

concentric: circular forms that share the same center

concinnitas: a term borrowed from ancient rhetoric by Alberti to describe a careful combination of elements into a harmonious whole

consoles: in classical architecture, S-shaped brackets that traditionally support a shelf, lintel, or other minor horizontal element

context: a building's immediate environment; can be physical or cultural

Corinthian: the most elaborate Greek classical order with an acanthus-leaf-covered capital

cornice: a projecting horizontal ornamental molding decorating the top of a wall

cortile: in Italian architecture, an open interior courtyard, usually surrounded by columns or arches

cultural capital: forms of knowledge and taste that shape social identity and establish status

curtain wall: a building envelope attached to a structural frame that provides enclosure but does not support vertical loads

dentil: a small cube-shaped projection placed in a row directly beneath the cornice of various classical orders; from Latin for "tooth"

disegno: Italian for "drawing" or "design"

dolmen: a megalithic structure in which multiple vertical monoliths support a horizontal one

domus: an ancient Roman aristocratic townhouse

Doric: the simplest and heaviest of the Greek classical orders

duck and decorated shed: Robert Venturi and Denise Scott Brown's two theoretical categories describing how buildings communicate, either through three-dimensional form or separate signage

elevation: orthographic drawing showing a building's vertical surfaces

empiricism: the belief that knowledge is acquired through sensory interaction with the physical world

engaged column: a full or partial column that is physically attached to a wall

entablature: horizontal beam or lintel spanning a row of classical columns

entasis: in classical architecture, a slight bulge in a tapering column shaft, typically about one-third above the base

Eucharist: a ritual enactment of Christ's Last Supper

façade: a surface providing a building's exterior "face"

fascism: early twentieth-century political movement that is authoritarian, nationalistic, and anti-democratic, typically emphasizing a common ethnic identity, heritage, and strength through unity and obedience

favela: housing settlement outside large South American cities; usually built by residents, often illegally, using salvaged materials

feminism: belief that abilities are not determined by sex, and that opportunities should not be limited by sex

firmitas: structural stability or soundness; part of the Vitruvian triad, along with utilitas and venustas

flying buttress: in Gothic architecture, an exterior strut that transfers loads from the roof to a vertical pier

foliate: having leaf-shaped forms

forum: in ancient Roman cities, an open space for civic and public life

frieze: horizontal strip of imagery; in architecture, typically carved in low relief

genius: Latin for "spirit" or "divinity," often associated with an individual's qualities or talents or a mechanism that seems animated; since the early modern era, an individual with unique and exceptional talents and abilities

genius loci: Latin for "spirit of a place"

gentrification: gradual process whereby private investors transform an urban neighborhood in disrepair and inhabited by lower-income residents into one dominated by a wealthier population

ghetto: urban neighborhood restricted to a marginalized minority population, typically with substandard conditions

glacis: an open, sloped area surrounding urban fortifications to deny cover to invading troops

groin vault: ceiling form produced by two barrel vaults that intersect each other at right angles

guttae: small cone-shaped projections along the bottom of the triglyphs in a Doric architrave

gynaeceum: area of an ancient Greek house reserved for women

harmika: a square-shaped, low-walled structure on top of a stupa

hierarchy: a structural arrangement where certain elements are more important than others

hypostyle hall: a room filled with closely spaced columns

icon: in Peircean semiotics, a visual sign that communicates through visual resemblance of its referent

ideal city: design for a community that expresses both aesthetic and social ideals

ideology: an overarching system of beliefs about how the world works, or should work

impluvium: sunken basin to collect rainwater in the atrium of an ancient Roman house

index: in Peircean semiotics, a visual sign that is produced through physical contact with its referent

Ionic: one of the three ancient Greek orders whose capital features two large volutes

iwan: a large arched niche in Islamic architecture

kondo: a large worship space in a Buddhist sanctuary ("Golden Hall" in Japanese)

lineaments: Alberti's term for a building's overall formal dimension (geometric forms, organization of spaces and volumes)

loggia: a roofed porch with openings framed by columns or arches on at least one side

longitudinal plan: a design in which elements are balanced around a long, lateral axis

mandala: sacred diagram in Buddhist and Hindu tradition, combining squares (symbol of the earth) and circles (symbol of the heavens)

mandir: a Hindu temple (Sanskrit for "home")

manifesto: a declarative statement of principles for a movement, usually intentionally provocative

mastaba: ancient Egyptian monumental tomb consisting of a raised mud-brick mound with a flat top and sloping sides; from Arabic for "table"

mausoleum: a monumental building housing an individual's tomb

McMansion: a single-family home that is larger and more luxurious than the average, but still intended for a mass market

megachurch: a Protestant Christian church with a membership of many thousands

megalith: a single large stone used in construction

menhir: a megalith placed upright in the ground

mihrab: a niche for the Qur'an in the qibla

minaret: a tall tower associated with a mosque, from which the call to prayer is sung

minbar: a raised platform for reading scripture and preaching in a mosque

modernism: cultural movements begun in the nineteenth century that focus on the expression of new realities, typically through innovative artistic forms

monument: a structure built to preserve a cultural memory

modular: system consisting of small, consistently sized units

mortise and tenon: in construction, a joint consisting of a projection (*tenon*) in one member inserted in a corresponding void (*mortise*) in another member

mosque: public prayer hall for Islamic worship

node: in urban planning, a point where multiple streets intersect

obelisks: thin, vertical monolithic stone monuments with a tapering square cross-section and pyramidal top erected by ancient Egyptians in front of pylons at temples

organic: in urbanism, an irregular city structure that appears to have evolved gradually and has few straight streets or geometrically precise open spaces

orthographic projection: a scale drawing that presents all physical and visual elements of a structure as if "projected" onto a flat surface

pagoda: in Buddhist architecture, a tower-like structure with multiple, vertically stacked roofs that protects sacred relics or scriptures

palazzo: any urban, multi-story structure in Italy; a townhome for an aristocratic family during the Middle Ages and later

paper architecture: designs that only exist as images, not physical buildings

paradigm shift: Thomas Kuhn's term for a radical change in a field's intellectual framework

parti: in the Beaux-Arts educational system, a diagram showing the scheme for a building design in plan

party wall: a solid wall shared by two separately owned properties

patrician: an ancient Roman aristocrat

patron: a powerful person who sponsors the work of an artist or architect; in ancient Rome, a wealthy politician who protected other, less powerful people ("clients").

pediment: triangular space formed by the gable end of a roof

peripteral: in Greek architecture, a structure surrounded by a row of free-standing columns

peristyle: a row of columns surrounding a structure or open space

perspective: various methods of drawing that convey how three-dimensional forms in space appear to the eye

phenomenology: philosophical investigation of how sensory, mental, experiential, and other subjective phenomena filter knowledge about the world

piano nobile: Italian for "noble floor"; the first floor above street level in a palazzo, which contained the most formal rooms for receiving visitors

piazza: Italian term for an open, public urban space (*square* in English, *place* in French, *plaza* in Spanish, *Platz* in German)

picturesque: compositional strategy based on variety and asymmetry inspired by both Chinese garden design and seventeenth-century French landscape painting; later considered a Romantic aesthetic category

pier: a vertical architectural support, usually with a cross-section that is not round (see column)

pilasters: decorative vertical elements attached to a solid wall that echo classical columns in profile but are flat and project only slightly from the wall surface

plan: orthographic projection showing a structure's walls and spaces as a horizontal slice viewed from above

plastic: a material that can be easily molded

plebian: a member of ancient Rome's working class

podium: in ancient Roman architecture, a high platform supporting a temple

polemic: a provocative statement intended to incite controversy and debate

portico: in classical architecture, an open porch supported by columns

post-structuralism: late twentieth-century intellectual movement that argued against any stable and objective meaning in language

pozzolana: naturally occurring cement from deposits of volcanic ash near Mt. Vesuvius in Italy; used for concrete construction by ancient Romans

precedent: a prior work of architecture providing a model for a later work's design

proletariat: working-class people; in Marxist thought, usually industrial and agricultural laborers

pylon: a solid wall with battered sides at the entrance of an ancient Egyptian temple

qibla: in a mosque, a wall that faces toward Mecca and contains the mihrab

rationalism: term used to describe modernist work in early twentieth-century Italy

redlining: a U.S. Federal Housing Authority practice designating an area unworthy of government mortgage insurance guarantees, typically because it had non-white residents

referent: in semiotics, the content or message communicated by any sign

reinforced concrete: modern concrete system with embedded metal bars or mesh to withstand tensile forces

restrictive covenants: neighborhood rules that exclude residency or purchase by specific ethnic or racial groups

ribbed vaults: in medieval architecture, ceiling vaults with thick ribs along the length of the joint where surfaces meet

Romanticism: eighteenth-century aesthetic movement that emphasized subjective, emotional reactions to works of art

rustication: surface treatment of masonry wall that visually emphasizes each block as a separate unit

scorpio: ancient weapon that launched darts; a smaller, more agile version of the ballista

section and township: surveying units used to divide new territory in the early United States; a *township* was 6 miles on each side, containing thirty-six 1-mile-square *sections*

selective definition: the view that only certain buildings or designs should be labeled "architecture"

semiotics: academic study of how signs function

sengu: ritual rebuilding of the Inner Shrine at Ise in Japan every twenty years since 690

shikara: highest tower of a Hindu temple

Shinto: traditional, indigenous Japanese religion centered on the worship of ancestors and natural forces

sign: in semiotics, any visual phenomenon that is used to communicate an idea

single-family home: a free-standing house intended for occupancy by one group of related people

slum: neighborhood with poorly maintained, substandard housing

social condenser: in the early Soviet Union, an architectural project intended to eradicate traditional values and inculcate socialist ones through its design and programming

socialism: belief in public ownership of a society's economic resources, most famously advocated by Karl Marx

speaking architecture: translation of the eighteenth-century French concept (*architecture parlante*) that architectural form and design should visually explain a building's purpose

stadium: in ancient Greece and Rome, a long, narrow open space surrounded by tiered seating for athletic events

stoa: in ancient Greek architecture, a long, narrow roofed portico enclosed on one side with a row of columns opposite

streetcar buildout: a suburban area along a streetcar line with dense housing for working-class residents

structural rationalism: the belief that architectural form should visually explain a building's physical and material character

studiolo: in a Renaissance palazzo, a private study adjacent to the bedroom

stupa: a solid domed structure built over the remains of the Buddha

style: a distinctive set of visual qualities that result from a common approach to design across multiple works

sublime: in Romantic aesthetic theory, something that induces an intense response in the viewer, who feels awed, powerless, and overwhelmed

symbol: in Peircean semiotics, a sign with an arbitrary, socially determined relationship with its referent

synagogue: public worship space for a Jewish congregation ("house of assembly" in Greek)

tablinum: in an ancient Roman domus, the room opposite the main entrance, across the atrium, where family records were stored and the *paterfamilias* would receive visitors

temenos: in ancient Greece, a walled sanctuary containing temples

tenement: a long, narrow, multi-story apartment building in nineteenth-century New York City

terra cotta: fired, unglazed earthenware; from Italian for "baked earth"

theory: an explanation of a subject based on abstract, general principles

thermal mass: the capacity of a building envelope to absorb and store heat and thereby maintain a constant interior temperature in extreme climates

thesis-antithesis-synthesis: Hegel's model of intellectual progress; an original idea, a counter-idea, then a new idea reconciling the first two

torah ark: in a synagogue, decorative cabinet to house sacred scriptures

torana: a monumental gateway into sacred sites in India

trabeation: structural system consisting of horizontal beams supported by upright columns or piers

triglyph: rectangular tablet with vertical grooves defining three raised panels used on a Doric frieze

trilithon: three-megalith structure with a horizontal lintel supported by two upright stones

type: in architecture, a category of buildings that conform to a common and recognizable formal pattern

universalist definition: the view that all buildings should be labeled "architecture"

urban artifact: Aldo Rossi's term *fatto urbano* (also "urban fact") for a human-made element whose form contributes to a city's structure over a long span of time

urban fabric: a city's entire physical structure, encompassing buildings, streets, open spaces, and topography

urban renewal: in the twentieth-century U.S., a government-led transformation of a city neighborhood in disrepair, usually inhabited by lower-income residents, into one that conformed to an official development agenda, often defined in racial and socioeconomic terms

utilitarian: serving practical, direct needs

utilitas: utility or usefulness; part of the Vitruvian triad, along with firmitas and venustas

utopia: from Greek roots meaning both "good city" and "non-city," an idealized, perfect, and imaginary world

veneer: a thin decorative surface of fine material covering a plainer structure beneath

venustas: beauty or delight; part of the Vitruvian triad, along with firmitas and utilitas

vernacular architecture: "everyday" structures built by non-architects that constitute most of the built environment

villa: an ancient Roman farmhouse, later a country retreat

Vitruvian triad: Vitruvius' position that architecture must possess firmitas, utilitas, and venustas

Volksgeist: German for "spirit of the people"; Hegel's term for the cultural essence of an ethnically or geographically specific group

volute: spiral-shaped embellishment on Ionic and Corinthian column capitals

yeoman farmer: Thomas Jefferson's term for a landowner who supports himself by working property he owns

Zeitgeist: "spirit of the age"; Hegel's term for the essence of a cultural moment

BIBLIOGRAPHY

Ackerman, James. *The Villa: Form and Ideology of Country Houses*. Princeton, NJ: Princeton University Press, 1990.

_____. *The Architecture of Michelangelo*. New York: Viking, 1961.

Adams, Annmarie. "Gender Issues: Designing Women," in J. Ockman, ed. *Architecture School: Three Centuries of Educating Architects in North America*. Cambridge, MA: MIT Press, 2012.

Adams, Cassandra. "Japan's Ise Shrine and Its Thirteen-Hundred-Year-Old Reconstruction Tradition." *Journal of Architectural Education* 52, no. 1 (Sept. 1998): 49–60.

Alberti, Leon Battista. *On Painting: A New Translation and Critical Edition*. Trans. R. Sinisgalli. Cambridge: Cambridge University Press, 2011.

_____. *On the Art of Building in Ten Books*. Trans. J. Rykwert and J. Tavernor. Cambridge, MA: MIT Press, 1988.

Archer, John. *Architecture and Suburbia*. Minneapolis: University of Minnesota Press, 2005.

Aristotle. *Politics*. Trans. H. Rackham. Cambridge, MA: Harvard University Press, 1944.

Banham, P. Reyner. "A Home Is Not a House." *Art in America* (April 1965): 109–118.

_____. *Theory and Design in the First Machine Age*. New York: Praeger. 1960.

Barrie, Thomas. *Spiritual Path, Sacred Place: Myth, Ritual and Meaning in Architecture*. Boston: Shambhala, 1996.

Bauer Wurster, Catherine. *Modern Housing*. New York: Houghton Mifflin, 1934.

Blair, Sheila and Jonathan Bloom. *The Art and Architecture of Islam, 1250–1800*. New Haven: Yale University Press, 1994.

Bharne, Vinyak and Krupali Krusche. *Rediscovering the Hindu Temple: The Sacred Architecture and Urbanism of India*. Newcastle upon Tyne: Cambridge Scholars Publishing, 2012.

Bourdieu, Pierre. *Distinction: A Social Critique of the Judgement of Taste*. Trans. R. Nice. Cambridge, MA: Harvard University Press, 1984.

Brooks, H. Allen. *Le Corbusier's Formative Years*. Chicago: University of Chicago Press, 1997.

Burke, Edmund. *A Philosophical Inquiry into the Origin of Our Ideas of the Sublime and the Beautiful*. New York: Garland, 1971.

Cannon, Jon. *The Secret Language of Sacred Spaces: Decoding Churches, Temples, Mosques and Other Places of Worship Around the World*. London: Duncan Baird, 2013.

Carson, Rachel. *Silent Spring*. New York: Houghton Mifflin, 1962.

Cerdà, Idelfonso. *The Five Bases of the General Theory of Urbanization*. Madrid: Electa, 1999.

Ching, Francis, Mark Jarzombek, and Vikramaditya Prakash, *A Global History of Architecture*. Hoboken, NJ: John Wiley & Sons, 2007.

Choay, Françoise. *The Modern City: Planning in the 19th Century*. New York: Braziller, 1970.

Cohen, Jean-Louis. *The Future of Architecture Since 1889*. London: Phaidon, 2012.

_____. *Architecture in Uniform: Designing and Building for the Second World War*. Montréal: Canadian Centre for Architecture, 2011.

Coleman, Debra, Elizabeth Danze, and Carol Henderson, eds. *Architecture and Feminism*. New York: Princeton Architectural Press, 1996.

Collins, George R. *Camillo Sitte: The Birth of Modern City Planning*. New York: Rizzoli, 1986.

Colomina, Beatriz, ed. *Sexuality and Space*. New York: Princeton Architectural Press, 1992.

Conrads, Ulrich. *Programs and Manifestoes on 20th Century Architecture*. Trans. M. Bullock. Cambridge, MA: MIT Press, 1970.

Conway, Hazel and Rowan Roenisch. *Understanding Architecture: An Introduction to Architecture and Architectural History*. London and New York: Routledge, 1994.

Costanzo, Denise. "The Medici McMansion?" in D. Medina Lasansky, ed., *The Renaissance: Revised, Unexpurgated, Expanded*. Pittsburgh: Periscope Press, 2014.

Cuff, Dana. *Architecture: The Story of Practice*. Cambridge, MA: MIT Press, 1991.

Curtis, J. R. *Modern Architecture Since 1900*. Third edition. London: Phaidon, 1996.

Davies, Colin. *Thinking about Architecture: An Introduction to Architectural Theory*. London: Laurence King, 2011.

Doordan, Dennis. *Twentieth-Century Architecture*. New York: Harry N. Abrams, 2002.

Downing, Andrew Jackson. *The Architecture of Country Houses*. Reprint edition. New York: Da Capo Press, 1968 (1850).

Drexler, Arthur, ed. *The Architecture of the École des Beaux-Arts*. New York: Museum of Modern Art, 1977.

Droste, Magdalena. *Bauhaus 1919–1933*, Trans. K. Williams. Berlin: Taschen, 2002.

Eisenman, Peter. "Post-Functionalism." *Oppositions* 6 (Fall 1976): 1–4.

Ettinghausen, Richard, Oleg Grabar, and Marilyn Jenkins-Madina. *Islamic Art and Architecture 650–1250*. New Haven: Yale University Press, 2001.

Fathy, Hassan. *Architecture for the Poor: An Experiment in Rural Egypt*. Chicago: University of Chicago Press, 1973.

Fazio, Michael, Marian Moffett, and Lawrence Woodhouse. *A World History of Architecture*. Third edition. London: Laurence King, 2013.

Frampton, Kenneth. *Modern Architecture: A Critical History*. Fourth edition. London: Thames & Hudson, 2007.

Frank, Susanne S. *Peter Eisenman's House VI: The Client's Response*. New York: Whitney Library of Design, 1994.

Freire-Medeiros, Bianca. "The Favela and Its Touristic Transits." *Geoforum* 40, 4 (July 2009): 580–588.

Friedman, Alice T. *Women and the Making of the Modern House: A Social and Architectural History*. New Haven and London: Yale University Press, 2006.

Frontinus, Sextus Julius. *The Two Books on the Water Supply of the City of Rome*. Trans. C. Herschel. Boston: Dana Estates, 1899.

Ghirardo, Diane. *Italy: Modern Architectures in History*. London: Reaktion Books, 2013.

———. *Out of Site: A Social Criticism of Architecture*. Seattle: Bay Press, 1991.

Giedion, Sigfried. *Space, Time and Architecture: The Growth of a New Tradition*. Cambridge, MA: Harvard University Press, 1941.

Goethe, Johann von. "On German Architecture," in H. F. Mallgrave, ed., *Architectural Theory, Volume I: An Anthology from Vitruvius to 1870*. Malden, MA: Blackwell Publishing, 2006.

Grafton, Anthony. *Leon Battista Alberti: Master Builder of the Italian Renaissance*. Cambridge, MA: Harvard University Press, 2000.

Greenough, Horatio. "American Architecture" in *Form and Function: Remarks on Art, Design and Architecture*. Berkeley: University of California Press, 1947.

Gropius, Walter. "Tradition and Continuity in Architecture." *Architectural Record* 135 (May 1964): 131–136; (June 1964): 133–140; v. 136 (July 1964): 151–156.

Guo, Qinghua. "Yingzao Fashi: Twelfth-Century Chinese Building Manual." *Architectural History* 41 (1998): 1–13.

Hale, Jonathan. *Building Ideas: An Introduction to Architectural Theory*. Chichester: Wiley, 2000.

Harris, Dianne. *Little White Houses: How the Postwar Home Constructed Race in America*. Minneapolis: University of Minnesota Press, 2013.

Hart, Vaughan. *Paper Palaces: The Rise of the Renaissance Architectural Treatise*. New Haven: Yale University Press, 1998.

Hays, K. Michael, ed. *Architecture Theory Since 1968*. Cambridge, MA: MIT Press, 1998.

Hearn, Millard Fil. *Ideas That Shaped Buildings*. Cambridge, MA: MIT Press, 2003.

Heidegger, Martin. "Building, Dwelling, Thinking" in *Basic Writings from Being and Time (1927) to The Task of Thinking (1964)*. New York: Harper & Row, 1977.

Hollein, Hans. "Absolute Architecture" in U. Conrads, ed., *Programs and Manifestoes in 20th-century architecture*. Trans. M. Bullock. Cambridge, MA: MIT Press, 1970.

Hübsch, Heinrich. "In What Style Should We Build?" (1828), in H. F. Mallgrave, ed. *Architectural Theory, Volume I: An Anthology from Vitruvius to 1870*. Malden, MA: Blackwell Publishing, 2006.

Hudson, Karen E. *Paul R. Williams: Classic Hollywood Style*. New York: Rizzoli, 2012.

Hurwitt, Jeffrey. *The Athenian Acropolis: History, Mythology and Archaeology from the Neolithic Era to the Present*. Cambridge: Cambridge University Press, 1999.

Huyssen, Andreas. *Present Pasts: Urban Palimpsests and the Politics of Memory*. Stanford: Stanford University Press, 2003.

Hyman, Isabelle and Marvin Trachtenberg, *Architecture: From Prehistory to Postmodernity*. Second edition. New York: Prentice Hall, 2003.

Ingersoll, Richard and Spiro Kostof, *World Architecture: A Cross-Cultural History*. New York: Oxford University Press, 2013.

Jacobs, Jane. *The Death and Life of Great American Cities*. New York: Random House, 1961.

James-Chatraborty, Kathleen. *Architecture Since 1400*. Minneapolis: University of Minnesota, 2014.

Jarzombek, Mark. *Architecture of First Societies: A Global Perspective*. Hoboken, New Jersey: John Wiley & Sons, 2013.

Jencks, Charles. *The Language of Post-Modern Architecture*. New York: Rizzoli, 1977.

Johnson, Paul-Alan. *The Theory of Architecture: Concepts, Themes & Practices*. New York: John Wiley & Sons, 1994.

Kostof, Spiro, *A History of Architecture: Settings and Rituals*. New York: Oxford University Press, 1995.

Kostof, Spiro, ed. *The Architect: Chapters in the History of the Profession*. Oxford: Oxford University Press, 1977.

Kruft, Hanno-Walter. *A History of Architectural Theory from Vitruvius to the Present*. Trans. R. Taylor, E. Callander, and A. Wood. New York: Princeton Architectural Press, 1994.

Kuhn, Thomas. *The Structure of Scientific Revolutions*. Chicago: University of Chicago Press, 1962.

Lambert, Phyllis, ed. *Mies in America*. Montreal: Canadian Centre for Architecture, 2001.

Larson, Magali Sarfatti. *Behind the Postmodern Façade: Architectural Change in Late Twentieth-Century America*. Berkeley: University of California Press, 1993.

Laugier, Marc-Antoine. *Essay on Architecture*. Trans. W. and A. Herrmann. Los Angeles: Hennessey & Ingalls. 1977 (1753).

Le Corbusier. *Toward an Architecture*. Trans. J. Goodman. Los Angeles: Getty Research Institute, 2007.

_____. *The City of To-Morrow and its Planning*. Trans. F. Etchells. New York: Dover, 1987.

_____. *Towards a New Architecture*. Trans. F. Etchells. New York: Dover. 1986.

_____. *The Athens Charter*. Trans. A. Eardley. New York: Grossman Publishers, 1973.

Leach, Neil, ed. *Rethinking Architecture: A Reader in Cultural Theory*. London and new York: Routledge, 1997.

Ledoux, Claude-Nicolas. *l'Architecture considérée sous le rapport de l'art, des moeurs et de la législation*, ed. Ramée. Reprint edition. Princeton: Princeton Architectural Press, 1983 (1847).

Levine, Neil. *The Architecture of Frank Lloyd Wright*. Princeton: Princeton University Press, 1996.

_____. *Modern Architecture: Representation and Reality*. New Haven and London: Yale University Press, 2009.

Levy, Matthys and Mario Salvadori. *Why Buildings Fall Down*. New York: W. W. Norton, 1987.

Lima, Zeuler Rocha Mello de Almeida. *Lina Bo Bardi*. New Haven: Yale University Press, 2013.

Ling, Bettina. *Maya Lin*. Austin, TX: Raintree Steck-Vaughn, 1997.

Loos, Adolf. "Ornament and Crime" in U. Conrads, ed., *Programs and Manifestos on 20th-Century Architecture*, Trans. M. Bullock. Cambridge, MA: MIT Press, 1970.

Lu, Duanfang. *Third World Modernism: Architecture, Development and Identity*. New York: Routledge, 2011.

Lynch, Kevin. *Image of the City*. Cambridge, MA: MIT Press, 1960.

Mallgrave, Harry Francis. *Modern Architectural Theory: A Historical Survey, 1673–1968*. Cambridge: Cambridge University Press, 2005.

_____. *Gottfried Semper: Architect of the Nineteenth Century*. New Haven: Yale University Press, 1996.

Mallgrave, Harry Francis, ed. *Architectural Theory, Volume I: An Anthology from Vitruvius to 1870*. Malden, MA: Blackwell Publishing, 2006.

Mallgrave, Harry F. and Contandriopoulos, eds. *Architectural Theory, Volume II: An Anthology from 1871 to 2005*. Second edition. Malden, MA: Blackwell Publishing, 2008.

Marinetti, Filippo Tommaso. "The Foundation and Manifesto of Futurism," in C. Harrison and P. Wood, eds. *Art in Theory 1900–2000: An Anthology of Changing Ideas*. Malden, MA: Blackwell Publishing, 2003.

Martini, Francesco di Giorgio. *Francesco di Giorgio architetto*. Milano: Electa, 1993.

Marx, Karl. *Capital: A Critical Analysis of Capitalist Production*. New York: Appleton, 1889 (1867).

_____. *The Communist Manifesto*. Trans. and ed. F. L. Bender. New York: W. W. Norton, 2013 (1848).

McCarter, Robert and Juhani Pallasmaa. *Understanding Architecture*. London: Phaidon, 2012.

McDonough, William and Michael Braungart. *Cradle to Cradle*. New York: North Point Press, 2002.

McHarg, Ian. *Design With Nature*. Garden City, NY: American Museum of Natural History, 1971.

McKenzie, Judith. *Architecture of Alexandria and Egypt, 300 BC –AD 700*. New Haven: Yale University Press, 2007.

Middleton, Robin, ed. *The Beaux-Arts and Nineteenth-Century French Architecture.* Cambridge, MA: MIT Press, 1982.

Middleton, Robin and David Watkin, eds. *Architecture of the Nineteenth Century.* Milan: Electa, 1980.

Mitchell, George. *The Hindu Temple: An Introduction to Its Meaning and Forms.* Chicago and London: University of Chicago Press, 1977.

Mitrović, Branko. *Philosophy for Architects.* New York: Princeton Architectural Press, 2011.

Moore, Rowan. *Why We Build: Power and Desire in Architecture.* New York: Harper Design, 2013.

Morris, A. E. J. *History of Urban Form before the Industrial Revolutions.* Harlow, England: Pearson, Ltd., 1994.

Müller, Hans. *Ancient Architecture.* Milan: Electa, 1980.

Mumford, Eric. *The CIAM Discourse on Urbanism, 1928–1960.* Cambridge, MA: MIT Press, 2000.

Mumford, Lewis. *The City in History: Its Origins and Transformations, and its Prospects.* New York: Harcourt and Brace, 1961.

Nevett, Lisa. *Domestic Space in Classical Antiquity.* Cambridge: Cambridge University Press. 2012.

_____. *House and Society in the Ancient Greek World.* Cambridge: Cambridge University Press, 1999.

Nicoloso, Paolo. *Mussolini Architetto: Propaganda e paesaggio urbano nell'Italia fascista.* Turin: Einaudi, 2008.

Nietzsche, F. *Twilight of the Idols.* Trans. T. Common. Dover Publications, 2012, http://www.myilibrary.com.ezaccess.libraries.psu.edu?ID=567271 (accessed 3 December 2014).

"Obituary: Philip Johnson," *The Telegraph,* 28 January 2005, http://www.telegraph.co.uk/news/obituaries/1482161/Philip-Johnson.html (accessed 2 December 2014).

Ockman, Joan, ed. *Architecture School: Three Centuries of Educating Architects in North America.* Cambridge, MA: MIT Press, 2012.

_____. *Architecture Culture 1943–1968: A Documentary Anthology.* New York: Rizzoli, 1993.

Parcell, Stephen. *Four Historical Definitions of Architecture.* Montreal: McGill-Queen's University Press, 2012.

Perrault, Claude. *Ordonnance for the Five Kinds of Columns after the Method of the Ancients.* Santa Monica: Getty Center for the Study of Art and the Humanities, 1993.

Pevsner, Nikolaus. *An Outline of European Architecture.* New York: C. Scribner's Sons, 1948.

Rendell, Jane, Barbara Penner and Iain Borden, eds. *Gender Space Architecture: An Interdisciplinary Introduction.* London and New York: Routledge, 2000.

Riley, Terrence and Barry Bergdoll, eds. *Mies in Berlin.* New York: Museum of Modern Art.

Rossi, Aldo. *The Architecture of the City.* Trans. D. Ghirardo and J. Ockman. Cambridge, MA: MIT Press, 1982.

Roth, Leland. *Understanding Architecture: Its Elements, History and Meaning.* Third edition. Boulder: Westview Press, 2014.

Rowe, Colin. *The Mathematics of the Ideal Villa and Other Essays.* Cambridge, MA: MIT Press. 1976.

_____. "The Mathematics of the Ideal Villa: Palladio and Le Corbusier Compared." *Architectural Review* 101 (1947): 101–104.

Ruskin, John. *The Stones of Venice*. London: Smith, Elder & Co., 1851–1853.

Rybczynski, Witold. "The Bilbao Effect." *Atlantic Monthly* (September 2002).

Rykwert, Joseph. *The Dancing Column: On Order in Architecture*. Cambridge, MA: MIT Press, 1996.

Saint, Andrew. *The Image of the Architect*. New Haven and London: Yale University Press, 1983.

——. *Architect and Engineer: A Study in Sibling Rivalry*. New Haven and London: Yale University Press, 2007.

Sant'Elia, Antonio. "Futurist Architecture" in U. Conrads, ed., *Programs and Manifestos on 20th-Century Architecture*. Trans. M. Bullock. Cambridge, MA: MIT Press, 1970.

Schleier, Merrill. "Ayn Rand and King Vidor's Film 'The Fountainhead': Architectural Modernism, the Gendered Body and Political Ideology." *Journal of the Society of Architectural Historians* 61, 3 (Sept. 2002): 310–333.

Schulze, Franz. *Philip Johnson: Life and Work*. New York: Knopf, 1994.

Scott Brown, Denise. "Learning from Pop." *Casabella* 359/60 (December 1971): 15–23.

Sebag, Paul. *The Great Mosque of Kairouan*. Trans. R. Howard. London, Collier-Macmillan, 1965.

Sitte, Camillo. *City Planning According to Its Artistic Principles*. Trans. G. R. and C. C. Collins. New York: Random House, 1965.

Smith, Korydon, ed. *Introducing Architectural Theory: Debating a Discipline*. New York and London: Routledge, 2012.

Speer, Albert. *Inside the Third Reich: Memoirs*. Trans. R. and C. Winston. New York: Macmillan, 1970.

Steinhardt, Nancy Shatzman. *Chinese Imperial City Planning*. Honolulu: University of Hawaii Press. 1990.

Sudjic, Deyan. *The Edifice Complex: How the Rich and Powerful Shape the World*. London: Allen Lane, 2005.

Suetonius Tranquillis, C. *The Divine Augustus*. Trans. E. S. Shuckburgh. Cambridge: Cambridge University Press, 1896.

Sullivan, Louis. *Autobiography of an Idea*. New York: Dover, 1956 (1924).

——. "The Tall Office Building, Artistically Considered." *Lippincott's Magazine* 57 (March 1896): 403–409.

Sykes, A. Krista, ed., *The Architecture Reader: Essential Writings from Vitruvius to the Present*. New York: George Braziller, 2007.

Tavernor, Robert. *On Alberti and the Art of Building*. New Haven and London: Yale University Press, 1998.

Twombly, Robert. *Power and Style: A Critique of Twentieth-Century Architecture in the United States*. New York: Hill and Wang, 1995.

Van Zanten, David. *Building Paris: Architectural Institutions and the Transformation of the French Capital, 1830–1870*. Cambridge: Cambridge University Press, 1994.

Vasari, Giorgio. *The Lives of the Most Excellent Painters, Sculptors, and Architects*. Trans. J. C. and P. Bondanella. New York: Oxford University Press, 1991.

Venturi, Robert. *Complexity and Contradiction in Architecture*. New York: Museum of Modern Art, 1966.

Venturi, Robert, Denise Scott Brown, and Steven Izenour. *Learning From Las Vegas*. Revised edition. Cambridge, MA: MIT Press, 1977 (1972).

Verma, Som Prakash. *Taj Mahal*. Oxford: Oxford University Press, 2012.

Vidler, Anthony. *Histories of the Immediate Present: Inventing Architectural Modernism*. Cambridge, MA: MIT Press, 2008.

_____. *Claude-Nicolas Ledoux: Architecture and Social Reform at the End of the Ancien Régime*. Cambridge, MA: MIT Press, 1990.

Viollet-le-Duc, Eugène-Emmanuel. *Discourses on Architecture*. Trans. B. Bucknall. New York: Dover. 1987 (1872).

Vitruvius. *The Ten Books on Architecture*. Trans. I. Rowland. Cambridge: Cambridge University Press, 1999.

_____. *The Ten Books on Architecture*. Trans. M. H. Morgan. Cambridge: Harvard University Press, 1914.

Wagner, Otto. *Modern Architecture: A Guidebook for His Students to This Field of Art*. Trans. H. F. Mallgrave. Santa Monica, CA: The Getty Center, 1988 (1896).

Wallace-Hadrill, Andrew. *Houses and Society in Pompeii and Herculaneum*. Princeton, NJ: Princeton University Press, 1994.

Watkins, C. and Ben Cowell. *Uvedale Price: Decoding the Picturesque*. Woodbridge: Boydell. 2012.

Wharton, Annabel. *Selling Jerusalem: Relics, Replicas, Theme Parks*. Chicago: University of Chicago Press, 2006.

Whitely, Nigel. *Reyner Banham: Historian of the Immediate Future*. Cambridge, MA: MIT Press, 2002.

Wilkins, Craig L. "Race and Diversity: African Americans in Architecture Education," in J. Ockman, ed., *Architecture School: Three Centuries of Educating Architects in North America*. Cambridge, MA: MIT Press, 2012.

Wittkower, Rudolf. *Architectural Principles in the Age of Humanism*. London: Academy Editions, 1949.

Woods, Mary N. *From Craft to Profession: The Practice of Architecture in Nineteenth-Century America*. Berkeley: University of California Press, 1999.

World Commission on Environment and Development, *Our Common Future*. Oxford: Oxford University Press, 1987.

Wright, Gwendolyn. *USA: Modern Architectures in History*. London: Reaktion Books, 2008.

_____. *Building the Dream: A Social History of Housing in America*. New York: Pantheon Books, 1981.

_____. "On the Fringe of the Profession: Women in American Architecture," in S. Kostof, ed., *The Architect: Chapters in the History of the Profession*. Oxford: Oxford University Press, 1977.

Zanker, Paul. *The Power of Images in the Age of Augustus*. Trans. Alan Shapiro. Ann Arbor: University of Michigan Press, 1988.

INDEX